OUR THEATRES IN
THE EIGHTIES

Also by Sheridan Morley:

A Talent to Amuse
Review Copies: London Theatres 1970–74
Shooting Stars: Plays and Players 1975–83
Marlene Dietrich
Oscar Wilde
Sybil Thorndike: A Life in the Theatre
Gertrude Lawrence: A Bright Particular Star
Gladys Cooper
Tales from the Hollywood Raj:
The British in California
Katharine Hepburn
The Other Side of the Moon:
The Life of David Niven
Spread a Little Happiness:
A History of the British Stage Musical
Elizabeth Taylor
James Mason: Odd Man Out

AS EDITOR:

The Noël Coward Diaries (with Graham Payn)
Noël Coward and his Friends
(with Graham Payn and Cole Lesley)
Theatre 71, 72, 73, 74
The Theatre Addict's Archive
Punch at the Theatre
The Stephen Sondheim Songbook
The Theatregoer's Quiz Book
Bull's Eyes: The Memoirs of Peter Bull
Noël and Gertie: A Stage Anthology
Out in the Midday Sun:
The Paintings of Noël Coward

OUR THEATRES IN THE EIGHTIES

SHERIDAN MORLEY

Illustrations by William Hewison

A John Curtis Book
Hodder & Stoughton
LONDON SYDNEY AUCKLAND TORONTO

FOR RUTH

British Library Cataloguing in Publication Data
Morley, Sheridan, *1941*–
Our theatres in the eighties.
1. Great Britain. Theatre, history
I. Title
792.0941

ISBN 0-340-50979-1

Preface copyright © 1990 Sheridan Morley
Copyright © 1980–89 Punch Publications
Copyright © 1989 *International Herald Tribune* and
© 1989 the *Sunday Telegraph*

Illustrations copyright © 1980–89 Punch Publications
Reproduced by permission of *Punch*

First published in Great Britain 1990

All rights reserved. No part of this publication may be reproduced or transmitted in any form or by any means, electronic or mechanical, including photocopying, recording, or any information storage and retrieval system, without either prior permission in writing from the publisher or a licence permitting restricted copying. In the United Kingdom such licences are issued by the Copyright Licensing Agency, 33–34 Alfred Place, London WC1E 7DP.

The right of Sheridan Morley to be identified as the author of this work has been asserted by him in accordance with the Copyright, Designs and Patents Act 1988.

Published by Hodder and Stoughton,
a division of Hodder and Stoughton Ltd,
Mill Road, Dunton Green, Sevenoaks, Kent TN13 2YA
Editorial Office: 47 Bedford Square, London WC1B 3DP

Photoset by Rowland Phototypesetting Ltd,
Bury St Edmunds, Suffolk

Printed in Great Britain by St Edmundsbury Press Ltd,
Bury St Edmunds, Suffolk

Contents

Preface	1
1980	9
1981	25
1982	39
1983	51
1984	77
1985	97
1986	123
1987	153
1988	177
1989	209
Index	235

Preface

IN THE PREFACE to the first volume of his collected theatrical criticism, *Our Theatres in the Nineties*, Bernard Shaw looked back briefly at some of the issues which had been troubling him as a theatre critic in the immediate past. These were, in no particular order, the ongoing absence of a National Theatre, the tendency of certain star actors (unnamed, but almost certainly Irving, a perpetual target of GBS at this time) to overlay productions with the self-importance of their own personalities, and the vain search for significant new drama with some sort of social message amidst the dross and gloss of the West End.

We seem, a hundred years on, to have solved the problem of the National Theatre by at least building one: star actors may be back in the ascendent, though they are not yet prepared (as Irving was) to dismiss the services of a director altogether; and as for the search for new dramatists of consequence, the situation would seem to be much the same as ever.

The message would appear to be that the lot of a drama critic is never likely to be a happy one, so long as he (or all too seldom she) sees the job as having any direct influence on the state of theatre. But Shaw was the only one of us who ever really gave it up for anything better, and even he would in later life look back almost wistfully to the days when his opinions could at least guarantee him the attention of a seductive actress for a moment or two. The rest of us nowadays usually have to be content with an outraged letter from a subsidised theatre's press office, or the invitation to yet another doom-laden press conference announcing the closing of a studio stage or an entire Barbican because of further cuts in official aid. But we can at least be certain, as Shaw was, that the job is not a negligible one, and that from time to time a critic can be almost as useful as, if not a dramatist, then at the very least an odd combination of stage manager and advance-bookings expert. It was Jack Buchanan who once asked a local Midlands drama critic how well his new *Goodnight Vienna* musical would do in

Birmingham: 'About as well,' murmured the drama critic thoughtfully, 'as a musical called *Goodnight Birmingham* would do in Vienna.'

The decade that started theatrically enough with Mrs Mary Whitehouse trying to imprison or, at the very least, heavily fine Howard Brenton and the director of his *The Romans in Britain* for having Romans attempt to bugger Druids on the stage of the National Theatre no less, the decade that ended with the Royal Shakespeare Company in the face of a £3 million deficit having to announce an at least temporary closure of the two stages it had so proudly opened at the Barbican only seven years earlier, was perhaps not one of constant limelit celebration. But this was, nonetheless, the decade when we conquered the very heartland of the American musical on Broadway with a series of spectacular invasions from *Cats* all the way through to *Phantom of the Opera*, rather as though a team of American actors had set up home in Stratford-on-Avon and begun to monopolise the Shakespeare industry there. It was the decade when an Arts Minister in a Conservative Government (Richard Luce) finally began to accept that his administration should perhaps be paying rather more into theatre and the other performing arts across London and the entire nation than one small German town annually gives to its opera house.

It was the decade when principles of Thatcherite self-help led the Royal Shakespeare Company to seek the sponsorship of Royal Insurance, and when Jeffrey Archer's Playhouse Theatre awoke from years of use as a radio studio only to find itself promptly rechristened the MI Group Playhouse in recognition of a £½ million donation from a city insurance house. It was the decade of such virulently anti-City plays as Caryl Churchill's *Serious Money*, but also the decade when the theatre had to go more and more often to the City cap in hand for some sort of survival subsidy or sponsorship.

As 1990 dawned, the West End alone was facing a £300,000 increase in its rates charges, ticket prices for certain hit musicals had gone up to £25, while at least one major fringe theatre (the Royal Court Upstairs) had to close its doors for lack of financial support. At the other end of the commercial and artistic spectrum, more hit musicals were making more money at home and abroad than ever before, and, when Andrew Lloyd Webber decided that he wished to reclaim his Really Useful Group from the stock market on which he had floated it in 1986, the price placed on the value of the group and, therefore, on his own worth as a composer was just over £77 million.

As I write this it occurs to me that I am celebrating (though others may well not be) the start of my twenty-fifth year as a London drama critic: five of those years were spent on the *Tatler*, thirteen on *Punch* and eleven where I still am, at the *International Herald Tribune*. I should perhaps

PREFACE

explain, before you start to worry about the arithmetic, that there has been some overlapping within that time. But what, even after two decades in the reviewing business (for such it is: let no one kid you we are professors of drama), gives me the courage or even the right to publish a third collection of my theatrical notices?

First of all, perhaps, the fact that I have yet again managed to collect them. At a time when productions still disappear on the night they take the scenery and the posters down, it seems to me quite extraordinary that the British film industry, one which by its very nature gets preserved on videotape and celluloid all the time, has an entire institute devoted to its memories, while we in the theatre have little more than a rather academic museum in Covent Garden. Researching the first nights of the 1980s thus becomes, unless you are lucky enough to have access to Ian Herbert's invaluable fortnightly mailings of *London Theatre Record*, a matter of ransacking press cuttings in distant newspaper libraries, where they are often mis-filed or inadequately indexed. Over the years some of us have, indeed, tried to rectify the situation with hardback theatre annuals, usually coming to financial grief in either the third or fourth year of publication.

So there is, perhaps, something to be said for trying to turn the garbled messages I have scribbled to myself in the dark on the backs of theatre programmes (and when will some management be kind enough to supply a blank page opposite the cast list for just such a purpose, an invention I

We've had Writer's Theatre, Actor's Theatre, Director's Theatre. In 1986 we'll have Mechanical Scenery's Theatre. (All Timber)

3

would rate second only to that of the deaf-aid sound circuits among really useful theatrical breakthroughs?) into the occasional volume for the shelves, especially as precious few of my colleagues seem to get around to it these days, though in postwar years almost every London critic did an annual anthology.

But a collection like this can, in just over 100,000 words, make no claim to complete coverage of a decade. I reckon to write at least 1,000 words a week on London first nights, which means that what you have here is about one-fifth of the decade's theatregoing. It is also light on the first two years of the Eighties, because some reviews of mine from 1980–82 have already been republished elsewhere. But looking through these collected reviews, all drawn from *Punch* and the *International Herald Tribune*, it does immodestly seem to me that you do get some sort of an idea of what it has been like, in Kenneth Tynan's celebrated definition of our calling, to be in certain theatres on certain nights.

I would hope the recording of the events has always been accurate, but would make no such claim for the total reliability of the opinions, unless of course you happen to agree with them. No drama critic is ever right or wrong, and it is only around Broadway, with the ludicrous monopoly situation of the *New York Times*, that a review is taken as holy writ. Over here, in a vastly healthier press climate, there are perhaps a dozen of us writing for major daily or weekly papers about the British stage, and we do indeed form what would pass for most high court judges as a reasonable jury: the bias is perhaps still overly male and overly Oxbridge circa 1965, but the chances of total agreement on any show are remote. You will usually find among us as many opinions about a play as there are writers of those opinions, and our power to make or break a show is therefore mercifully almost non-existent on an individual basis. I say mercifully, because this allows each and every one of us to write precisely what we believe about a show without having to worry, as do our *New York Times* colleagues, about whether or not we are throwing people out of gainful employment or bringing about the total economic collapse of the theatre we are supposed to be reviewing.

When I started to write about plays and players, I was twenty-eight and deeply in love with both; I am now forty-eight and no less in love with them, which is not to say that both the theatre and I haven't changed in the meantime. There is still some magic around, and a great many mistakes; change does not bring total improvement or disintegration, it usually just brings change.

Certainly the habits of theatregoers are changing all the time: despite a cut-price ticket booth in Leicester Square originally aimed at the back-packing young, West End audiences continue to look older, more affluent and more foreign as the years go by. The native playgoer, the one with the

PREFACE

wife and the kids and the mortgage and nowhere much to put the car, let alone enough money left over to pay for the dinner and the babysitter after investing in tickets, is more inclined to fall back on his friendly local fringe or neighbourhood playhouse, be that at Leatherhead or Islington, Guildford or Shepherd's Bush, rather than risk the environmental nightmare of an evening in central London.

Equally, buildings such as the National and, for all its design faults, the Barbican have begun to realise the virtues of bookshops, art galleries, restaurants and theatres all under one roof, leaving one to wonder how long it can be before such huge central London playhouses, as for instance the Theatre Royal, Haymarket, currently open for only maybe three out of an average twenty-four hours, have to overcome the local licensing laws and turn themselves into all-day bars and restaurants in order to justify the ground rent.

As the decade progressed, more and more signs of joint ventures became apparent: subsidised companies would link up with commercial managements to arrange West End transfers of hit shows from the South Bank, while it was not unusual by the end of the 1980s to see the names of three producers in partnership over the title of even a two-character show.

Producers such as Michael Codron went into real estate, managing theatres as well as individual shows, while actors such as Kenneth Branagh, the late Sir Anthony Quayle and his successor at Compass, Tim Pigott-Smith, went into management at least partly in order to counteract what they saw as decades of an over-dominant directors' theatre. Branagh encouraged a trio of other star players, Dame Judi Dench, Derek Jacobi and Geraldine McEwan, to follow his lead in directing their fellow players, but those who saw something radically new in all of this perhaps need to be reminded of the actor-manager years of the 1930s and 1940s, when leading players of the calibre of Gielgud and Olivier would regularly form their own managements around the West End.

Shakespeare seemed to come not as single spies but in battalions: 1980 saw four *Hamlets* (among them Jonathan Pryce and Frances de la Tour) and three *Richard IIIs*, while 1988 gave us three Prosperos (among them Michael Bryant and John Wood) and four *Twelfth Nights*. Sir Peter Hall rendered up the National Theatre to Richard Eyre and David Aukin (the first successful director/producer duopoly in subsidised theatre, and one I would guess most likely to be copied elsewhere, not least at the RSC) and Trevor Nunn gave over the RSC to Terry Hands, who, attempting to pass a parcel that threatened all too often to explode in his face, had by the end of the decade managed to announce his own retirement, but, as yet, no successor willing to take up an increasingly poisoned chalice of impossible artistic management.

The Old Vic closed in 1981 with a reported deficit of £½ million, but reopened three years later with a magnificent facelift by the Canadian millionaire shopkeeper, Ed Mirvish, and a policy, under Jonathan Miller, of obscure classical revivals, which often put the better subsidised repertoire houses further up and downstream to intellectual shame. John Osborne memorably noted that all plays at the Royal Court seemed to be written by a man called Les and directed by a man called Ron. The Pope turned out to be a playwright in 1982, though not enough of one to keep *The Jeweller's Shop* running too long, and Alan Ayckbourn, undaunted by the fact that it took the National Theatre three months and £25,000 to build a river on stage for his *Way Upstream* (one which burst its banks so that 6,000 gallons of water poured downstage), finished the decade by writing a play largely set in a swimming-pool.

Thelma Holt almost single-handedly kept the notion of Peter Daubeny's World Theatre Seasons alive, Elizabeth Taylor brought to *The Little Foxes* all the animation traditionally associated with Madame Tussaud, and an obsession with the peculiarly English tradition of gay Cambridge traitors brought us Julian Mitchell's *Another Country*, Alan Bennett's *Single Spies* and, most under-rated of all, Robin Chapman's *One of Us*.

It was the decade when the giants started to leave us: Michael Redgrave, Ralph Richardson, Laurence Olivier, while Gielgud at eighty-six alone remains as a reminder of the most remarkable generation of classical players ever born to the British theatre. On a lighter note, the musical triumphs of Lloyd Webber and Boublil/Schonberg (as marketed worldwide by Cameron Mackintosh, who took *Les Misérables* alone into something like forty cities from Toronto to Tokyo) tended to mask such more localised achievements as that of Willy Russell, who in *Blood Brothers* gave us England's only true rival to *The Threepenny Opera*, and Howard Goodall, whose *The Hired Man* suggested a promise as yet unfulfilled.

Periodic panics about the exchange rate of sterling, or the habits of American tourists in staying at home during Libyan or other terrorist crises, caused the West End to remain in its usual states of euphoria or deep depression. On the suburban fringe, both the Bush and the Tricycle arose Phoenix-like from the flames of their own fires, while the Orange Tree in Richmond embarked on an elaborate expansion, proving that smaller need not always be better.

This book has, I fear, no moral, no message, not even a few hints for aspiring critics: it just explains what I have been doing with the last 1,500 nights of my life and why I'll be going back into the dark of the stalls for another decade or three.

It is also about time I paid some sort of tribute to my erstwhile colleague Bill Hewison, art editor of *Punch* for most of the years that I was its arts editor and for many before that; almost alone, he sustains the tradition of

PREFACE

theatre drawing done from the stalls rather than the photographs, and, if you are going to spend most of the evenings of your life sitting next to a man making lightning thumbnail sketches in the dark, I can think of no funnier or kinder or better companion. Maddeningly, these drawings usually manage to say more about an actor, a setting or a production than I can achieve in the thousand or so words around them.

Sheridan Morley

1980

NOT THE MOST WONDERFUL OF THEATRICAL YEARS, indeed one famous for its on-stage disasters, though in fact neither the O'Toole *Macbeth* (at the Vic) nor the Brenton *Romans in Britain* (at the National) were as bad as the critics said. Both were a great deal worse. Elsewhere, specifically in the West End, managers were looking so far backwards over their nostalgic shoulders as to be in imminent danger of breaking their necks: the year of Richard Rodgers's death

Peter O'Toole *as Macbeth*

brought us *Oklahoma!* and *Pal Joey* back, but it also brought us back Noël Coward (*Private Lives*), Mary Pickford and Lillian Gish (*The Biograph Girl*), Gilbert and Sullivan (*Hinge and Bracket*), Victorian melodrama (*The Streets of London*), Tom Lehrer (*Tom Foolery*), Terence Rattigan and Lillian Hellman at the National, and Charles Dickens at the Aldwych.

Indeed so desperate was the Society of West End Theatre to find a Best New Play worthy of award this year that they gave their prize to *Nicholas Nickleby*, which was neither new nor a play, though undoubtedly the best theatrical event of the year. Like Busby Berkeley's Hollywood in the Depression 1930s, Trevor Nunn's Royal Shakespeare Company was this year battling inflation and a slump with ever bigger and better productions – among them not only the eight-hour *Nickleby* extravaganza but a nine-hour John Barton *Greeks* (an epic unfairly already forgotten in the rush to honour *Nickleby*) and a double helping of Alan Howard as Shakespearian *Kings Richard II* and *III* at Stratford.

The National had, by contrast, a somewhat low-key year, unless you counted the Cutler–Whitehouse yapping over the *Romans*, which neatly sidetracked the issue into censorship when it should really have been about an appalling failure of management; that apart, its successes were in getting Peggy Ashcroft back on to the boards after a four-year absence in an eminently respectable revival of Hellman's *Watch on the Rhine* and in getting Michael Gambon up to starring status in John Dexter's superlative revival of *Galileo*, while its failures included a curious thermo-nuclear saga called *Thee and Me* and the baroque miscasting of Alec McCowen as the old schoolmaster in Rattigan's *Browning Version*. There was also a curious failure to recognise that Alan Ayckbourn's sprawling and very minor *Sisterly Feelings* comedies could only be justified in taking up a couple of nights a week of the Olivier space by the crudest box-office measurements, and here again there was a terrible absence of anything very new.

What we had, all over the British theatre, was a crisis in management: once you had listed Trevor Nunn at the RSC, Alan Strachan at Greenwich, Giles Havergal at Glasgow and Michael Elliott at Manchester, it was actually very hard to think of any other subsidised theatre in Britain that was being run as well as it could or should have been, and non-subsidised theatres were by their very natures not being run at all, they were merely being leased out much after the fashion of rooms in a seaside boarding-house, over-expensively and often for short stays only.

A number of good theatrical managements came to avoidable ends: Bill Bryden left the Cottesloe, where he had given the National its only really sustained run of success since the new building opened, Peter Gill left the Riverside, and the Lyric, Hammersmith, had (until December's arrival of Peter James from Sheffield) sorely lacked a visible and flamboyant administrator. In

1980

building terms we appeared to have lost the Astoria for ever as a theatre, but the May Fair, after nine months in the dark, made a spectacular return to life at the end of the year with Bertice Reading in concert and looked set to stay in business as a commercial theatre once again.

Perhaps the most important development of a financially difficult and (for shows) disastrous year was the belated realisation by commercial managements that, instead of fighting each other for customers, they would do better to band together against such common enemies as falling tourism, scandalous VAT charges, an increasingly sordid West End environment and an over-strong pound. Thus, and only ten years after it was first mooted, we at last had the cut-price ticket booth in Leicester Square and some indication that the commercial theatre was prepared to fight for a life it appeared to have already almost abandoned.

Elsewhere it was a year of isolated but powerful delights: Sondheim's *Sweeney Todd* at Drury Lane was shamefully mistreated by most critics and therefore ignored by theatregoers, but would eventually emerge as one of the most important and influential musicals of the century; Ralph Richardson, that greatest of all National treasures, was back in the West End (at the Comedy) in David Storey's fragile but poetic *Early Days*; Glenda Jackson (as *Rose*) and Frances de la Tour (as the crippled musician in *Duet For One*) and Tom Courtenay and Freddie Jones (in Ronald Harwood's Wolfit play *The Dresser*) all gave the kind of performances that would be remembered long after the year was over.

Three untimely deaths took from us the actress Rachel Roberts, the critic Kenneth Tynan and the playwright David Mercer; in those terms it was an unusually sad year, but the general air of doom and despondency in which it started proved to be (if only a little) premature. The most that could be said about the London theatre in 1980 was that it survived largely intact, but that was no mean achievement.

Georgia on my Mind

Any week which brings new comedies by Michael Frayn and Peter Nichols, plus, even in these troubled times, a complete Soviet theatre company from Georgia, to say nothing of a kind of one-man promenade concert devoted to Sir Thomas Beecham and (venturing northwards) a stunning revival of *Oklahoma!* has to indicate that maybe the British theatre is not yet as terminal a case as many at the recent Drama Awards presentation were inclined to believe.

At the Round House the Rustaveli *Richard III* is quite simply a Georgian epic. Clearly this theatre company relates to Moscow in much the same way that the Abbey Theatre, Dublin, relates to London, which is to say hardly at all. Political objections (such as the opening night's mini-demonstration) are therefore largely irrelevant: Georgia appears to be a law unto itself, and nowhere is this better expressed than in Robert Sturua's vast, sprawling pageant of a production. Its star, Ramaz Chkhikvadze, appears to be the local Donald Wolfit: his is a matinee-idol Richard, only very faintly misshapen and inclined to head straight for the nearest spotlight and stay there while the rest of the company form respectful circles around his bravura turn. But Sturua has had some vastly good ideas, not least the use of Queen Margaret as prompter and stage manager, the permanent shadowing of Richard by an unusually sinister Richmond, and the final struggle between these two men literally draped in a torn map of Britain. It's a performance that Barnum, Bailey and Cecil B. de Mille might have considered unrestrained, but joky and electrifying and illuminating by turn and coming complete with a superlative score by Gia Kancheli; there's been nothing quite like it in our (or I suspect any other) theatre in my lifetime, and we owe the Georgians a considerable debt of fascination and gratitude.

Pieces of Atrium

Of the ten plays that make up the current cycle of *The Greeks* (Royal Shakespeare Company at the Aldwych) seven are by Euripides, one is Homer as adapted by John Barton, one is by Aeschylus and the tenth is an amalgam of Sophocles, Euripides and Aeschylus. Already, therefore, it should be apparent that what we have here is a kind of instant guide to classical drama, one cobbled together by Mr Barton himself and his translator Kenneth Cavander to provide a nine-hour theatrical epic. Such epics are not of course unknown to the RSC or to Barton: in 1964 they did *The Wars of the Roses*.

But there all such comparisons must end: where in the *Roses* we had a sustained narrative, here we have ten totally separate plays ranging in

1980

style and tone from magnificent sacrificial tragedy (*Iphigenia in Aulis*) to campy comedy of the old Giraudoux 'classics can be fun' school (*Helen*). Wisely the RSC chose to show the entire cycle to the critics on a single marathon day, and that is far and away the best arrangement for general audiences too. Seen across three separate evenings, the problems of the weaker plays would become all too apparent: seen together, they cease to have such individual failings and become part of one great rolling event.

And the event is all: for the actors, for Barton himself (and finally at the end of the first day for the audience too) the applause was to denote that we had all got through it together. There was something both moving and fascinating about starting out a day at ten in the morning watching a group of giggling Greek girls gathering at Aulis to watch the great ships depart for Troy and ending it at eleven at night with these same women, ravaged by seventeen years of sacrifice and war and bereavement and murder and rape and madness, being told by one of the Gods who have destroyed their lives that, all in all, the best idea is compromise.

On John Napier's bare, dust-bowl set, a company of forty work their way through the saga in the simplest possible terms: Barton and Cavander have gone for a prose style of stark simplicity to match both the setting and the acting. *The Greeks* is not a day of metaphor or of subtlety. Instead, everything is up front, laid out before you from Astyanax to Zeus like some appalling tapestry of blood and revenge. For Agamemnon, having butchered his own child, to tell his grieving wife as he sets off for Troy that he 'may be some time' is admittedly a little anti-climactic, but it is in keeping with a pageant which, by its very nature, has to lurch from idle gossip about the Gods to the equivalent of *Hamlet* Act V within a matter of minutes.

What we have here, then, is the cartoon-strip history of the classical world, one which can incorporate characters as diverse as the dizzy blonde Thetis (Annie Lambert) apologising to her son Achilles for having been so forgetful about his heel, and the massively tragic Clytemnestra (Janet Suzman), who, having killed Agamemnon (John Shrapnel) for what he did to their daughter, is then in turn butchered by her own children, Orestes and Electra, who have (in one of the rare production mistakes of the epic) been allowed to grow up into modern-dress urban guerrillas.

Such occasional errors of judgement arise from the same source as much of what is best about Barton's production: an utter determination never to bore or confuse or forget its audience. Gone forever are rows of chorus ladies chanting in white sheets; gone too are the unwieldy and stagey translations of the past. It is something of a surprise, even so, to discover about eight hours into the epic that Helen was never living in Troy at all, and that Iphigenia never got herself sacrificed either: the whole of the Trojan Wars have been some terrible black joke perpetrated by the Gods. But people have lived and died through them, some have even survived them, and that too is what *The Greeks* is all about. Like forty ancient mariners, the RSC company fix you with glittering eyes and proceed to tell you their terrible tales. But, thanks to Suzman and Shrapnel, to Billie Whitelaw, to Mike Gwilym and Lynn Dearth, and to a whole host of supporting players including Judy Buxton, Eliza Ward, Tony Church and Oliver Ford Davies (and to Nick Bicât's score), the parade passes by in fine fettle. True, its final sequence runs downhill so fast that even the cast seem breathless, but if you take my advice and see *The Greeks* at one sitting that will only appear as the inevitable anti-climax to the war itself.

Greenwich Mean Time

Arguably the greatest comedy written in the English language since *The Importance of Being Earnest* (which preceded it by thirty-five years), *Private Lives* is a technical exercise of immense difficulty for two superlative light comedians plus a couple of stooges. It contains the second most famous balcony scene in the whole of dramatic literature, but precious few actual jokes ('Women should be struck regularly, like gongs' is more of an aphorism and anyway now considered somewhat unfeminist) and almost no action of any kind. A couple of divorcees on second honeymoons meet accidentally at a hotel in the South of France, decide they prefer being married to each other rather than their new partners, and run away together to Paris. And that, across three entire acts, is more or less that.

When Noël Coward first sent the play to Gertrude Lawrence, for whom he'd written it as a kind of apology for not casting her in his *Bitter Sweet* on account of her voice not being good enough for its score, her wired reply was 'Nothing that can't be fixed'. 'The only thing to be fixed', replied Noël, 'will be your performance,' and from there they started rehearsals, watched over by Robert Montgomery and G. B. Stern in the villa Gertie had appropriately rented on Cap Ferrat.

It was the summer of 1930 and, when they first opened in London (opening also the Phoenix Theatre), one critic wrote that it was like watching 'buckets of filth being thrown around the stage'. But Aimee Semple McPherson (also at the first night, sitting next to Lawrence of Arabia) approved, and Lawrence added that he had closely examined the script and failed to find in it 'a single redundant syllable'.

Noël and Gertie only played it for twelve weeks in London and another twelve on Broadway, Coward's boredom threshold in performance being somewhat low; he never played Elyot again, she only played Amanda once, for a week in 1940 at a summer theatre on Cape Cod. So the whole 'Noël

1980

and Gertie' legend rests on twenty-four weeks and a scratchy gramophone record on which the great love scene is reduced to about three and a half minutes, mainly about the flatness of Norfolk and the potency of cheap music. But since their time scarcely a month has passed without *Private Lives* being staged somewhere in the world and usually fairly badly. The last major London revival was a decade ago, with Robert Stephens looking uneasy and his then wife Maggie Smith unaccountably doing impressions of Kenneth Williams.

Now, however, praise be, the Greenwich Theatre have come up with a winner, thanks largely to their casting of a lady called Maria Aitken, who, since the premature retirement of Kay Hammond and equally premature death of Kay Kendall, is the nearest our stage has ever come to that leggy, aristocratic jokiness which was Gertrude Lawrence's peculiarly evanescent stock in trade. Miss Aitken makes a perfectly ravishing Amanda and the miracle is that Michael Jayston, cast against type as Elyot, manages to keep up with her, largely by reminding us of the underlying

Private Lives Maria Aitken *as Amanda Prynne* and Michael Jayston *as Elyot Chase*

seriousness and sadness of a play about two people who find it impossible to live apart and equally impossible to live together.

The director at (and of) Greenwich, Alan Strachan, was involved in both the great Mermaid Theatre nostalgia songfests, *Cowardy Custard* and *Cole*, and this new production exudes a kind of 1930s confidence. True, it is a little anachronistic to have Elyot at the piano do a rendering of *These Foolish Things*, which was actually written some months after the play, but beyond that the period accuracy is well-nigh faultless and Ian Collier in the old Laurence Olivier role makes a splendidly blustering stooge, as does Jenny Quayle playing the unfortunate Sybil (so christened to allow Elyot to utter his immortal 'Don't quibble, Sybil'). It will be sad if this production does not find a central London home for the summer, not least because of Miss Aitken's rare ability to stand around like an elegant alcoholic lamp-post.

Rough Knight

Playwrights from Chekhov all the way through to Clifford Odets have succumbed to the temptation to write the one about the old actor nearing the end of his days in states ranging from nostalgia through alcoholism to penury. Reflections in a dressing-room mirror have always had this understandable Pirandellian fascination; if what the actor does for a living is by definition unreal, how real can the rest of his life hope to be?

Now, at the Queen's Theatre, we are asked to consider a specific case history. In his programme note the dramatist Ronald Harwood is eager, some might say rather too eager, to have us understand that though his new play *The Dresser* is partially about Sir Donald Wolfit (for whom Harwood spent five postwar years working as dresser) it is not wholly or solely about him. Nor, Mr Harwood hastens to add, should we assume that 'Her Ladyship' in the play bears any relationship to Lady Wolfit.

Yet a great deal of this play cuts closer than such absolute comfort in the programme might indicate; the fact that Harwood has collected here a vast range of backstage jokes (mostly concerning *King Lear*) and cobbled them together into a kind of Garrick Club benefit night does not detract from his searing insights into Wolfit and the nature of the actor-manager in decline.

In that sense, *The Dresser* is a tragedy, a long day's journey into would-be knight at the end of which we are left with a mixture of relief and sadness that the days of tacky Shakespearian provincial touring have long gone. The title character is immortally well-played by Tom Courtenay as a waspish, intermittently savage homosexual manservant all too well aware that his task is not just to dress this Lear but also to play his offstage Fool. The old actor, a no less impressive or important performance from

1980

Freddie Jones, is therefore the other half of this odd-couple relationship. Back from the brink of a nervous breakdown and heading rapidly for on and offstage death, 'Sir' (as he is known throughout the play) is admittedly a collage job. There are bits of Martin Harvey in there, and not a little of Bransby Williams and Robert Atkins as well.

The running joke is that we are in the midst of a 1943 air-raid; the Luftwaffe are thus providing the sound effects for this *King Lear*, and Herr Hitler has left Sir with a company comprised solely of 'old men, cripples and nancy boys' with which to carry the immortal words of the Bard out into the number three touring dates around England. It is not, however, made clear how much (if any) better Sir's company would have been in peacetime, and, although Harwood may have had (as he says) the intention of recreating the 'magnificent tradition' of such old tours, he has allowed his impressions of company characters to degenerate into novelettish glimpses of lovelorn spinster stage-managers or angry young rebels.

Actors will recognise a lot of truth in the two central characters, both of whom theatregoers of thirty and up could easily have encountered as late as 1960; but with the exception of Lockwood West (marvellous as the old 'play as cast' company man hauled in to give his Fool due to the unexplained but all too obvious police detention of Mr Davenport-Scott) the rest of the characters are mere caricatures sent on, like those in Sir's company, to 'keep your teeth in and serve the playwright'.

In the end *The Dresser* is a very schizoid play, hugely entertaining but reflecting only Harwood's own inability to decide whether his love or his hatred for the last generation of the great overactors should emerge strongest. Suitably enough, therefore, the performance is all: Courtenay and Jones are a stunningly good double act, so good that it is already impossible to imagine that any of the many actors doubtless already longing to get their hands on this play will ever be better. The idea of a *Lear* being acted both on-stage and off is also stunningly effective; it is in the trappings, in the play's willingness to incorporate a whole treasure trove of green room wit and wisdom, that some of the power of *The Dresser* is lost. Harwood seems to have been torn between saying something historically very interesting about the way our theatre has changed, and creating a lovable old wreck married not to 'Her Ladyship' (to whom he has declined marriage on the grounds that the prerequisite divorce from a first wife might injure his fading chances of a knighthood) but to his equally wrecked dresser. For all that, *The Dresser* remains the most quintessentially theatrical play we have had since Osborne's *Entertainer* fully twenty years ago.

Class Struggle

At a time when the West End theatre is starved of economic shows, when indeed the May Fair Theatre is actually closing because of a shortage of same, it is a gesture of eccentricity bordering on the loony for the Royal Shakespeare Company to stage Willy Russell's *Educating Rita* at their Warehouse in Covent Garden. For what we have here is an eminently commercial two-character comedy, better indeed than most comedies currently on offer in the West End, which has nothing at all to do with the RSC and still less to do with the experimental nature of the Warehouse. Moreover there is a Pavlovian critical reflex whereby a play opening at, say, the Fortune or the Ambassadors is treated totally differently from a show opening at the Warehouse, and had Mr Russell gone to either of the former homes I suspect reaction to his play would have been a great deal warmer.

True, *Educating Rita* owes a lot to *Butley* and a great deal more to *Pygmalion*; it concerns a jaded university lecturer (Mark Kingston) into

Educating Rita Mark Kingston *as Frank* and Julie Walters *as Rita*

whose study one morning swans an Open University pupil wanting nothing more nor less than a total literary education. He who has hitherto had to suppress a deep desire to throw pupils through windows suddenly finds himself with the perfect recipient for his words of wisdom; she (quirkily and twitchily and marvellously played by Julie Walters from the Victoria Wood tele-musicals) progresses from a state of unholy ignorance to one of such utter intellectual and social confidence that she finally has no need at all of her teacher.

What we have here, therefore, is both a comedy and a tragedy; Mr Russell (he of *John, Paul, George, Ringo . . . and Bert*) has some good jokes and, though he has borrowed his two main characters from earlier and better plays, he gets a lot of good fun and even some moments of real drama by throwing them together and watching them operate on each other. Mike Ockrent's production is swift and fluid, and in Rita's getting of wisdom there is something both hilarious and very touching. Her tutor, naturally enough, prefers her ignorant even if this does mean she approaches E. M. Forster with a thirteen-amp plug on account of his 'only connect'; she, on the other hand, cannot wait to put her little learning into action and the end result is an inevitable reversal of roles once we have been through the confrontation immortalised by first Shaw and then Lerner–Loewe as *I can do bloody well without you*. True, Mr Russell has yet to find his play an effective end, but for all that *Educating Rita* is a lot of fun.

Young Nick

There are a number of stunningly theatrical moments in the Royal Shakespeare Company's epic new nine-hour dramatisation of *Nicholas Nickleby* at the Aldwych, but none better than the final one: after all those loose ends have been interminably tied into one of Dickens's most sentimentally happy endings, the recently married young Nicholas strides down to the footlights and scoops up into his arms one of the destitute lads who have newly been freed by him from the dread Dotheboys Hall. This is not, as some of my critical colleagues would have you believe, merely the gesture of a man about to adopt some poor and unwanted orphan. There is a look of such inner rage on the face of Roger Rees (as Nicholas), and the child is held out to the audience with such defiance, that it is clear he is being offered up as a symbol of poverty and illness and corruption, and as a reminder that, when all is said and done, even at such length as here, there are no happy endings.

At which point we'd better go back to the beginning. This *Nickleby* project has been around the RSC for more than two years now: it first emerged partly out of a suggestion by Peter McEnery that Dickens was about due for stage treatment other than those of Lionel Bart and Emlyn

Williams, and partly out of an accidental discovery that Dickensian dramatisations are a regular feature of subsidised-company repertoires in the USSR. So if there, why not on home territory?

One reason is of course the sheer scale of the venture: *Nicholas Nickleby*, as dramatised by its cast and stitched together by David Edgar, requires a cast of fifty and nine hours to say nothing of a score (by Stephen Oliver) which would not have disgraced a David O. Selznick movie, and a set (by John Napier and Dermot Mayes) which has entailed the virtual rebuilding of the Aldwych proscenium.

If the question is do we actually need a stage *Nickleby*, the answer must, I believe, be yes; if the question is do we need one at quite this length, the answer gets a bit more uncertain. Since the 1940s movies of David Lean (and *Nickleby* must have been the only one that starred neither Alec Guinness nor John Mills) Dickens has been musicalised out of all existence; *Nickleby* itself has twice been plundered, once for a tele-musical called *Smike!* and on another occasion by the Sherrin–Brahms team, who limited themselves, as I recall, to two major sequences, Dotheboys Hall and the Crummles touring players. Both these sequences are, of course, in the first third of the book and there's no denying that by the break in the present production, roughly four hours in, there's a distinct feeling that we've had not just the best of it but virtually all there is worth remembering about the story. We've by then had Mr Squeers (marvellously leeringly played by Ben Kingsley) and we've had the old actor-manager Crummles (equally definitively intoned by Graham Crowden) leading us up to a brilliantly camp first-half finale in which the RSC disguised as the Crummles company solemnly perform the happy-ending version of *Romeo and Juliet*.

If you plan to take in only one part of *Nickleby*, therefore, it has got to be part one; part two, though much more densely packed with characters and sub-plots, is something of an anti-climax unless you believe, as the directors Trevor Nunn and John Caird clearly do, that the event is all and that you have to experience it wholesale, preferably in one day-long sitting. It is an understandable belief, particularly if you happen to be running a company of fifty eager character actors only about half a dozen of whom have had enough to do in part one; but it is here that the sheer intractability of much of the material begins to defeat everyone. Dickens was himself of course no stranger to theatre; not only did he effectively create on American recital tours the notion of the one-man show, he also himself witnessed pirated stage versions of the school scenes from *Nickleby*, which were being staged even before he'd completed the rest of the part-work novel. Had he wanted to make *Nickleby* a play rather than a novel he could very well have done so; what stopped him, by all accounts, was a realisation that themes of poverty and injustice can only effectively be staged in the very narrowest frames of reference. Once you take the whole of London as your canvas, and a hundred and fifty of its citizens as your characters, realistically the stage cannot be expected to cope.

Still, anyone who has recently witnessed *The Greeks* or the closing minutes of *Once in a Lifetime* will tell you that the RSC is currently in a Cecil B. de Mille frame of mind, and it has led here to a patchwork tapestry offering (at best) performances like that of Edward Petherbridge as the gently decaying Newman Noggs and (at worst) sequences which appear to have been staged exclusively for an RSC Christmas staff treat. There is a lot of self-indulgent pantomime performing going on here, but there is also a lot that is as powerful and valuable as the performance of John Woodvine playing the evil Ralph Nickleby. His suicide, and the quieter yet infinitely sadder departure of Crummles and his diminished troupe for America, are pictures which will linger like those of Boz. With maybe ninety minutes shaved off its overall running time and some minor performances toned down, *Nickleby* as a whole might be equally triumphant; as it is, we are left to reflect that outside of Russia the RSC must be the only theatrical company capable of such a massive endeavour as this.

Fiasco Time

Now that at least some of the dust has settled around the O'Toole *Macbeth* (at the Old Vic, and arguably the greatest Shakespearian catastrophe since the burning of the Globe) we may perhaps be allowed to ask ourselves certain questions not only about how the whole thing was allowed to happen in the first place but also about what it portends for the by no means assured future of the Vic itself.

The problem here is not just that a 1960s film star eager to clamber back into a theatrical lifeboat has been allowed to take the entire ship's crew down with him, though it is in this context perhaps worth noting that when Burton found himself similarly eager to get back to the American stage this summer he went back not in the long-threatened *King Lear* but instead in the musical *Camelot* as a way of getting himself back into condition. The real problem here is one of management.

Since Peter Hall pulled his National Theatre team out of the Vic in 1975 virtually nothing of any real value has happened there; occasional touring and children's companies have been allowed to come and go, Prospect made it a temporary home where they did an adequate Jacobi *Hamlet* and an appalling McCowen *Antony and Cleopatra*, and in casting around for a resident director at the beginning of this year the board came up with Timothy West, an interesting and valuable character actor with remarkably little experience of administration or regular theatrical production. In this context the Vic board decision (and I sometimes think our theatre will die not of VAT or falling tourism or the strengthened pound, but quite simply of theatre boards) made about as much sense as giving Chichester to Keith Michell, though that too, may I remind you, was once done by a board.

What has emerged from the Waterloo Road these last few days has been the realisation that the Vic cannot be saved by a 1960s film star who comes on stage, arch as the admiralty, to convey to us a state of deep trance-like inadequacy bathed in a glow of amber lighting of the kind MGM used to accord Esther Williams underwater. Nor can it be saved by an administrator who believes that, having taken money over the counter on O'Toole's name and then attacked O'Toole's work, he is not then morally obliged to hand back all the money. Nor can it be saved by an administration who believe that pre-publicity and pre-selling are any substitute for a coherent policy of casting and production. Even Harry Lauder, to whose memory Mr O'Toole made constant rehearsal allusion, could have run the Vic better than that.

There are directors around (indeed one of them, Frank Dunlop, is working rather less than five hundred yards from the stage door) with the vision and the energy to save the Vic by imposing upon it some sort of coherent reason for continued existence. If none can be found with sufficient experience, then it might be as well to turn the Vic over to a permanent theatre museum where future generations could perhaps learn from the mistakes of the past. One of which, of course, is this production.

Dublin Troubles

The surprising thing about *Juno and the Paycock* (now in a masterly revival by Trevor Nunn for the Royal Shakespeare Company at the Aldwych in celebration of the O'Casey centenary) is how little it turns out to be about its apparent theme. Set in 1922 in the two-room tenement home in Dublin of Juno Boyle and her 'Captain Jack', the strutting pub-peacock husband of the title, it was described by O'Casey himself as 'a play about the calamitous Civil War in Ireland, when brother went to war with brother over a few insignificant words in a Treaty with England'.

And so, in its final moments, this is indeed a play about the original Irish troubles. But only then. For two preceding acts we have, in fact, been treated to an altogether different play, a comedy of Irish manners centred around the 'Paycock' himself, marvellously comically played by Norman Rodway. In his refusal to go to work, in his sudden twinges of mythical leg pains, in his phony blustering and makeshift memoirs, in his love-hate relationship with his treacherous neighbour Joxer (played in a fine double-act with Rodway by John Rogan) are the beginnings of every

1980

twentieth-century British television success from *Coronation Street* to *George and Mildred*.

It was in the nature of O'Casey's brilliance to accept that neither the Abbey in Dublin nor audiences elsewhere would in 1924 accept a play of unremitting gloom about the then still current Troubles. Better to give them a comedy, '*Macbeth* as viewed from the Porter's lodge', and then gradually turn it back on the customers so that the laughs would freeze on their lips. And still, half a century later, those laughs freeze.

It is only at the end of the second act that it happens: a sudden shadow of a gunman in the doorway, and Juno's already twitching son is led away to certain death. Now we learn why he has spent the first half of the play in a state of shock: not just to be the butt of his father's scorn, but because he knows he has betrayed a rebel and is to die. And that is just the beginning of the end. The legacy which Juno and the Paycock have been counting on to pay for their furniture turns out to be a mirage; their daughter's boyfriend then leaves her both pregnant and unmarriageable even to the one man (finely played by Frank Grimes) who does truly love her.

When, therefore, the Paycock gets back from the pub with Joxer in the play's chilling final scene, it is to a total unawareness that his son has been killed, while his daughter and wife have left him in search of a home for the new and illegitimate child. He is now, and for ever, with Joxer: their comedy has become a tragedy of death and destruction, and they still don't know it.

In an immensely distinguished cast (Marie Kean turns up momentarily as the grieving neighbour) Judi Dench plays Juno with infinite courage; surrounded by the genuine Irish, her accent occasionally wavers and she still lacks the earth-mother quality that perhaps wrongly we have come to expect of a true Juno. But this is a performance that will mature and grow, and, when it has, we shall have at the Aldwych one of the finest O'Casey revivals I have ever seen.

1981

A YEAR NOT OF MASSIVE ECONOMIC DESPAIR but of persistent gloom and a curious lack of excitement or enthusiasm; after the Arts Council cuts of last winter, perhaps the greatest theatrical achievement was sheer survival, and in that context it's good to note that the major casualties were fewer than forecast. True, we lost the Old Vic as a permanent classical house and further out towards the fringe the Round House, Riverside and the Mermaid all lost a lot of ground in straitened circumstances. In the West End, too, many houses were too dark for too long, but what seemed to be most lacking was any real sense of a coherent policy for the 1980s.

Certain theatres still seemed to have a definable idea of what they were doing and where they were going: David Aukin at Hampstead and the management of the Bush were, for example, both still managing on minimal budgets to run playhouses where there was a distinct style. Equally, the RSC was still rolling superlatively along tracks laid down twenty years earlier by Peter Hall, while ironically it was the failure to build just another set of such tracks that was besetting the National under Hall. And not only the National; what, now, was the purpose or policy of the Royal Court? Or of the Lyric, Hammersmith? Or of the Young Vic? All these and more were forced economically to succumb to a random hit-and-run or flop-and-fail policy.

Outside London, larger theatres from Chichester north to Nottingham and Leicester seemed to find some sort of salvation in a lot of big old musicals often complete with big old stars, while the good news from inner London was the turning of the Fortune into a home for the best of the Fringe; meanwhile precious few other central London managements wanted to risk their investors' money on any but the very safest of bets; like publishers, impresarios were running for cover at the first breath of cold air.

For all the noble noises sounded by its organisers, the West End was still a wasteland of crumbling theatres, surly box-office managers, overpriced bars and impossible parking. It took Broadway more than a decade to realise that its only hope of salvation was a deal with the City of New York on matters environmental and social as well as economic and theatrical; it was apparently going to take London theatre managers even longer to do a sensible deal with their proprietors (who should bear at least half the show risk), the GLC and the Metropolitan Police.

So much for what was wrong with 1981 in the theatre; what was right with it included the first major Irish play since O'Casey (Brian Friel's *Translations*) and a couple of smashing comedies, Nell Dunn's female Turkish Bath chatterama (*Steaming*) and Jack Rosenthal's backstage *Smash*, which for reasons still unclear never got further in than Richmond.

From awards announced by December it was clear that Mark Medoff's deaf-liberation *Children of a Lesser God* was set to scoop the pool, though (like *The Miracle Worker*) more for its cause than its actual writing. In sheer performance terms I could not think of a better production all year than Michael Blakemore's revival of *All My Sons*, though it was run a very close second by Harold Pinter's production of Simon Gray's English-With-Tears school play *Quartermaine's Terms*. What was especially remarkable on both these stages (the Albery and the Queen's) was that the level of company playing achieved with a group of actors who met only in rehearsal a month before opening was actually much higher than anything achieved this year by either of our major permanent companies.

1981

On the musical front *Cats* was a clear winner, and indeed the first homegrown musical we could send to Broadway with a feeling of pride rather than deep embarrassment; Michael Crawford proved himself the best three-ring-circus in town as *Barnum*, but London curiously rejected one of the best Broadway scores in years, perhaps because *The Best Little Whorehouse in Texas* was a less than ideal title for the Drury Lane billboards.

Two of the best individual performances of the year undoubtedly came from Daniel Massey in the National's *Man and Superman* and Dorothy Tutin in the Greenwich *Deep Blue Sea*, though had Edna O'Brien's *Virginia* been less of a literary-lunch monologue and more of a play then Maggie Smith would have been in that league too. John Wells as Denis Thatcher turned in an excellent topical cabaret of the old *That Was The Week* tradition, though I reckon the best comedy performance in town was that of Simon Callow as the unbelievably randy Beefy in Donleavy's superb *Beastly Beatitudes of Balthazar B*.

Disappointments of the year included Ustinov's lacklustre embassy comedy *Overheard* and the failure of *The Accrington Pals* to make it beyond the Warehouse. Appalling mistakes of the year included Richard Huggett's belief that he could play Evelyn Waugh and Emile Littler's that he could fill the Palace with Colin Welland's old school play. I am still undecided whether *The Sound of Music* or *Childe Byron* or *Her Royal Highness?* was actually the most mind-bendingly awful evening I'd had in a theatre all year, though I firmly believe that all three may well have been contenders not only for Worst of the Year but also for Worst of the Decade.

On the brighter side, 1981 was also the year of Manchester's *Duchess of Malfi*, Brighton's *Brothers Karamazov*, C. P. Taylor's haunting Nazi musical *Good* and, at the Court, a lyrical Irish *Seagull* as well as (at the National) John Dexter's superb *Shoemaker's Holiday*. All in all, a fair old mix.

Altered Egos

Not since the mid-1940s, when Mary Chase first produced her invisible rabbit out of the Broadway hat in *Harvey*, has there been the invention of a stage device quite so neat as that provided by Peter Nichols for his new *Passion Play*, now in an agile RSC production by Mike Ockrent at the Aldwych. The device is quite simply that of the alter ego: both main characters have by intermission appeared on stage in duplicate, so that while James and Eleanor are man and wife, visible to each other and neighbours, Jim and Nell are their consciences, inner souls and confidants, visible only to themselves and of course to us. Two characters, four actors.

So far so splendid, especially when you consider that the RSC has for Mr Nichols wheeled in a massively impressive guest-star quartet consisting of Billie Whitelaw, Eileen Atkins, Benjamin Whitrow and Anton Rodgers, the first two playing Eleanor and the second two playing James in their public and private incarnations.

The trouble, however, and this seems to have gone unnoticed in an elsewhere generally ecstatic press, is that, although he has found himself a superlative stage device, Mr Nichols doesn't seem to have found himself anywhere much to put it. *Passion Play* is a depressingly soap-operatic account of a marriage on the rocks, desperately lacking the humour and the nostalgic insights of his earlier plays and oddly lacking, too, in any real developments of either plot or character.

James is a restorer of and dealer in paintings; Eleanor sings in the choir at the Albert Hall, thereby allowing James to start an illicit affair with the mistress of a deceased buddy while listening to radio broadcasts in order to ascertain the precise time of his wife's return home.

There's also a vindictive widow (Priscilla Morgan) who keeps Eleanor informed of James's infidelities, plus the aforementioned mistress (Louise Jameson), the two splendid alter egos, and a number of extras whom the RSC, unlike any West End management, has been able to provide as party guests, restaurant diners, figures in one of Eleanor's nightmares and generally to fill out Patrick Robertson's huge and elegant setting, which would appear to be representing a town house in Blackheath roughly the dimensions of Windsor Castle.

As if exhausted by his invention of the doppelgangers (whom I long to see in a stronger play) Mr Nichols has fallen back on the hoariest of plot devices: the wife only discovers that the mistress is still having an affair with her husband when she mentions his visit to Switzerland and the mistress lets slip the word Zurich. The wife then says, 'But I never mentioned Zurich,' for all the world like an inspector in the last reel of a British B picture of the 1940s.

Passion Play much resembles Pinter's recent *Betrayal* in that a stage device (there it was to begin at the end and work back to the beginning) is allowed to take the place of any real depth of feeling or personality; though Nichols writes passionate speeches about the death of marriage and the birth of lust, they fall interchangeably from lips it is very hard to care about. Thus we have a very clever but at heart curiously arid attempt to deal with the destructive powers of sex and marriage set against a lapsed-Christian background (she sings the Matthew Passion, he restores religious paintings) which ends up in lines like 'You're overlooking the fact that I love this man', lines that would not sound out of place in *Crossroads* if only anybody there could remember them.

But Whitelaw-Atkins and Whitrow-Rodgers work so well together as aspects of the same two people that one ends up hoping they will abandon the increasingly turgid mechanics of a will-they-won't-they-stay-together plot and just settle for being a couple of marvellous double acts in search of a play.

She Woolf?

Before writing *Virginia* (Theatre Royal, Haymarket) Edna O'Brien, we are told, threw herself to the Woolfs and spent several months 'immersed' in the writings of the blessed Virginia. The result of such immersion is much what you'd expect: a distinctly soggy play apparently written underwater and with a somewhat blurred vision of the subject. As an evening in the theatre, *Virginia* is saved by a remarkable and massive star turn from Maggie Smith, who has recognised and rightly received acclaim for one of the great modern opportunities given to an actress. She never leaves the stage, seldom draws breath, constantly commanding and galvanising attention in what is clearly not only a homecoming but also soon to be an award-winning performance after her five years in Stratford, Ontario.

The trouble is, though, that we have here a solo show rather than a play: true, there are two other actors (Nicholas Pennell doubling Virginia's father and husband, and Patricia Conolly doing a somewhat bossy Vita Sackville-West), but they are at best shadows, often left standing upstage with their backs to us, decorating a set by Philip Silver, who seems to have reached the eccentric conclusion that Virginia spent much of her life living in an otherwise deserted Japanese restaurant.

It is, therefore, as though we are at some form of literary lunch where Virginia Woolf has been asked to address us for a couple of hours on the subject of her life and Bloomsbury times; there is no real drama here, no confrontation, no development. Instead, a Sunday-supplement canter through the known facts of her life which takes for granted that we know most of them anyway. Thus, at the outset, the sound of rushing water is presumably meant to convey to us an instant image of Virginia sinking gently, pockets stone-filled, into the River Ouse. The trouble is, of course, that theatregoers unacquainted with her tragic end might simply assume that she had left a tap running somewhere, and Miss O'Brien's particular brand of precious, hothouse intensity makes one long for that celebrated Alan Bennett parody, the one about him being distantly related to the Woolfs through some Alsatian cousins and therefore meeting the great lady herself, hot and sweaty from a hard day's reading in the London Library and proud holder of the *Evening Standard* award for the Tallest Woman Writer of 1927.

There is a terrible kind of reverence at work in Robin Phillips's static production, a coy and cloying adoration of Virginia which is only rescued by occasional moments of acid having more to do with Miss Smith's delivery than Miss O'Brien's remarkably dormant critical faculties. To hear Virginia deliver a line like, 'I had known there were buggers in Plato's Greece but it never occurred to me there could be buggers in our drawing room at 46 Gordon Square,' is to realise how much better this play would have been if written with a little more humour and a little less unquestioning adoration. There are also strong indications that Miss O'Brien has got the character of Vita wrong in several crucial respects; doubtless she would argue that she is not in the documentary business. My regret is that she's not really in the playwriting business either. The result is a fey glimpse of Virginia through a glass darkly.

Possum Power

Andrew Lloyd Webber's *Cats* (at the New London) is a vivid and marvellous gesture of transatlantic defiance; for years we have been told by Broadway that, though we might have our Royal Shakespeare and our National, the one thing the London theatre lacked was an ability to do an all-dancing show. Now, and not before time, comes the answer; like Bob Fosse's *Dancin'*, this is a choreographer's benefit, and not even a bomb scare could silence the cheering that rang through the auditorium on opening night.

True, this production leaves nothing to chance; customers taking their seats in at least half the stalls are, during the overture, transported in those seats on a circular conveyor belt around the set in pure Disneyland fashion so that the mound of dustbin rubbish which threatened to obscure all other views suddenly becomes the backdrop for the dance festival that is to follow. *Cats* has no plot, no book, no storyline; it is simply an arrangement of twenty of T. S. Eliot's *Old Possum* poems for dancers and orchestra, a revolutionary dance drama which, though occasionally both arch and twee, is vastly more often breathtaking in its confidence and ambition.

1981

As cat-dancers poured through the auditorium, stroking the napes of unsuspecting necks and arching their backs for the next showstopper, it became clear that neither Lloyd Webber nor his director Trevor Nunn had attempted more than a celebration of Eliot's original verses; yet within those limits they have created a world total and unique, a world in which Gus the Theatre Cat can recall lost years at the Lyceum, Macavity can be not there and Mr Mistoffoles can bring back old Deuteronomy from behind a magic scarf. Number after number tears the place apart: Wayne Sleep doing the Jellicle Ball, Paul Nicholas as a rock-star Rum Tum Tugger, Elaine Paige doing the haunting, repetitive *Memory* and Ken Wells as Skimbleshanks form the starriest all-singing all-dancing team in town, but in the end *Cats* is the utter and total triumph of one single talent. Not Mr Lloyd Webber, who has already written many better scores, nor yet Trevor Nunn, whose direction is to say the least unobtrusive; but for Gillian Lynne as choreographer. *Cats* is a show which not only brings the New London to full and proper life for the first time in its eight-year history but also, and again for the first time, proves that Britain can now muster thirty show dancers as talented, versatile and energetic as any team ever fielded on Broadway or in Hollywood. And all that while remaining entirely faithful to the weird mix of menace, melancholy and mayhem that exists in the original poems. *Cats* is a total and utter feline delight; it will doubtless lead more than nine other lives in more than nine other cities, but if the New London needs a new show much before 1985 I shall be more than a little surprised. Smash hits don't come more smash than this one.

On the Map

We are in Donegal, the town of Baile Beag known to the English as Ballybeg; it is 1833, and a party of initially friendly redcoats has come over to chart the countryside and anglicise the local place names. Ireland is to be conquered not by the sword but by the map; there is to be a process of 'erosion', whereby English will replace Gaelic first as a language and second as a way of life. So starts Brian Friel's new play *Translations* (at the Hampstead Theatre), arguably the most important drama to have come out of Ireland both theatrically and historically since the death of O'Casey, and one which deals not only with the roots of the present conflict but also with the cornerstones of the Irish character. For we are not just anywhere in the village; we are in a hedge school, one of those secret corners which as early as the beginning of the nineteenth century had already begun to harbour those who objected to the banning by the English of Catholic education.

Presiding over the occasional classes there, in a massively welcome return to the stage, is Ian Bannen as the drunken old pedant who is better in Latin or Greek or Gaelic than he is in English, and whose pupils are similarly uninclined to learn the language of the map-making redcoats. Already, therefore, we have a problem of interpretation and non-communication, though at first it seems no matter. A local girl who speaks no English falls in love with an English soldier who speaks no Gaelic; in an infinitely touching love scene they communicate only through the alternate place-names of the surrounding district, she speaking the originals while he intones the translations of the title.

But then, abruptly and inexplicably, the soldier disappears and as the play ends his captain is threatening to lay waste all the surrounding fields until he is found; within a matter of days, for the play takes place over less than a week, a group of harmless map-readers has become an invading army willing to devastate the fields that are their owners' only means of support. What began as a John Ford comedy of Irish misunderstanding has become a tragedy of epic proportions, one which is to last a hundred and fifty years and bring us up to the present time. But the importance of Friel's play does not just lie in its awful topicality; what matters here is that he has taken the old Abbey stereotypes, the drunken schoolmaster and his Joxer friend and the young lovers of folk comedy, and created for them a tapestry altogether new and chilling. The result is an ordnance survey of Irish humanity in which the present is shaped by the past and the map-maker becomes map-destroyer; Donald McWhinnie's production and the cast of ten led by Stephen Rea who join Bannen make this the most haunting and powerful new play of the year.

Ring Master

When the curtain fell on the first night of *Barnum* (at the London Palladium) Michael Crawford was treated to an eight-minute standing ovation, the longest I have ever heard given to an actor in this country and one which so moved a leader-writer on the *Daily Mail* that the following morning readers of that paper were solemnly informed in an editorial that, if more people in this great country of ours could be more like Mr Crawford, an end to our present little local economic and social difficulties could be arranged.

The idea of a nation led by song-and-dance men or women does admittedly have certain charms; America has settled for Ronald Reagan, when they could have had Ray Bolger, but over here a tap-dancing premier hoofing it down Whitehall to unveil statues to Walter Crisham and Jack Buchanan before executing a swift buck and wing on the tarmac at Heathrow en route to a conference choreographed by Gillian Lynne might well succeed where all else and Mrs Thatcher have failed.

What the *Mail* writer curiously missed, however, is a further analogy:

like politics itself, *Barnum* is a massive, only more successful, confidence trick and at this point it becomes necessary to separate the very genuine achievement of Mr Crawford from the somewhat phonier but still dazzling achievement of the show.

After six months in a circus school in New York, he has conquered the (fairly) high wire, mastered a certain amount of juggling and found the courage to slide down a rope anchored some fifty feet above stage and stalls; for an actor with a known affection for stunting (notably in the *Some Mothers* TV series) this is still a remarkable conquest, and what makes Crawford considerably more fascinating in the role than was Jim Dale on Broadway is that he retains the very real possibility of failure. Every moment of the show therefore becomes a cliff-hanger; whether intentionally or not, he gives the constant impression that his entire circus may be about to fall apart at the seams of the big top and, when it doesn't, the mixture of relief and exultation that spreads first across his face, then

Barnum Michael Crawford *as Phineas T. Barnum*, William C. Witter *as Ringmaster* and Deborah Grant *as Charity Barnum*

across the stage and finally out into the auditorium becomes a wave of sheer theatricality the like of which you will find nowhere else in town or country.

Where Jim Dale's Broadway *Barnum* is a ringmaster in constant command, Crawford's is more like a circus-struck teenager who has suddenly been given the uniform and told to try it for size. The fact that both these interpretations suit the show equally well may suggest that the guy ropes supporting the structure of *Barnum* are a little loose, and indeed they are. Though there still are indications in the score (notably in the second-half number *Black and White*, one which will, I suspect, be largely incomprehensible to anyone without a working knowledge of Barnum's desire to be a city planner) that the musical was originally meant to be a more faithful reflection of the man's infinitely complex and often contradictory life, most of this has now been sacrificed to the stunting. Biographical details are therefore now not so much sketchy as invisible, and we are left with what is effectively a three-hour finale incorporating some smashing big-band numbers, some brilliant solo stunts from Crawford and the rock-solid belief that everybody loves a circus parade.

To prove Barnum's contention that there was a sucker born every minute, and that people will watch anything just so long as you give them somewhere to watch it, the penultimate first-half closer is sung largely in Swedish and the midget Tom Thumb turns out to be about five foot ten.

But at a time when all too many people are starting to think that Bertram Mills must have been Hayley's father, *Barnum* does at least manage a celebration of the spirit of circus; though it misses chance after chance to tell us who Phineas Taylor Barnum really was, and though it declines any *Cabaret*-like attempt to define a theatrical form through its performers or its audience, and though in its journey from Broadway it has become somehow more muddled and fluffy, this is still a great sawdust singalong made unforgettable by the energy, tenacity and bravura of its central performance, one admirably supported by Deborah Grant as Mrs Barnum and by Cy Coleman's oom-pah-pah score.

Goodbye Dolly

There are going to be precious few members of the National Theatre audience not aware in advance of the outcome of Tom Stoppard's latest comedy *On The Razzle* (Lyttelton); it's the one about the two grocery clerks having a day out in the big city, and it was first written by John Oxenford in 1835 London as a one-acter called *A Day Well Spent*. A few years later Johann Nestroy turned it into a full-length Viennese comedy, but it first came to modern notice in 1938, when Thornton Wilder rewrote it for America as *The Merchant of Yonkers*; fifteen years later, for Wilder

1981

was not a man to waste much, he added a new central character and got another Broadway hit comedy called *The Matchmaker*. That in turn became *Hello Dolly!* and what we have now at the National is a return to the Nestroy in an admittedly somewhat faithless translation by Tom Stoppard.

It is then in a mood of *déjà revue* that the play needs to be approached and has indeed been staged; as if aware that the original vehicle was getting a little overcrowded and rusty, the director Peter Wood has had some razzle-dazzle production ideas, not the least of which is the casting of Felicity Kendal as one of the male clerks. There is no textual reason for this, nor indeed is there much of a reason why our most distinguished comic dramatist should have been spending his recent time cobbling some new jokes into a dog-eared plot; but in a remarkable triumph of energy and eccentric invention the old engine is cranked up again and made to run one more time.

On the Razzle Dinsdale Landen *as Zangler*, Michael Kitchen *as Melchior* and Felicity Kendal *as Christopher*

From the moment of Dinsdale Landen's first appearance as the master grocer, three-time winner of the Johann Strauss medal for duck-shooting but unable to separate his niece from his knees, at least phonetically, it is clear that we are already some way over the top. Mr Landen pitches his performance as a vaudeville turn somewhere halfway from Groucho to Chico Marx, and the rest of the company are left to follow his suit, a baroque affair which jingles his approach long before he actually camps into view. Abandoning, mercifully, the original local Viennese allusions Stoppard has come up with a wordplay of his usual daunting, dazzling, Scrabbled and scrambled brilliance. Some of the jokes, notably the one about Alpha and Omigod, might look better in a crossword but by the time, two hours later, that we've reached, 'He'll alter you before the dessert, no, no, I mean he'll desert you before the altar,' most lines of resistance have long since been worn down.

In that sense Stoppard's turn is about as outrageous as Landen's: 'I woke up this morning feeling like a new man so I went out and got one.' 'Personal servant, is he?' 'Yes, a bit,' is dialogue that doesn't leave a lot of room for comment, and *On The Razzle* has the precisely correct air of a bank holiday, one on which a hitherto fairly studious writer has suddenly been allowed his turn as a stand-up comic. 'One false move,' says Landen early in proceedings, which are eventually to involve a ladder, a sex-mad coachman and a maid who appears to have wandered in from Feydeau to clean up the rest of the jokes, 'and we could have a farce on our hands,' and that is of course exactly what we get. There's not much sense of Vienna, or the grocery trade, or escape from suburban routine, and without those elements it is true that the running jokes stop running somewhere around the middle of the third and last act. At that point I did start missing the songs a bit, and thinking about how brave it is of Mr Wood to try the running-waiter gags that Gower Champion made such magic in *Hello Dolly!* without having a choreographer, a score or any dancers, let alone Carol Channing on that legendary staircase. But if you want to see how it's possible to balance twenty-five people on nothing more than a dictionary and the realisation that with enough puddings on the table there's even a joke in just desserts, then this dazzling evening is the one to go for. National Christmas treats are coming around a little early this year.

Miller's Tale

One of the larger mysteries of the postwar London theatre has been its failure to come to terms with the greatness of Arthur Miller; the National has in fifteen years managed just one revival of *Death of a Salesman* and two of *The Crucible*, the RSC has not managed even that, and commercially we still await London premieres of *After the Fall* (1967) and everything Miller has written thereafter.

But now, to Wyndham's in a stunningly powerful production by Michael Blakemore, comes the first London revival in more than thirty years of the play that made Miller's name and established the guidelines of his work: *All My Sons* is about guilt and family and survival in small-town America, and in its central figure, Joe Keller, the guy that knowingly sold the cracked cylinder heads that sent twenty-one pilots and his own airman son to a flaming death, we have already the beginnings of Willy Loman. Joe too (played here by Colin Blakely in a performance of such controlled brilliance that even the armpits seem to sweat on cue) is out there working the territory on a smile and a shoeshine, and like *Death of a Salesman* this play too is *Our Town* rewritten in acid and poison and blood.

Doubtless Miller had a more lofty model than Thornton Wilder; the fallen tree that stands centre stage as a symbol of Joe's fallen son, the conscious use of family patterns established by O'Neill many years earlier, the lengthy prose soliloquies all suggest a pattern of classical Greek tragedy compressed within the fences of the archetypal mid-Western backyard. Even the neatly arranged sets of neighbours, one couple living each side of Joe, are no more than onlookers, a chorus of ordinary people brought up against one extraordinary happening in the past that all for different reasons would like now to forget.

In that sense *All My Sons* is a play of deep cynicism about postwar America's ability to kill in the name of commerce, and about its belief in the overriding and all-forgiving importance of family loyalty. But Miller is on about something else here too; like Ibsen in both *The Wild Duck* (which this play much resembles) and *Enemy of the People*, he is on about a community within which one individual is holding up too many mirrors for the others, mirrors which eventually have to get smashed if that community is to survive. On that level, what separates *All My Sons* from *The Crucible* is that at curtain fall Joe has the grace, or perhaps just enough panic, to take his own life before others start doing that for him.

Yet the supreme achievement of Blakemore here has been to take an *ad hoc* company, few of whom have ever worked in the American theatre or with each other before, and mould them within a month's rehearsal period into a deeply convincing community; you may hear the occasional creaking of Miller's three-act, three-hour plotting, you may wonder whether the notion that all postwar affluence is bloodstained loot might not be a little simplistic, but you will not easily forget the look in Rosemary Harris's eyes as she finally comes to terms with the tragedy she has helped to write, nor the moment when Colin Blakely as her Joe finally and all too late accepts the parental responsibility of the title. This is the American postwar tragedy, and we shall not see it better played in the foreseeable future.

Out at Greenwich, Julian Mitchell's *Another Country* is a new play intelligently and intriguingly derived from some recent newspaper headlines. A year or so ago, during the Blunt spy scandal, journalists the world over leapt to the easy and understandable conclusion that Cambridge in the late 1920s and early 1930s was the breeding ground for upper-class homosexual treachery. Mr Mitchell takes a somewhat different view; he reckons that characters are formed, and even ideals selected, some time before arrival at undergraduate status and that therefore we should root around further back, into the British public schools that sent those men to Cambridge. Thus we have here a play about the schooldays of Guy Burgess; true, the school in the play is not specifically Eton, and the character is called Guy Bennett, but beyond that Mitchell has not made much attempt to disguise his subject matter. Like two other recent and similarly titled plays, Alan Bennett's *The Old Country* and Trevor Griffith's *Country*, this is a drama about the way that modern England comes ready-wrapped in old school ties. In allowing only one of his cast of ten (David William as a camp pacifist lecturer) to be over seventeen on stage, and in setting the entire piece within the school, Mitchell has taken some considerable theatrical risks, but Stuart Burge's fluent production meets that challenge very well, and the result is an enthralling school play which establishes that every single requirement for the trade of traitor (ambition, disillusion, cunning and a talent for hypocrisy) is amply matched by the requirements of a good British public school. Shades of the prison house are beginning to close fast around these golden lads of the Thirties, among whom Rupert Everett (as the Burgess character) and Joshua le Touzel (as the one modelled on John Cornford) are especially impressive.

1982

A YEAR WHICH SAW THE ARRIVAL of the Royal Shakespeare Company at the Barbican, major new plays from both Pinter and Stoppard and the storming of Broadway with *Plenty* and *Cats* and *Good* can hardly be described as a disastrous one for the British theatre in general. Yet 1982 also saw a moment in early October when no fewer than twelve (or just over one in three) main and central London playhouses were dark, with four of those actually for sale; it saw the permanent loss of Riverside Studios, which had operated continuous World Theatre seasons of a kind long since abandoned by the RSC, and it saw the demise of the Talk of the Town and the Astoria as cabaret theatres. It saw an American (James Nederlander) buy the Aldwych and a Canadian (Ed Mirvish) buy the Old Vic. It saw theatre budgets being slashed all over the country as Arts Council grants failed to keep pace with inflation, and it saw an increasingly desperate determination in the commercial West End to rely on old stars and even older musicals to keep theatres open. It was perhaps symbolic that the one really successful theatrical campaign fought this year had nothing to do with the present or future of the British theatre but was solely concerned with its past in the saving of the British Theatre Museum.

But annual theatrical reports are too often inclined to descend rapidly into non-specific accounts of doom and gloom, and it might make sense to start with a few facts. By my reckoning, in London alone, no less than 286 shows opened this year; some of those were in the repertoires of the two big culture palaces run by the National and the RSC, some were in the pubs and clubs, a few were even in the West End. Some moved into their second year, some barely made it to the end of their first week, and a few only ever meant to stay a day or two on some prolonged tour north to or south from the Edinburgh Festival.

All the same, no city which can open nearly 300 productions in twelve months can claim to be in terminal theatrical trouble, whatever the depredations of a Government which seems to regard actors, in so far as it regards them at all, as a useful sub-division of troop entertainment. It is true that we had an Arts Minister (Paul Channon) to whom at the age of five a play was dedicated by Terence Rattigan; it would have been even better if he had not sometimes given the impression that it was also the last play he ever saw.

The essential problems had not in fact changed much since last year: a West End which suffered increasingly from inner-city decay, so that its traditional local audiences found it hard to get to, harder still to park in, expensive to attend and unattractive to visit, while the tourists who once took their place in the golden early 1970s were also coming to much the same conclusion – theatregoing, like charity, should begin either at home (in this case with cut-down television versions of such archetypal stage classics as *Nickleby*) or else in a local playhouse where the costs and the inconvenience could be at least cut by half. Meanwhile a once-thriving pub circuit was now also severely strapped for cash both over the counter and backstage, while increasingly any money spent too visibly at the National or the Barbican (the river-boat disaster that was Ayckbourn's *Way Upstream*, for instance, or the brave attempt at an angry pantomime in the Barbican *Poppy*) began to look dangerously like profligacy.

Like Mrs Thatcher and her once-famous kitchen larder, the British theatre was now desperately about storing and preserving and cutting back: in a world where *The Mousetrap* could run thirty years on a shoestring, who needed epic adventures in great stagecraft? The answer was of course that we did: in a time of recession, as Busby Berkeley discovered in the Hollywood 1930s, there's nothing quite like an extravaganza but try telling that to the banking theatre managers of Shaftesbury Avenue. The success of *Guys and Dolls* was of course living proof

1982

that Berkeley was right, but then again *Guys and Dolls* was playing maybe two nights a week at most on a heavily subsidised stage at the National.

So much for the doom and gloom I was trying to avoid; on the credit side this was the year of Pinter's superb triple bill *Other Places*, the year of Stoppard's untypical and therefore hugely under-rated *Real Thing*, the year of Jonathan Miller's stunning theatrical farewells with the Anton Lesser *Hamlet* and the English National Opera *Rigoletto*, this last far and away the best musical in town. For new work it was also the year (at the Royal Court) of Terry Johnson's intriguing Marilyn Monroe play *Insignificance*, and for performances it was the year of Joss Ackland's Falstaff, Judi Dench's amazingly youthful Lady Bracknell, Michael Gambon's Stratford King Lear and Anna Massey and Yvonne Bryceland in Edward Bond's (also much under-rated) *Summer*.

It was also the year when Barry Humphries in his Dame Edna drag managed to turn Drury Lane into a massage parlour of the human spirit, bestowing like some manic Mother Teresa a compulsory barbecue upon selected unfortunates from the audience who had already forfeited their shoes and much of their dignity in an evening which made even Elizabeth Taylor in *The Little Foxes* seem almost credible by comparison.

Enough there to keep the drama-critical mind alive for a year, and sometimes not just alive but also blown.

Taylor Made

January being the awards time of year, when critics are in an unusually giving vein and actors and dramatists required in return to give some of their finest renditions of surprise, humility and gratitude on podiums rather than stages, most of my Fleet Street colleagues seem to have decided that either Brian Friel's *Translations* (at the National from Hampstead) or Peter Nichols's *Passion Play* (briefly at the Aldwych) was the best new play of 1981. In both those selections they are of course deeply mistaken.

Far and away the best new play of last year was one which turned up in the RSC repertoire at the Warehouse for a very few performances in the autumn and has now just reopened there for what will, I trust, be a much longer stay, though tragically this return to the RSC repertoire comes just a month after the sudden and early death of its writer C. P. Taylor. Having now a second chance to see his *Good* confirms my belief not only that it was the major achievement of his remarkable playwriting career, but also that it will live long after some current award-winners have been forgotten.

A chamber concert in death and destruction, pitched somewhere halfway from *Cabaret* to *Pennies From Heaven*, *Good* tells the story of a semi-detached German professor called Halder, played in a performance of exquisite other-worldliness by Alan Howard. In the four months since I first saw Howard blinking myopically through this role I have been trying to think why it seemed so strongly reminiscent, and of precisely what, since the performance is unlike anything else I have ever seen Howard do for the RSC; seeing the play again this week it finally dawned on me that what he is doing here is precisely what Mr Howard's uncle Leslie used to do in such English films of the early 1940s as *Pimpernel Smith*, the creation of a character so totally self-absorbed that new rules have to be invented for his integration into the surrounding society.

In *Good* that society is the immediately pre-war Germany; Halder is a well-meaning academic who happens to have written somewhat casually a novel suggesting that in certain special circumstances euthanasia might not, on balance and all things considered, be such a terribly bad idea. Hitler gets to hear of the book, and across six years from 1933 Frankfurt to 1939 Auschwitz, we follow Halder's decreasingly dreamlike involvement with the Nazis. On stage throughout the evening is a company of ten actors and five musicians, though only Halder and we can ever hear the band: they exist in his head, a permanently portable palm court quintet who play everything from *A Night in Monte Carlo* to *You Are My Heart's Delight* in ever-increasingly ghastly jovial counterpoint to the book-burning and the Jew-baiting and the euthanasia that take up more and more the centre of the stage. And then, at the last, when Halder starts to run Auschwitz for Eichmann, not especially because he wants to but just because it seems the thing to do at the time, the band finally becomes a reality and it is of course a band of Jewish prisoners.

Taylor himself called *Good* a comedy with music, and in the blackest possible way that is perhaps what it is; but it's also a play about the power of popular music, about the infinite possibilities of self-delusion, and about the daft notion of virtue in the abstract. Halder is not essentially evil, and he's not just obeying orders, at least not in the beginning; nor is he especially ambitious, or corrupt, or stupid, or afraid. Like Don Quixote (and predictably he ends up at the Auschwitz railway station reading just that) he would wish the world to pull its socks up and prove benevolent, and if his contemporaries do at the moment seem a little over-inclined to set fire to books and Jews, well then perhaps sooner or later they might

Good Alan Howard *as Halder*

give up and go home and all will be vaguely right again under a German heaven.

In one sense, *Good* has a lot in common with both *Arturo Ui* and *The Good Soldier Schweik*; where Brecht showed us Nazi history as a comic strip, Taylor shows it to us in the form of a concert by some Bavarian mountain ensemble; true, they are still playing *September Song* a decade or so before it was written, which is curious given the minutely detailed historical documentation offered us by the programme, but, that apart, this Howard Davies production seems to me as near faultless as any of the 1980s thus far. It boasts an immensely strong cast, with Domini Blythe and Penelope Beaumont among the women in Halder's life and Joe Melia in the performance of his career as the wry Jewish friend who insists on injecting reality into Halder's otherwise engaged existence. Not since the Trevor Nunn/Ian McKellen *Macbeth* almost five years ago has the RSC come together on a small-scale production of such intensity and triumph, and their achievement has been to turn what might have veered towards nightmare farce ('I'm in love with you and the children, but I'm not a hundred per cent sure about Hitler,' says Halder to his wife in one of his few moments of lucid doubt) into a play about moral compromise and political uncertainty. Halder's sole aim is survival without harm to others; when that aim is seen to be impossibly idealistic, he has no other. All that's left him is the band, and the band plays on; Howard's final shocked realisation that it has come to life in the midst of death is a stage image as powerful as any you will find in any contemporary theatre.

Greater Loesser

The National looks set for a long Runyon. Fully ten years after Olivier's ill health caused him to abandon his plan to play Nathan Detroit, the stage that bears his name at last has its *Guys and Dolls* and with it, I would guess, the first mass populist box-office smasheroo sell-out in the often troubled history of Hall's South Bank administration. In that sense the wait of a decade has been worthwhile, and true to Damon Runyon's gambling instinct the success has been achieved at odds of about eight to five against.

Guys and Dolls may be one of the true classics of the Broadway musical but it is a curiously intransigent show to stage; its songs are its plot, its characters are its action, and in the end it lives or dies by its choreography and its cast's understanding of the original Frank Loesser/Abe Burrows three-cent opera convention.

In this case the casting has been brave to foolhardy: of the four principals, Bob Hoskins (as Nathan) is more Hammersmith than New York Broadway, Julia McKenzie (as Adelaide) is patently too great and

1982

good a singer ever to have been confined to the crummy Hot Box nightclub, Ian Charleson (as Sky) is years too young and innocent, and Julie Covington (as Sister Sarah) oddly lacks the requisite Major Barbara fervour. The fact that all four manage to rise above these character drawbacks is due partly to the aforementioned choreography (and if there is a single triumph in this evening it is that of David Toguri), and partly to the vast amount of help they receive from a contrastingly perfectly-cast supporting team.

I never expect to see a better Nicely-Nicely Johnson than David Healy, nor a more sinister Big Jule than James Carter; Bill Paterson as Harry the Horse, Barrie Rutter as Benny and Harry Towb as Brannigan are equally superb down to their patently aching feet, and what was always a company show (the title song and the second-half showstopper are both sung by minor characters) becomes in Richard Eyre's brisk production a victory of mass stagecraft over individual turns.

From its filmic opening titles, which sensibly haul the memory back into the Warner Brothers' black-and-white 1940s from the false Goldwyn Technicolor image of Brando and Sinatra, right through to John Normington doing *More I Cannot Wish You* quite beautifully, this is a

Guys and Dolls David Healy *as Nicely-Nicely Johnson*, Bob Hoskins *as Nathan Detroit*, Julia McKenzie *as Miss Adelaide* and Julie Covington *as Sarah*

production in which the whole is always greater than its parts. It is a tapestry of small-time losers and big-band numbers, and, though Eyre's overall concept may lack the acid edge of the recent Half Moon revival, it manages to fill the Olivier stage with the brassy sound and tacky soul of Runyon's Broadway.

There is, however, one point about this success which my critical colleagues seem curiously willing to overlook, and at the risk of incurring yet again the wrath of Sir Peter Hall I would like to point it out. A smash hit at the National Theatre is not precisely the same thing as a National smash hit; this revival has been achieved by a director and a choreographer totally new to the National with a cast among whose four principals only one has ever before played a leading role on a main National stage. In that sense *Guys and Dolls* is a triumph for the National in just the way that the recent *My Fair Lady* revival was a triumph for the Adelphi Theatre; it is not a show which emerges (as, say, did the RSC's *Nickleby* or *Swan Down Gloves*) from the bowels of the company, nor is it one which says anything about the nature or existence of a National policy on musicals.

Elizabeth Regina

In a Victoria Palace programme note much recommended for quiet reading during those all too frequent moments when the plot of *The Little Foxes* proves less than entirely gripping, the producer Zef Bufman (an ex-First Lieutenant in the Israeli Army commandos, and therefore ideally trained for the portage of Elizabeth Taylor to London) reveals that Lillian Hellman's creakingly ancient melodrama was only selected for Miss Taylor's stage debut after both *Hay Fever* and *Who's Afraid of Virginia Woolf?* had been carefully considered. Noël Coward and Edward Albee have had a remarkably lucky escape.

The Hellman deep-South saga, one dedicated to the notion that the family which decays together stays together, will perhaps be familiar from an original Broadway performance (in 1939) by Tallulah Bankhead and a film two years later which starred Bette Davis. Both those ladies had a redoubtable quality of performance evil which lifted this turn-of-the-century *Dallas* into a soap-opera of distinction; few will forget Miss Davis watching Herbert Marshall (as her invalid husband) dying at her feet after she has graciously declined to pass him the medicine bottle.

Miss Taylor, however, after years of formative training in some MGM charm school, is unable to scale those melodramatic heights, and indeed the big scene of the husband's death now happens offstage; we are left therefore with a lady who in certain studio-like conditions (notably the final confrontation with her daughter) can manage to be powerful, but who for the rest of a long evening is hopelessly unable to relate to a stage full of other characters. Admittedly she has not been much helped by a set which looks as though it is on the last legs of a long bus-and-truck tour and a supporting cast who look much the same; seldom can so many B villains from minor television movies have been assembled on the same stage at the same time, and it is intriguing that the one actress who distinguished this revival when it first opened on Broadway last year (Maureen Stapleton as Birdie) has now disappeared from the cast-list.

The result is a curiously tacky, crumbling and dilapidated evening, much like watching *Gone With The Wind* in an Atlanta cinema shortly after the burning; Miss Taylor gives a very small performance inside a very large costume, unlike the rest of the company, who give very large performances inside a restricted playing area caused largely by the fact that whenever their star enters they retreat upstage as if in the presence of minor Balkan royalty. All in all, an evening for stargazing rather than stardom.

The Barbican Chronicles

I have seen the Barbican and it works; difficult to find your way to, harder still to find your way about inside, it nevertheless contains at the heart of its concrete maze a gem of a theatre, eleven hundred seats large, yet retaining a feeling of intimacy and acoustic privacy which the builders of the Olivier must now be gnashing their teeth over. It is indeed to rejoice in the architecture of the playhouse, and of John Napier's stunningly carpentered set, that I'd recommend an early visit to Trevor Nunn's inaugural production of *Henry IV* parts one and two and suggest that you see the two plays (as is possible on certain summer Saturdays) across one single seven-hour day.

Part One, judged alone, is a massive disappointment; Nunn seems content to use it as a primer, bringing to the text none of that flair or intellectual discipline that one remembers from the Terry Hands and Peter Hall excursions into this same Stratford territory over the past two decades. Instead the play is left there, sprawled out across the wide stage while the cast amiably ramble around both apparently in search of a map. As a pageant to show off the new RSC premises it is just about all right, as a rediscovery or enlightenment of the text it seems remarkably lacking in both style and coherence. Only Timothy Dalton's starry Hotspur begins to approach the sense of personal danger that can bring these battlefield chronicles to life; the rest of a distinctly undercast and understrength company seem to have settled for a plod through the text in traditional Shakespeare for schools fashion.

But then, and this is why I suggest the full day, as Part Two begins to pull itself into shape (and it is admittedly a vastly better play) the old virtues of the company tradition begin to reassert themselves; Joss Ackland's muted Falstaff, Gerard Murphy's long-haired Hal and Patrick Stewart's unobtrusive Henry IV start to make sense as characterisations, and by the time we reach Ancient Pistol (Mike Gwilym in marvellously manic form) leading the company in a rooftop chase across the set, what has been up to then a dull and defiantly unspectacular history lesson is suddenly galvanised into the kind of life and excitement that typifies the RSC at their epic *Nickleby* best. What began as an example of adequate stage-management becomes, as the newly crowned Henry V finally rejects his Falstaff, a triumphal arrival in the heart of both real and stage City.

Treble Chance

The National Theatre is currently offering a complete and utter guide to one of its own directors, Harold Pinter, which should on no account be missed despite the fact that the usual appallingly incompetent NT scheduling means that it is only available for four doubtless already sold-out performances in the whole of November. The guide comes in the form of three short plays on the Cottesloe stage, directed by Peter Hall himself and played under the overall title *Other Places*. The first of these plays, *Family Voices*, has already been around a bit both on BBC radio and as a National platform performance last year; the other two are, however, totally new and, taken together, cross-cast across one single evening, they add up to a remarkable insight into Pinter past and present.

Family Voices is the one about the letters, written but probably never posted, of a mother and son and recently deceased husband/father; these are spoken aloud, radio-style, by Anna Massey and Nigel Havers with Paul Rogers as the third voice from the grave, and there is no attempt here at any real dramatisation. It remains a radio play, but one of intense fascination because it re-caps all the familiar Pinteresque themes of his past plays, from *The Room* through *The Caretaker* to *The Homecoming*: menace is here, and non-communication, and sinister sexuality, and the re-arrangement of truth depending on who is to speak next. Half-heard whispers from the past are mingled with screams of reality from the present to form a vocal tapestry that might in a less reverential atmosphere seem almost a parody of Pinter circa 1965.

But then, for the second play, we go even further back, back in fact to the Harold Pinter who first made his name writing revue sketches for Kenneth Williams in shows like *Pieces of Eight*. Here, in a new play called *Victoria Station*, is a sudden return to that eerie jokiness: its only two characters are a minicab controller (Paul Rogers again) and his luckless driver, wonderfully played by Martin Jarvis. The cab and its driver are, we're told, deeply lost; there may or may not be a body on the back seat and, if there is, it may or may not still be alive. That, oddly enough, doesn't much matter; what does is the sense that the world may suddenly have come to an end leaving one cab driver and his organiser desperately trying to make some sort of sense out of what they have got left. Brilliantly staged by Hall so that we only ever see Jarvis through the windscreen of a real on-stage car, while Rogers set in an office high above him goes gradually to pieces in perfect counterpoint to his driver's increasing calm, this is a double act of considerable skill, which comes as a sharp reminder that Pinter can still do the jokes.

But both these plays are really only curtain-raisers for the last, *A Kind of Alaska*, which instead of harking back to past triumphs suggests that Pinter is in fact now moving forward into some altogether new direction. In the first place, and extremely unusually for him, the play is derived from a book, and a book of medical fact. Oliver Sacks's *Awakenings* was a 1974 account of the arousal from years of catatonic lethargy of a large number of sleeping-sickness patients, brought back to life by the wonder-drug L-Dopa. Pinter shifts the location to England and considers the awakening of just one patient, played by Judi Dench in what has to be the performance of even her remarkable career.

She plays Deborah, who at the age of sixteen fell into sudden and total coma; some twenty-nine years later, she awakes to find her doctor (Paul Rogers now going for the treble) and her sister (Anna Massey) watching over her, beginning the attempt to explain how she has come to lose three decades of her life in sleep.

But what makes *A Kind of Alaska* so haunting is the technique Pinter has devised for telling the story from Deborah's own eyeline; 'You've aged substantially,' she tells her sister and it is an accusation, as if she had put on weight in all the wrong places. This is a play about the unfreezing of the body while the mind remains desperately unable to thaw out quite so fast, and Judi Dench's ability to conjure up the soul and voice of a teenager in the body of a woman nearly fifty should win her just about every one of this winter's acting awards.

Real Magic

When they come to write the textbooks on Tom Stoppard, if they haven't already started, his new *The Real Thing* (at the Strand) is the play that's going to give them the most trouble since it fits almost no preconceived notion of the kind of playwright he is thought to be. It is not, for instance, a brilliantly Scrabbled wordplay like *Rosencrantz* or *Jumpers*; nor is it as socially or politically committed as *Night and Day* or *Every Good Boy*, nor even as quickfire comic as a sketch like *The Real Inspector Hound*.

Instead it's a romantic comedy of a tragic nature, corresponding perhaps most closely to less successful attempts in this same field recently made by our other two leading British dramatists, Harold Pinter (in *Betrayal*) and Peter Nichols (in *Passion Play*). Like them, it's a story of rearranged marriages and furniture in the affluent London architect-and-actor belt; in its first Cowardly moments we get what appears to be a stylish comedy of bad manners, full of cuckoo-clock jokes about Old Basle and Swiss Frank, but no sooner are we getting used to those *Private Lives* than we realise that they're not what the play is about at all. We are in fact watching a play-within-a-play and its central characters are about to fade away since their only real function is to introduce us to the two people the play is really about, who just happen to be their offstage marital partners in real life and who are therefore *The Real Thing* if you're still with me.

But *The Real Thing* is also love, and divorce, and jealousy, and innocence, and anguish and in writing about all of that within the context of a marital drama about an actress and a playwright Mr Stoppard has come up with the warmest and the most touching play he has ever written. In a purely artistic sense, this is also an autobiographical play since it is about a dramatist trying to write a play about indescribable love; it is a stunning variant on the eternal square (since both central characters, wonderfully well played by Roger Rees and Felicity Kendal, have other marital and professional partners whom we are allowed to meet and often to like as much as we like them) and it is also shot through with sudden and splendid laughs; while rehearsing his forthcoming appearance on *Desert Island Discs*, the playwright recalls an earlier brush with the musical classics: 'I was taken to Covent Garden to hear Callas in a foreign musical without dancing; people were giving kidneys to get tickets.'

Buried somewhere deep in *The Real Thing* are also some marvellous insights into the nature of the theatre in which its central characters work: 'If you get the right words in the right order,' says the dramatist, at a time when he is signally failing to do so, 'you can nudge the world.' *The Real Thing* is not, perhaps, going to nudge the world: but it is going to nudge a lot of people into a realisation of what theatre and love and betrayal are all about, and for that we should be more than grateful. It is a play which lends some much-needed dignity and life and purpose to a West End that is currently desperately in need of all of that, and Peter Wood's production is a miracle of discreet stagecraft: not only in his central casting of Kendal and Rees, but also in performances from Jeremy Clyde and Michael Thomas and above all Polly Adams, he has drawn together the best teamwork in town.

1983

A VOLATILE NOT TO SAY MERCURIAL YEAR in the London theatre: around the middle of February there were no fewer than twelve theatres dark, roughly one-third of the mainstream total. Not all that remarkable by Broadway standards, where this year was catastrophic anyway, but for London still a postwar record and therefore distinctly unnerving. But no sooner had the doom-and-gloom articles appeared in the press than the theatres began to open up again and the papers at least temporarily to close down: in early December there was not a single empty theatre in London, though there were a few empty news-stands.

Nevertheless, like a very early heart attack, the warning signs were there: by midsummer no fewer than five theatres had changed ownership, always a sure indication that somebody somewhere is getting a little uneasy: intriguingly those changes added to the number of North American landlords in the London theatre. And there were other signs that we crept closer to the Broadway of circa 1970, with a record number of old musicals back in town – *Oliver!* with its original stage and screen star Ron Moody, Danny La Rue dragging up and back *Hello Dolly!*, a pale shadow of the movie *Singin' in the Rain* at the Palladium and a sizeable number of other musicals as well as a first-ever pantomime at the National, and a flight back to *Peter Pan* at the Barbican. In a nation gone big on nostalgia, a very dead English movie star played by a fairly alive American stage star might well be a good recipe for 1984: Liza Minnelli as Jessie Matthews, perhaps?

But if that's the kind of Christmas Past with which the year ended, what about the rest of it? 1983 was a time of major performances rather than major plays, and feminists might like to note that for the first time in my memory women had total charge of Shaftesbury Avenue, from Judi Dench at the Lyric (*Pack of Lies*), past Hannah Gordon at the Apollo (*Country Girl*), *Daisy* at the Globe, Penelope Keith at the Queen's (*Hay Fever*), Liz Robertson at the Palace (*Song and Dance*) and then around the corner to Jane Lapotaire at the Cambridge (*Dear Anyone*). All strong and memorable performances to set beside the actors of the year: Derek Jacobi in a remarkable Barbican quadruple (a youthful Prospero, a stylish Benedick, a disappointing Peer Gynt, but above all a marvellously swashbuckling Cyrano); Antony Sher literally beneath him in the Barbican Pit with an equally impressive double as Tartuffe and his creator Molière (in the Bulgakov stage biography); two returning giants, Peter Ustinov in *Beethoven's Tenth* giving us a play the way lesser hosts give dinner parties and Rex Harrison back to his old Shavian best as Shotover in *Heartbreak House*; Jack Shepherd leading a cast of travelling salesmen in Mamet's brilliantly manic *Glengarry Glen Ross*; our newest theatrical knight Sir Michael Hordern along with Tim Curry (and Geraldine McEwan) in the most stylishly-cast rediscovery of the year, *The Rivals*; Sher again, weaving a path through David Edgar's socialist epic *Maydays* at the Barbican; and of course the great Merlin of the stage we this year lost, Ralph Richardson making an eerie departure in a de Filippo play about his beloved fireworks, but also a play in which suitably enough nothing was quite what it seemed. With Richardson gone, those *Inner Voices* are never going to sound the same again.

In a year when there was more drama in Peter Hall's Diaries than on any one of his stages, a year when the National dug up Jean Seberg only to bury her again under the weight of an amazingly inept Hamlisch musical, a year when the major subsidised companies were by no means always or even often those giving best value for box-office money, there were faint but reassuring signs of a rebirth of the West End and a return to an actors' theatre. Both Maria Aitken and Albert Finney formed management companies dominated by players rather than directors, while Ray Cooney's Theatre of Comedy (though by the end of the year it had

1983

led to nothing much more than one good farce and a singularly tacky *Aladdin*) showed signs that the commercial theatre had at least learnt how to group itself into multi-stage companies which could take on the subsidised houses at their own gargantuan game.

The closing weeks of a year not strong on major new drama nevertheless brought Athol Fugard's *Master Harold and the Boys*, another cry for the beloved country, but one of personal and haunting anti-apartheid power and one which (alongside *Woza Albert!*) confirmed the Market Theatre Company's tremendous strength. The end of the year also brought a massively disappointing stage debut by Dennis Potter (*Sufficient Carbohydrate*), but as against that a wickedly astute comedy by Brian Thompson at the Bush: *Turning Over* came to us with a marvellous kind of topicality just as we were about to be colonised by the television screening of three major Indian Raj epics, and it worked on so many levels of internal BBC satire and external midlife truth that it deserved a vastly longer and wider life than its month on the fringe.

But in the end, no year that gave us Willy Russell's brilliantly black Liverpudlian musical *Blood Brothers*, Christopher Hampton's following of Brecht and the Manns from the tyranny of Nazi Germany to the tyranny of the Warner Brothers (*Tales From Hollywood*) and A. R. Gurney's account of the final buzzing of American WASPs (*The Dining Room*, one of several Greenwich hits unaccountably denied a transfer) can be called disappointing or undistinguished: especially when it also gave us Frances de la Tour and Ian Bannen in O'Neill's great lament for his alcoholic brother (*Moon for the Misbegotten*), Alan Bates in Osborne's *A Patriot For Me* and intriguing new plays about the poets of the First World War (*Not About Heroes*) and the nuclear physics of the potential Third (*The Genius*). All that and the Royal Court's haunting *Falkland Sound* as well as renewed London life for Peter Nichols's thoughtful pantomime of the opium wars (*Poppy*): 1983 may well turn out to have been the kind of year the future calls vintage.

Designs for Living?

Caryl Churchill's *Top Girls*, back briefly at the Royal Court from a Broadway triumph, has been hailed by at least one of my critical colleagues as 'the best play ever written in Britain by a woman': up against *Richard of Bordeaux*, even up against *Dusa, Stas, Fish and Vi*, that seems to me a risky claim, not least because it begs one of the play's most central issues which is the precise definition of female achievement in a male world. Even if we accept it, we have still to face the fact that *Top Girls* is essentially not one but three excellent short plays.

The first is a table-top discussion between some legendary historical figures, not least Pope Joan and the Victorian explorer Isabella Bird, about the precise nature of feminine survival and at what cost through the ages. The second is a tough little documentary set in a modern employment agency featuring some case-histories of ambitious management secretaries. And the third is a tight, taut and marvellous domestic drama about two sisters, one of whom abandons her baby to the other in a bid for professional and personal freedom. True, these plays are all linked by one character: Marlene (Gwen Taylor), the giver of the dinner party, is also the manager of the employment agency and the sister who has abandoned her baby. True, too, the other six women all double up so that the debate about feminism and freedom continues across centuries and counties throughout the two-hour evening. But in the end, we have still got three short plays even if they do all contribute to one central theme.

Top Girls is not a stridently feminist work of propaganda: instead it's an immensely carefully weighted argument, starting in Shavian debate and gradually narrowing down to domestic particulars, about the cost of emancipation and equality. What makes it so powerful is a curious kind of passionate detachment that Caryl Churchill has achieved through her start in history, and what makes it such a splendidly powerful evening is the group playing of a wonderfully strong cast in Max Stafford-Clark's hugely powerful production.

At the Bush, Doug Lucie's *Hard Feelings* is billed as 'a viciously funny play set in Brixton in 1981' and that seems no violation of the theatrical trades' descriptions act, though it doesn't tell you the whole story. What Mr Lucie has done here, exactly half a century on from Noël Coward, is to come up with a modern *Design for Living*, in which six characters are used to hold a mirror up to the nation and the times which have bred them.

But we are not into documentary reality: the riots of that Brixton summer happen way off-stage and affect only one of the characters. He, Tone (Stephen Tiller), is anyway a butch journalist outsider, using the group's milk bottles for anti-police missiles; though ironically it is also he who gives the others their only real glimpse of a moral code.

1983

Then there's Viv (Frances Barber) whose parents have given her the house and with it a final, chilling, proprietorial authority over all of its inhabitants; there's also Annie (Diana Katis from the marvellous Oxford undergraduate film *Privileged*), who's a laid-back model dabbling in pornographic movies; Rusty (Ian Reddington), a new-romantic singer whose tragedy is a successful father and an inherent talent for disaster; Jane (Jennifer Landor), a Jewish solicitor expecting to be forgiven for it; and Baz (Chris Jury), a Sheffield wimp hoping to end up as something big on the managerial side of frisbees.

These characters are Mr Lucie's play: they lunch at Routiers, shop at Camden Lock, wonder whether to rename their house Dunthinkin and gaze in wonder at Tone, the newcomer, a born-again pagan with a deep, understandable fear of Sir Geoffrey Howe. He (Tone) is the only one of the group not to have been through Oxford, and there too Mr Lucie is, I think, trying to tell us something of the incestuous dangers of a university education. His play is an acidulated, acerbic and often very funny look at power and property and the self-destructive mechanism therein. Like Evelyn Waugh in *A Handful of Dust*, he's trying to show us how laws of the jungle can still apply in a jungle of the cities, and he's on about the clan mentality. By the time all *Hard Feelings* have been expressed, some of the members have been ignominiously expelled from the group, but Queen Viv remains at least outwardly unharmed and presumably soon to start on the long march to Downing Street.

It's a play about greed and selfishness and insecurity and racial intolerance, made all the more powerful by its refusal to allow a Brixton brick in through the window. Mr Lucie's only weapon is (like Caryl Churchill's) that of language, and he too uses it with the economy, confidence and wit of a dramatist of twice his age and experience. He also deserves some sort of special award for allowing *Casablanca* to play on a video screen in full view of his audience for most of the second act; how many other dramatists would let in that sort of competition, and how many of those would win through to the point where I wasn't even looking at the set when Bergman and Henreid sang the *Marseillaise*? Mr Lucie is a writer to watch for in the future, and *Hard Feelings* is a play to see now; it runs on at the Bush until the first week of March.

Vivat Rex

In the ten years or so since Olivier gave up the National and most other great stars gave up the West End, we have grown accustomed – for better and often for worse – to an essentially academic theatre where the writers and directors reign unchallenged. Faced with a Bernard Shaw revival such as that of *Heartbreak House* now at the Theatre Royal, Haymarket, my critical colleagues therefore look instinctively to see what the director rather than the actors have brought to it, and as a result of that one-sided quest John Dexter's new production has been unfairly attacked for lacking the ensemble coherence of a recent National revival by John Schlesinger.

But this is to deny not only the flamboyant and marvellously quirky theatricality of what Dexter has produced, a theatricality which Shaw would have been among the first to recognise and grudgingly approve; it is also to deny the remarkable achievement of the new production in bringing Rex Harrison back into his own. Twenty-five years on from *My Fair Lady*, years which he has spent working in a fair amount of old rubbish, Harrison is at last home in his rightful Shavian territory and if this definitive Captain Shotover doesn't get him the knighthood then nothing will. Sure he is a little fluffy on some of the longer speeches, and there are indeed moments when he appears to be neither coming nor going, but merely hovering like some benign Prospero over a British isle that is still full of noises and somehow no longer very magical. Yet all of that is a perfect role description of Shotover himself, and when Harrison gets himself into the great speech about England ('The Captain is in his bunk, drinking bottled ditchwater; and the crew is gambling in the forecastle. She will strike and sink and split. Do you think the laws of God will be suspended in favour of England because you were born in it?') it is to be reminded with a sudden shock of what an extraordinary talent we have allowed to disappear over the Atlantic in these last forty years.

The play, admittedly, remains more of a problem: Shaw seems to have thought he was writing an English *Cherry Orchard* (the subtitle is 'a fantasia in the Russian manner on English themes') and come up instead with an Edwardian *Hay Fever* in which the true star apart from Shotover is the house itself, a house where hearts and nations can be broken with equal ease while the inhabitants debate the virtues of selling your soul to the devil in Zanzibar. Around Harrison in this rambling structure, apparently run up by an unholy alliance of Ben Travers and Turgenev, Dexter has assembled one of the starriest casts even the Haymarket has recently enjoyed: Diana Rigg looking like Lady Ottoline Morrell is Hesione, Rosemary Harris is an aristocratic Ariadne, Paxton Whitehead (as Hector) is back to these shores after twenty years in Canada and still sounding uncannily like Jonathan Miller, Simon Ward is a twit-of-the-year Randall Utterword and the indomitable Doris Hare is the aptly-named Nurse Guinness. You might, if you were very lucky, see a more intelligent production of this play sometime in the next half-century; I doubt you will ever see a more quintessentially theatrical one.

1983

Rival Merits

Like some great European opera house, the National Theatre bursts out in periodic triumph with the arrival of newcomers: whereas Royal Shakespeare Company productions tend to improve in direct proportion to the length of time they have been in the repertoire and their players within the company, the National is at its best with guest stars. Consider the team (Ian Charleson, Julia McKenzie, Julie Covington, now alas all departed again) who came in for *Guys and Dolls* last year and consider now the team that has come in for *The Rivals* on the Olivier stage: Tim Curry, Patrick Ryecart (from *Balthazar*), Anne Louise Lambert (from *Draughtsman's Contract*), Edward Petherbridge and – returning after long absences – Sir Michael Hordern and Geraldine McEwan. Like the *Guys and Dolls* team, they sweep on to the Olivier stage like some invading army under the superlative command of Peter Wood to give us what must surely be the definitive postwar revival of Sheridan's Bath nights.

Assessed on its casting alone, this production could have happened at the Theatre Royal, Haymarket: it does not stem from any recognisable National tradition or company strength, nor is there any discernible reason why many of the company should have met before the first rehearsal a few weeks ago. But what justifies this production as a National treat is the way that Mr Wood has managed to open it up for the Olivier stage. For too long, *The Rivals* has been imprisoned within a box set: now, in John Gunter's marvellous reconstruction of eighteenth-century Bath terraces and façades and meadows, it sprawls across the vast open spaces of the Olivier so we feel we are actually stationed somewhere in the city centre as the action unfolds around us, instead of peering in through the windows of the usual boxed-in setting.

The other great reason for hastening to the Olivier is the sight of Sir Michael Hordern celebrating his new knighthood with a wondrous comic turn, one which sets him up against Geraldine McEwan's Mrs Malaprop in one of the great double-acts of our time. While Sir Michael, who is fast becoming as dotty on stage as Sir Ralph, fumbles and witters and harrumphs his way through an exquisitely judged Absolute, Geraldine McEwan does for the word-blind Mrs Malaprop precisely what Judi Dench recently did at the National for Lady Bracknell – she pulls her down a generation and reclaims her for reality from the further reaches of old-bag lunacy to which Irene Handl and others have recently consigned her. Around these two blazing stars, Mr Ryecart (as the younger Absolute) and Mr Curry (as Bob Acres) and above all Edward Petherbridge (as the lovelorn Faulkland) made South Bank debuts of extreme distinction, and if the female playing of Lydia and Julia is inclined to seem a little thinner, that is perhaps only to be expected given the standard of frantic comedy achieved by the men.

About these triumphant *Rivals* there seems little critical doubt or dissent: about Willy Russell's *Blood Brothers* (at the Lyric) it has to be said that a fair number of my colleagues have got it very wrong indeed. With certain honourable exceptions, notably the *Guardian* and *Mail*, they have either despised or dismissed what is undoubtedly the most exciting thing to have happened to the English musical theatre in years. *Blood Brothers* is essentially a folk opera, a Liverpudlian *West Side Story*, about twin brothers who grow up on opposite sides of the social tracks without realising their fraternity until one inadvertently kills the other.

Like Sondheim's *Sweeney Todd*, this is an angry musical about blood and death and social corruption: Russell (the author of such gentler shows as *Educating Rita* and *John, Paul, George, Ringo . . . and Bert*) has here written and composed a marvellously grainy, tough and very black show which suggests that the musical can still be used by the British as a contemporary theatrical form of considerable power. Dominating *Blood Brothers*, and singing most of its best songs, is Barbara Dickson as the back-street mother of eight who gives her ninth child away to the rich woman whose house she cleans. The boy then grows up in affluence, knowing his twin brother only as a back-street playmate: as, however, we move from the 1950s through into the 1980s, and as the Depression then comes, times turn more violent and what began as a three-and-sixpenny opera ends as full-scale musical tragedy.

What makes *Blood Brothers* such a triumphant evening, above and beyond the acid singing of Miss Dickson and the brilliant playing of the twins by George Costigan and Andrew Wadsworth, is Russell's realisation that a small cast, most of whom double and treble up (especially Andrew Schofield as the narrator who also goes from milkman to gynaecologist with the simple explanation that he has changed jobs) can form themselves into a hit squad capable of slamming this music across. In the end it's a show about superstition and age-old guilt and modern urban blight: but it's also one that drags the London stage musical kicking and screaming into the 1980s and for the impact of its production (by Chris Bond, original begetter of *Sweeney*, and Danny Hiller) it is, I reckon, unmissable and unbeatable.

A Patriot for Chichester

It was both noble and extremely intelligent of the National Theatre to give up their option on John Osborne's *A Patriot For Me* (for which they had no immediate production plans) and allow it to be seen at Chichester. For despite the reservations of that Sussex theatre festival's founding father, who has reputedly taken himself off to the West Country to avoid the embarrassment of seeing two men in a bed on the stage he apparently built for less deviant affairs, Osborne's epic drama of homosexuality and political treachery in the Austro-Hungarian army comes up for its first revival looking wonderfully suited to the broad sweep of that vast open stage.

The play's first production in 1965 at the Royal Court was among the first I ever reviewed, and although its only survivor at Chichester is George Murcell, still playing the Russian spymaster with a superbly sinister bluster, the play itself has lost none of its original power. True, we have now lost that Royal Court sense of decayed opulence – the cramped red-velvet auditorium and the proscenium arch somehow conveyed an atmosphere of seedy decline which admirably suited the officers' drag ball, and Nigel Stock is never quite able to summon up the flamboyance of the petticoated, cigar-chewing Baron in the role which brought George Devine's life and management of the Court to such an abrupt, flamboyant and tragic halt.

But Alan Bates as Redl, the 'patriot' of the title, is vastly more subtle and believable in the role than was Max Schell, even though lacking Schell's teutonic militance, and Ronald Eyre's new production has rightly taken advantage of Chichester's wide open spaces to turn an out-of-the-closet drama into a fully fledged operatic epic. With its cast of forty and its twenty-three scenes, many of them cross-fading, there is of course always the question of whether *A Patriot For Me* wouldn't work even better as the film I have always thought it was meant to be. But this slow-starting, episodic adventure story which builds into a full-scale military tragedy has always contained some of Osborne's best dramatic effects and here, from the very first duel to the inevitable gunshot three and a half hours later, we get a rich and rare theatrical treat.

It augurs well for John Gale's arrival at Chichester to share the administration with Patrick Garland that his rapid determination to do the play there has been followed by a triumph of casting. For the central character of Redl, though one of the longest in modern drama, is also one of the least rewarding: he exists, even in Alan Bates's poetic and thoughtful portrayal, as little more than a linkman to get us from one great character sketch to another and it is here that Eyre's production reaps such rich rewards. From Lucy Fleming as the Lemberg prostitute, Harry Andrews as an imposing if forgetful General, Sheila Gish as the icy Countess, David King as the army intelligence officer, Neil Stacy as the Judge Advocate and of course Murcell and Ronnie Stevens as the Russians, Eyre has drawn a series of brisk performances that would be the envy of any stage company in Europe.

Moreover in the time since this play was first seen, *A Patriot For Me* has acquired homosexual spy references all the way through to Blunt: playwrights as diverse as Alan Bennett (in *The Old Country*) and Julian

Mitchell (in *Another Country*, still at the Queen's) have taken up the theme in a more localised English or Soviet setting, so that in seeing Osborne's Austro-Hungarian chronicle now there is a sense of going back to the root cause of a lot of uniformed angst.

The gaiety of nations was not, I think, a phrase ever meant to refer specifically to the politics of homosexuality, but Osborne's ever strong sense of the outsider in a closed society, coupled with his ever evident distaste for the ravages that can be wrought on the human body, results in a curious alliance of Wildean wit and puritanical loathing. Eyre's final and brilliant curtain call, one which rightly echoes *La Ronde*, pulls together a series of historical and social echoes of increasing fascination, and if Chichester can only now maintain the momentum of the best start to a season there in at least the past decade, then there's real hope that once great theatre could return to sustained critical respectability.

At the Apollo, Victoria, though only for another week, *Liza Minnelli* is back in a new concert devised by Fred Ebb and considerably more show-busy than the *Liza With a Z* we were treated to a decade or so ago. Her audience here is a bizarre one, consisting apparently of people who have seldom before seen the inside of a theatre and therefore have considerable difficulty working out the likelihood of row G being behind row F; they also stand up and cheer a lot, presumably to free their kneecaps from the appalling constraints of the Apollo, Victoria, which seems to have been designed exclusively for deaf pygmies. The programme is a rip-off at three quid for some coy snaps of our star and no coherent writing about her of any kind, and she herself really might now be encouraged to pack in the old *Cabaret* routine, which has gone very grey.

But in Sondheim and Kurt Weill and *New York, New York* she is still electric, and if somebody would just package the tribute to her father's movie musicals properly then there could be a marvellous Hollywood sequence: her Oscar number is unbearably self-regarding, however, and the show itself seems only to have encores where most of the second half should be. Yet there is something so deeply touching about this elfin lady singing *Meet Me in St Louis*, because that was the number on which her parents first made professional contact, that I'd willingly go back and see her do it again. If you can't be so lucky, the album should be out by the summer.

Henry 8, Wolsey 10

The problem with *Henry VIII*, quite apart from the question of who wrote it and the fact that whoever did should have cut at least an hour of it (something the RSC have also, as usual, failed to do), is that the title role

1983

happens to be one of the least rewarding in the entire cast list of forty. Howard Davies, whose new production on the main Stratford stage is understandably enough the first in twelve years, has overcome some of the textual confusions with the help of David Edgar, the dramatist-editor who cobbled *Nicholas Nickleby* into shape for the company and is therefore accustomed to the staging of huge and unwieldy epics.

Davies has, however, compounded the title role difficulty by giving it to Richard Griffiths, a marvellously bulky light comedian, but a player who totally lacks a sense of monarchy or absolute power, and without any of that there is even less of a coherent play here than usual. Age is not the issue: Laughton in the classic Korda film and countless lesser actors in revivals of Bolt's *Man For All Seasons* have given us jovial young Henrys with hands not yet too badly stained by the blood from the scaffold. Nor does it matter that Griffiths is unusually quick on the jokes, though there are few enough of those around. What does matter is that never for a moment, not even in the final council chamber defence of Cranmer, can he inspire the remotest terror or authority, so that the play's vast, broken backed machinery of court intrigue seems to be grinding into intermittent action for no apparent reason. We get to meet a good court jester, but the King himself seems not to have bothered to show up for these festivities, and one cannot altogether blame him.

As a result, this becomes even more than ever Wolsey's play: in John Thaw's fine, Machiavellian party-political performance the Cardinal occupies virtually all our attention and such plot as there is never recovers from his final undoing. Only in his 'farewell to all my greatness' is there a moment when the language soars to the back of the circle and one gets an instinct of what this play might have been if Shakespeare and/or Fletcher had bothered to get it right. As it is, if history did not inform us that Elizabeth I died six years before its first production, one might assume the whole pompous pageant had been devised expressly to improve the sovereign's grant to the Globe.

Howard Davies's production is therefore a firework affair, illuminated by occasional flashes of brilliance and consigned to long periods in the dark. The sinister, tricksy and very good notion of having Henry and his court arrive at Wolsey's palace in death's heads (Henry's reign being characterised by death following a loss of heads) gets us nowhere much, since it is underscored by an irrelevant and apparently understandably embarrassed modern-dress band, who seem to have drifted on stage from a nearby Warwickshire folk-dancing festival.

Similarly, there is not much point in playing Buckingham's great scaffold speech as a vaudeville routine of the 'and here's another thing' variety if that is all the first half of the play has to suggest the terror and political chaos of Henry's reign. Cut-out sets run on overhead tracks suggesting a form of toy theatre, but then again Gemma Jones's memorably tragic Katherine (a worthy successor to Peggy Ashcroft's in 1971) works in a convention of utter reality. All in all, we have here a production which constantly echoes the uncertainties and confusions of the text without ever cutting us a path through its undergrowth. Within it are some performances of considerable disappointment (such as David Schofield's lacklustre Buckingham) and some of extreme fascination, not least Richard O'Callaghan's last act Cranmer and Oliver Ford-Davies as the local Vicar of Bray, forever clambering out of sinking political ships just too late not to be noticed. But Davies has failed to set the ghastly sycophancy of the last act tribute to the baby Elizabeth in any meaningful context, and though his production will doubtless settle down a lot before it reaches the Barbican next year, it will also have to find itself some sort of sustained centrifugal force.

Seeing *Falkland Sound* (at the Royal Court's Theatre Upstairs) on the first anniversary of the final battle for those islands and only a night or two after an election won, many would say, on the officially unspoken but still all-too-audible echo of the Falkland Spirit, was an educational and theatrical experience of considerable fascination. For the first half of this short and sharp and unforgettable evening consists quite simply of a

Henry VIII Richard Griffiths *as Henry VIII* and Gemma Jones *as Katherine of Aragon*

recital by two actors (Julian Wadham and Paul Jesson) of the letters of David Tinker to his father Hugh.

Tinker was a professional naval lieutenant killed in action on HMS *Glamorgan*: a middle-class, career sailor sent to right an Argentinian wrong who only discovered when he got into the South Atlantic the utter futility of laying down his own or anybody else's life for islands whose official British ownership could not possibly be sustained for more than a few more years.

Tinker's ultimate cursing of the war is all the more powerful because of his background, and Julian Wadham's performance of a Dartmouth scholar having his eyes opened at the last to the real meaning of the blip at the end of the radar screen of Britain's colonial history will have to be remembered at awards time.

The second half of the evening, subtitled *Voces De Malvinas*, is an altogether less satisfactory attempt to pull together five representatives of Falklands folk into the kind of aimless public debate usually chaired by Sir Robin Day on late-night television.

Ralph's Rockets

The Neapolitan plays of Eduardo de Filippo have come, in English translation, to mean Joan Plowright slaving over a hot stove while around her (in *Filumena* or *Saturday, Sunday, Monday*) was celebrated the full Catholic complexity of Southern Italian family life. *Inner Voices*, now in a British premiere on the National's Lyttelton stage, is therefore something of a surprise: in a translation by N. F. Simpson vastly more eerie and sinister than the two cosy Waterhouse–Hall jobs of the recent past, we have a thoroughly mysterious black comedy dating from 1948 and offering an altogether less lovable view of Neapolitan family tradition.

In form, the play owes much to Pirandello with whom, when young, de Filippo once worked: it concerns a loony old buffer, immortally played as to the manner born by Sir Ralph Richardson, who accuses his next-door neighbour of murder, only then to have to announce that the killing actually happened in a dream when he is confronted by a certain lack of evidence and a walking corpse. But that is just the beginning: de Filippo's play is not about an actual murder, but about the possibility of murder in a city where all decency has already been murdered by the war. He is writing here about the killing of, rather than a killing in, the family, and accordingly his old familiar characters start looking rather less lovable than usual.

There's Robert Stephens as the neighbour, fully prepared to kill the old boy if there really should be evidence of a prior death; worse still, there's Michael Bryant as the old boy's brother, already starting to deal behind his back in the bric-à-brac of the secondhand furniture store in which they live. It is this set, lovingly built in London by de Filippo's own designer, Raimonda Gaetani, that superbly summarises the clutter and confusion of his Naples – a city where everything and everybody is now for sale with the exception of one splendidly mad old uncle (Daniel Thorndike) who will now only communicate from his loft by means of fireworks.

Inner Voices is a hastily written, often shambolic but ultimately enthralling piece of eccentric drama about the killing of prewar faith and relative values, and in Mike Ockrent's admirably agile production Richardson, Stephens, Bryant and Thorndike come superlatively together to remind us of the great Olivier days when the National Theatre meant a group of resident star players instead of a cluster of disparate stages.

Comédies Françaises

Francophile Week at the Barbican: two major French stage classics in distinguished new translations by Anthony Burgess and Christopher Hampton, and given by Terry Hands and Bill Alexander the kind of productions that re-state the RSC's claim to be the most versatile and exciting acting company in the business. On the main stage, *Cyrano de Bergerac* is for all who love a parade. Mr Burgess first worked on the play as a Broadway musical for Christopher Plummer more than a decade ago and, though this is now a somewhat revised text, certain of the longer speeches sound as if they could have done with a musical accompaniment by Stephen Sondheim or at the very least Andrew Lloyd Webber. In the title role Derek Jacobi (who has been obsessed with Cyrano for nearly as long as Burgess) goes all out for the voice beautiful and the gorgeous profile: even the famously long nose is here trimmed to elegant and manageable proportions, while Hands's marvellously agile and active production is forever allowing its star to leap into the kind of poses that must have been used to advertise the play on its original turn-of-the-century posters.

What we have in *Cyrano* is a curiously sexless pageant dedicated to chivalry and mindless heroism: early critics thought it a useful antidote to the neuroses of Ibsen and Strindberg, and indeed it works much after the fashion of a Douglas Fairbanks silent movie: the words themselves are a kind of afterthought, almost a piano accompaniment, to a series of set pieces like the arrival of Roxane at the battlefront or the great death in the orchard, where both Cyrano and his virginal beloved seem to be drowning in a sea of fallen leaves.

Meanwhile, below stairs in the Pit, Antony Sher is a spellbindingly manic *Tartuffe* in a chamber production which casts off the old Catholic shackles of the Comédie Française and goes instead for black farce. Nigel Hawthorne's Orgon is, it's true, a trifle too subtly intelligent to be taken in by Sher's caped anti-crusader, but Bill Alexander keeps his actors moving at such a lick that you barely have time to rejoice in Sylvia Coleridge's cascading Madame Pernelle before you're off with Hawthorne under the table to investigate Tartuffe's sexual leanings: a breathless, up-front and very funny evening, which in Christopher Hampton's translation fairly belts through a plot the British might at last begin to find accessible.

In Regent's Park, the Open Air Theatre has as its first-ever musical, a version of Bernard Shaw's boxing farrago (*Cashel Byron's Profession*, an early novel he himself then dramatised as *The Admirable Bashville*) which wonderfully anthologises almost all the varied interests of its lyricist Benny Green. Echoes of Shaw, Wodehouse, Victorian pugilism and Gilbert and Sullivan, to say nothing of Islington historical footnotes and a song about the Gladstone bag, are cobbled together into a mindless but intermittently very entertaining evening. Mr Green and his composer Denis King have rightly seen that here is the flip side of *Pygmalion* (linguistically obsessive boxer declines to become English gentleman until married at the final curtain) and if they have failed to come up with another *My Fair Lady*, they have at least managed a title song which is the most merciless parody of a Broadway first-half closer I have ever heard. *Bashville* is Benny Green's second Shavian singalong, and though it lacks the dramatic strength of *Boots With Strawberry Jam* (fifteen years overdue for a London premiere) it does allow a good leading performance from Peter Woodward and mercifully gets the Park theatre away for a while from all that Pucking about.

At Hampstead, Dusty Hughes's *Bad Language* starts impressively enough as *Charley's Aunt* rewritten in blood: the structuralist wars of the late 1970s are cutting through a Cambridge college, where bodies fall on to student productions from first-floor windows, but there hasn't been a really good scandal since the Dean's Moroccan lover ran off with the silver. Sadly however, though Mr Hughes has got some wonderful beginnings for an undergraduate satire, he totally lacks any conclusions and not even an immensely talented cast led by Alan Rickman under Mike Bradwell's direction can hide the fact that there's a great gaping hole where the second act should be. Both *Hard Feelings* and the film *Privileged* have recently been around these ivy-clad walls with more success: the irony is that if Mr Hughes's own structuralism were half as sharp as his pen we'd have had the best college comedy since Frayn's *Donkey's Years*.

Hooray for Hollywood

Having spent much of my non-theatregoing time over the past few years researching and writing a book about British actors in California between the wars (*Tales from the Hollywood Raj*, book tokens gratefully received at the usual address), it was with a mixture of terror and fascination that I approached Christopher Hampton's similarly titled *Tales From Hollywood* on the open Olivier stage of the National.

Mercifully, we have not been ransacking the same cupboard: where my exiles in search of their place in the sun were Britons escaping nothing more dramatic than failed careers in provincial repertory theatres or over-protective families, Hampton's exiles are all middle European and on the run from Hitler. They include Brecht, the brothers Thomas and Heinrich Mann, Salka Viertel and Lion Feuchtwanger, and what one of our brightest and best dramatists has rightly seen is something both hilarious and tragic in the notion of the greatest literary brains in mid-century Europe having to flee the dictatorship of Hitler only to end up as slaves to the altogether different dictatorship of the Warner Brothers.

Tales From Hollywood (first played to a curiously grudging press in Los Angeles itself last year) is an episodic, sketchy, funny, often touching and sometimes marvellous play which suffers all the usual border-crossing problems of the drama-documentary. True, Hampton is at some pains to establish that we are here in a world of more fantasy than fact: his central character, the Austro-Hungarian playwright Ödön von Horvath (whose *Tales From the Vienna Woods* Hampton translated for the National in 1977) never in fact got to Hollywood at all, largely because on his way there he

Tales from Hollywood Michael Gambon *as Ödön von Horvath* and Ian McDiarmid *as Bertolt Brecht*

was killed by a falling tree in a thunderstorm on the Champs Elysées. Undeterred by such minor details of history, Hampton has pushed him on to California as a ghostly kind of narrator, there in Michael Gambon's splendidly wry performance to introduce us to the expatriate colony of fellow teutonic hacks trying to carve out a living by cobbling together junk screenplays in a nomad's land of donuts, dentistry and divorce.

Neatly sidestepping the shadows of Stoppard's *Travesties* (which imagined a similarly unreal literary gathering in 1916 Zurich) Hampton sets up a series of subplots worthy of *Dinner at Eight* or any other multi-stranded Hollywood saga of the period: thus we get a wonderfully hostile portrait of Brecht, a nasty glimpse of Thomas Mann desperately grafting away for a safe American professorship and ignoring the poverty and misery of his more distinguished elder brother Heinrich, the latter already locked into a disastrous marriage with the original nightclub singer from his *Blue Angel*, and even a brief glimpse of the Marx Brothers on their way to play tennis with Schoenberg.

A lot of that is of course straight Hollywood wartime history, right down to the famous *Variety* report on Hitler's march into Czechoslovakia highlighting a possible resultant three per cent loss of foreign film income worldwide. But Hampton is not a movie historian (if he were, he might have noted that some of the posters decorating Alison Chitty's set at the Olivier are anything up to five years out of period) and as a dramatist his main problem here is threading some totally diverse strands of social, political and literary history into a play that says something coherent about the nature of exile. In this, at the last, I have to say that I think he has failed; but along the way he has created such wonderful confrontations, whether between the Manns (Philip Locke and Guy Rolfe) or Horvath and Brecht (splendidly arrogantly played by a cigar-chomping Ian McDiarmid) or the elder Mann and his Lola (Billie Whitelaw), that the evening is still a constant delight.

Whether dealing in random one-liners (a rueful Mann noting 'my entire American reputation stands on the legs of Marlene Dietrich' or a Tarzan hurtling from the trees to announce 'Me Johnny Weissmuller, you Thomas Mann') or building up whole sequences of kaleidoscopic images from Marlene to McCarthy, Hampton has come up with what is probably the closest the theatre will ever get to the feeling of celluloid and literary decay that permeates Budd Schulberg's *The Disenchanted*. And California praise doesn't come much higher than that, at least not from this typewriter, though Peter Gill's very sparse and oddly unHollywood production suggests that Hampton might have been better served by the National's resident movie addict Bill Bryden.

Odets Here Is Thy Sting

Two great American plays in a single London week ought to be a cause for some sort of celebration, and let's start it with the senior of the two. Clifford Odets, for my money the most powerful and heartbreaking American dramatist of the 1940s that separated O'Neill from Miller and Williams, has always had a rough time in this country. His best play, *Golden Boy*, is largely remembered as an undistinguished Sammy Davis musical and even his *The Country Girl* (now in a hugely welcome revival at the Apollo, the first in thirty years of neglect) was originally mis-titled *Winter Journey* over here because it was thought that London playgoers would otherwise be daft enough to think they were seeing a modern-dress version of *The Country Wife*.

Even now, Odets remains so shamefully little known in Britain that he is bizarrely credited in the actual programme for *Country Girl* with also having written *The Big Knight* (presumably a Charlton Heston Crusades musical) rather than the unforgettable *Big Knife*. The sooner the National or the RSC start giving Odets the attention they give to Miller or Williams or even Kaufman-Hart, the sooner his classic status might begin to be appreciated.

But what we have to be going on with is at least a start, and for it all credit to the commercial management of Bill Kenwright. When I first saw what was then *Winter Journey* in 1953 (all right, so I was twelve. It's an impressionable age; so is forty-two) it struck me as the greatest backstage story of all time. Admittedly then we had Michael Redgrave as the old drunken actor and Sam Wanamaker as the young Kazan-type director determined to save him, if necessary, from his own wife as well as the bottle. But even at that time, and in that wonderful production at the St James's, the play was largely dismissed by the British press with the same tone of faint academic patronage that I find to my amazement creeping back even into the current reviews.

But just as the true title has now been restored to *The Country Girl*, so too has its true balance: Hannah Gordon has pulled the play back from the men in her life to herself, and in her outburst of early 1950s feminism you suddenly realise that she alone, her sacrifice of a life to get her husband back on the boards, is what Odets meant this play to be about. In this she's admittedly much helped by the undercasting around her: Martin Shaw, though an adequately butch juvenile lead, in no way suggests a great director at work and John Stride as the actor, though marvellous in his present tense, carries with him none of the essential feeling of a great lost past, so that you have to blink and look again when his performances are spoken of in the same breath as Walter Huston's and Alfred Lunt's. Both he and Shaw are, quite simply, too young and too contemporary in their styles for what is being asked of them: the old actor doesn't have to be

1983

Wolfit, but he does have to be a dried out giant clambering back up the mountains he has once conquered, and with Stride there is no sense of that original climb. Elsewhere the casting is no better: Simon Merrick needs to look and sound a lot more convincing if he is to be believed as a powerful Broadway producer instead of the manager of a small town rep, and there is nothing to suggest that the actress in the play has to be quite as terrible as she is here portrayed. Rightly, the director Robin Lefevre has indulged himself in some creaking scene changes to convey backstage life, but for Hannah Gordon, radiantly in tune with the full strength of this massively powerful play, the evening is an unqualified triumph. If all you know of *The Country Girl* is the movie for which Grace Kelly won her Oscar (presumably the miracle for which she is now approaching sainthood) then hasten along.

On the National's Cottesloe stage, Bill Bryden's world-premiere production of David Mamet's *Glengarry Glen Ross* is an equally unmissable transatlantic treat. Though the title might indicate some sort of highland fling, it refers in fact to the romantic naming of some worthless tracts of desert land which are being sold by crooks to suckers in Chicago. Mr Mamet himself once worked as a salesman of American real estate, and seems to have seen in that unnerving experience some sort of commercial metaphor for the life and death of his own nation.

But where Arthur Miller in his *Death of a Salesman* was concerned with the reality of one man out there on a smile and a shoeshine, David Mamet is more concerned with the society which allows such men office space. His play is a black, scatological, often uproarious farce about wheeler-dealers whose wheels have sprung punctures, and an all-British cast of seven have done it proud.

Flowering Cherry

The whirligig of time brings in strange theatrical revenges: when Lindsay Anderson first directed *The Cherry Orchard* at Chichester in an undistinguished 1966 season, he was accused by at least one critic (Mervyn Jones) of selling out his Royal Court heritage to 'a Haymarket tradition of famous actors and actresses which dispenses with any overall design or interpretation of the play'. Now, all of seventeen years later, Anderson has returned to the play and indeed taken it straight into the Theatre Royal, Haymarket, where sure enough it works very well indeed.

The theatre is of course rather better suited to the play than was Chichester, where the final locking-in of Firs always seemed a little strange given that the open stage had about half a dozen exits out of any of which he could have wandered: in Bernard Miles's wonderfully dotty new rendering he is well and truly shuttered up to die as they start to chop down the cherry trees, and we are left with the eerie double vision of an actor whose own theatrical heritage is also now in Mermaid jeopardy. But Anderson's new production is in no need of such nudges from real life: it builds and strengthens on its original Chichester roots, gaining immeasurably from many of the lessons that were learnt there. Back in 1966, you have to recall, they were still only a year or two away from the great Olivier–Redgrave triumph at Chichester with *Uncle Vanya*, and another Chekhov must have seemed an obvious winner. In fact it wasn't, largely because of Celia Johnson's deep unhappiness in the role of Madame Ranevskaya on the open stage, and the fact that she and Hugh Williams (as Gayev) seemed to be recalling *Brief Encounter* rather than the collapse of the Russian landed gentry.

Yet coming as it did less than a decade after the celebrated Moscow Art Theatre visit to Sadler's Wells had shown us how to get the cobwebs off Chekhov and play the real comedy instead of the phoney nostalgia, Anderson's original *Cherry Orchard* was the first to relate the play to local sensibilities: Tom Courtenay as an angry-young-man Trofimov and even the clenched elegance of the Johnson–Williams partnership suggested that you did not have to be Russian to forecast the coming of a revolution or regret the losing of a childhood nursery.

Anderson's return to the *Cherry Orchard* has recaptured a lot of that feeling: the only actor to survive into the present cast is Bill Fraser as a splendidly blustery Simeonov-Pischik, but in giving the role of Gayev to another West End comedian untrained in the major classics (Leslie Phillips) and in having Trofimov played once again by one of the most promising actors of the current new wave (Frank Grimes) his stage tracks are clearly laid in much the same direction. But apart from the proscenium arch, never more welcome, the real bonus this time around is Joan Plowright: in a radiant return to the live theatre after far too long an absence, her Ranevskaya is the first to challenge Peggy Ashcroft's in twenty years and is (unlike that other great Madame) rooted in a kind of warm local experience all too seldom achieved by the British in Chekhov.

When this Ranevskaya returns to her estate for the last time it is almost as a character out of Enid Bagnold or N. C. Hunter, whose ghosts still inhabit the Haymarket: she is all of our faintly loony aunts going back to the family attic for a final romantic root around the human bric-à-brac, and dealing along the way with aged and even loonier retainers. Thus we get not only Lord Miles solemnly addressing his legs as if they were recalcitrant children, but David Battley as the walking disaster Yepihodov and Margaret Robertson as a moustachioed conjuring governess. On the other side of the green baize door we get Joanna David and Cora Kinnaird in fine elegiac form as Varya and Anya, while hovering somewhere on the threshold is Frank Finlay's Lopakhin and here again the casting has been masterly.

Finlay and Plowright as a stage team go back a long way together, which means that we can take for granted Lopakhin's unstated devotion to the lady from whose estate he is about to evict her: but the purchase of the cherry orchard is not played here as the usual act of aggression in a class war. Instead, it is just one more inevitable event in a brisk social comedy of changing times and it is not until the play's ending an act later, with the suitcases in the hall and the tears oddly enough in the eyes of the one man not truly affected by the sale (the neighbouring Pischik) that we realise we are already past the watershed.

This is a production of rare and remarkable insights, superior in almost every way to the recent National Theatre revival; yet it is no discredit to the present performance of Bernard Miles that I left it inevitably thinking about the last Firs I had seen, Sir Ralph Richardson, whose sudden death was announced while I was in China. With that death we have lost perhaps not the Prospero but certainly the Merlin of our theatre: of the four great actor-knights of the British classical stage in this century, he alone dealt directly in magic. He was Priestley's supernatural inspector, and when he came to call you always knew that there was going on something rather more than met the eye. How wonderfully fitting that his final appearance should have been in a play about his beloved fireworks, but also a play which looked as though it was going to be about a man witnessing a murder and turned out in the end to be about nothing less than Italy at war. With Ralph gone, the 'inner voices' are never going to sound quite the same again.

Pacific Overtures

Though its belated removal from the Barbican to the infinitely more suitably Victorian surroundings of the Adelphi has been somewhat grudgingly noticed elsewhere, there's still not much doubt in my mind that Peter Nichols's angry pantomime *Poppy* remains the most adventurous and intriguing musical in town. True, it still doesn't altogether work, and if anything the cracks in the structure that were apparent a year ago in EC2 have actually widened as the show reaches WC2 with the injection of a great deal of pre-Broadway American money and the arrival of Onna White as choreographer, not to mention an almost all new cast, the one survivor from the original being Geoffrey Hutchings as an award-winning Dame, whose main contribution to the first night was to advance on the footlights and threaten anyone who refused to join in his audience singalong with two tickets to *Jean Seberg*.

But to understand what makes *Poppy* so consistently enthralling, indeed given its hallucinogenic theme one might say so addictive, we need (as no other critic has bothered to do) to set it in the context of much of the author's earlier work. Just as *The National Health* was built on the structure of television hospital soap-operas, just as *Privates on Parade* was constructed out of the old wartime revue fabric, so *Poppy* derives directly from a tacky English pantomime convention and just what Broadway audiences are going to unscramble from that, considering over there pantomime means only Marcel Marceau, remains to be seen. Not that *Poppy* is even now any stranger to confusion: two ladies left the theatre with me worrying about its conceivable links to the Armistice.

So, what we have here first of all is a pantomime, indeed one originally conceived not for the Barbican at all but for the infinitely seedier surroundings of the Theatre Royal, Stratford East. We have a Dame, a principal boy who is of course a girl (Antonia Ellis), the usual two-man horse, a principal girl who is really a girl and then we have the study of British opium-pushing in China a century ago, which is what the show is mainly all about. And that is where the troubles of *Poppy* really start. For not only can no pantomime sustain or contain all that Nichols wants to say about the appalling behaviour of the British in the Far East a century or so ago, but no pantomime nowadays conceived on this scale can possibly pay for itself unless it is built for something more than a ritual Christmas-holiday month at the Palladium. Accordingly *Poppy* has had to become a sort of panto-musical, and within less than three hours it now has to contain (a) all the trappings of Victorian pantomime, (b) all that Nichols wants to say about colonial corruption, and (c) massive Broadway dance numbers conceived by Onna White, who looks as though she hasn't been altogether happy since they last revived *Hit the Deck*.

Like Sondheim with *Pacific Overtures* (a remarkably similar and equally fascinating exercise in mismatched oriental form and content), Nichols suddenly finds himself here defeated by his own framework: *Privates on Parade* had a deep internal logic because its central characters plausibly belonged to the Malaysian touring revue company they were also parodying: *Poppy* never satisfactorily explains why pantomime should be the format for an attack on drug-running, and indeed styles are now so confused that at the end of the first half for no very clear reason we get a kind of underwater Esther Williams nude ballet projected on a screen at the back of the stage, as though left over from the last revival of *Oh! Calcutta!*

There is, as may already have been gathered, a very great deal going on here and some of it is smashing: set-piece numbers like *Rock-a-Bye Randy*, in which Idle Jack sings of his devotion to the pantomime horse before settling down to eat it during a Chinese siege, or *Sir Richard's Song*, in which the Dame explains to the Principal Girl that she can't marry the

Principal Boy because she's already his half-sister, are marvellously savage twists on the old pantomime convention and had *Poppy* managed to stay with that, all would have been superb. As it is, we get still a kind of terrible second half drift toward *The King and I* or *The World of Suzie Wong*, neither of which ever set out to be pantomimes, and, though the show has been tightened considerably since the Barbican, the recasting is a very mixed blessing indeed.

True, we do now get Alfred Marks as Obadiah Upward, marvellously cast to give the show a whiff of genuine Victorian tat: but as against that we've lost Stephen Moore (as Jack), Geraldine Gardner (as Dick) and Jane Carr (as Queen Victoria), all of whom have been replaced by infinitely blander musical performers who somehow fail to trace the show back to its legitimate dramatic roots. In a world of *Blondel* and *Dear Anyone* and *Cats* and *Dancin'*, it is true that here at last we have a musical with something sharp and original to say about the country from which it comes, and above all a show which has not locked all its brains in the heels of its tap shoes. In that sense *Poppy* is an unmissable treat: but it still has about it the look of a show on which not all the participants have come to the same conclusion about what they're setting out to achieve, and in the long march from the Barbican via the Strand to Broadway a show originally conceived for and about a Victorian greasepaint convention is perhaps bound to look a little uneasy about its various transplants.

Saint Jean?

There is so much wrong with the new National Theatre musical *Jean Seberg* that we had better start with what is even faintly right. There is in fact no reason why the National should not be world-premiering a big band show, indeed there are those of us who wish they had done it twenty years ago. Nor is there any reason why it should not be done with at least one hopeful eye on Broadway or even on the eventual participation of an American management like the Shuberts — how, had it not been for American money, would *Nickleby* or *Cats* ever have made it across the Atlantic? Nor again, in all fairness, is *Seberg* anything like the total fiasco forecast and even recorded after the first night by some of my more hysterical colleagues in the tabloid press. It is just not good enough for a huge number of eminently simple reasons.

The idea for the show, so far as it can be traced back to its roots, seems to have started with the young lyricist Christopher Adler (son of the *Pajama Game*'s Richard), who decided that in the fraught life of a minor American movie star there lay the makings of a musical. Seberg, like Garland and Monroe and Frances Farmer before her, is always a tempting subject for anyone who wants to rake over the American dream-into-nightmare scenario: a small town teenager from the middle of nowhere, as Marshalltown, Iowa, is generally located, she was selected by Otto Preminger from eighteen thousand eager applicants to be his *Saint Joan* in 1956. The film was predictably terrible: so bad, said one critic, that had Shaw been alive at the time it would have killed him. Instead it killed Seberg in Hollywood, though she did manage a European renaissance starting in 1961 with Godard's *Breathless* and drifting back downhill from there. She got into a catastrophic Romain Gary marriage, and a row with the FBI, which led her to exhibit her dead baby in a glass coffin to prove that it was white, a curiously racist act for a civil-rights pioneer. Five years ago they found her own body in the back of a car in Paris, where it had lain undiscovered for ten days: for a girl who had started out twenty years earlier as an overnight discovery there is, I suppose, some sort of poetic irony at least in that.

So Mr Adler has this admittedly somewhat hackneyed notion of a rags-to-riches-to-rags story and he takes it to Marvin Hamlisch. Now Mr Hamlisch has a couple of musical hits behind him (*Chorus Line* and *They're Playing Our Song*), but both are largely plotless so they still need some sort of a book for *Seberg*, and to get that they go to Julian Barry, who has cobbled together stage and screen lives of Lennie Bruce, yet another doomed American dream-into-nightmare specialist. At this point the three of them had, it seems to me, several options: they could have gone into an off-Broadway workshop where there was the native technical expertise to get *Seberg* into some sort of stage shape, or they could have gone to an acknowledged expert like Hal Prince or Michael Bennett, men who have spent their lives making seemingly intractable subjects sing and dance in the popular theatre.

Instead, and for reasons still unclear to me, they came all the way across the Atlantic to Peter Hall; when asked why, Mr Hamlisch said it was because he had seen *Amadeus*, though what he thought an immensely carefully crafted (by Peter Shaffer) drama about Mozart had to do with the musical life of Jean Seberg is not explained. What is known is that they came to the National because at this point in his contract Peter Hall could not work on *Seberg* elsewhere. But that does not make *Seberg* right for the National, least of all when you have to cast the central figure with no less than two actresses (Elizabeth Counsell and Kelly Hunter), both of whom look as though they would be vastly more at home doing the early life of Anna Neagle. Nor does it make Hall right for *Seberg*: when I once suggested that, on the track record of one Broadway flop (*Via Galactica*), Hall was not a man to be allowed near musicals, I was severely taken to task by an official from Glyndebourne who solemnly informed me that anybody who could direct an opera could direct a musical. The flaw in that argument is now, alas, sprawled out all over the Olivier stage: a musical is not a bit of a play and a bit of an opera. It is a wholly different theatrical form, and in this case a man of Hall's acknowledged success in the worlds of straight and operatic drama has clearly not (as his own Diaries indicate) the faintest idea about what makes a musical sing and dance.

Admittedly he has not been much helped by Adler, Hamlisch or Barry. Adler it is who gives Joss Ackland, playing Romain Gary, the immortal couplet, 'True I excel at my writing/But I'm hardly exciting'; Hamlisch it is who has here written a dozen numbers any of which could have gone into any other show at any other time in the last twenty years; and Barry it is who has conceived the daft notion of framing Seberg's story within the *Saint Joan* she once happened to play. It would have made as much sense to do the whole thing on an aeroplane as a tribute to her appearance in *Airport*. Joan was a saint who liberated France; Jean was a minor movie actress who failed to liberate herself.

True there are some incidental pleasures here, not least John Savident's wonderfully over-the-top caricature of Preminger as the Nazi that Otto once played in *Stalag 17*; there's also a song called *Dreamers* which will sound a lot better when it gets flogged off to Barbra Streisand. But what there is not, alas, is any real expertise: the three American visitors to the National do not seem to have brought with them any real authority, and as a result a gawkily and painfully English company stumble through an all-American life trying desperately to make it relate to something in their own largely non-musical experience. A two-hour no-interval show like this needs to be choreographed with the brilliance that Toguri brought to *Guys and Dolls* or Gillian Lynne to *Cats*: here the arthritic Irving Davies dances seem at best an interruption, and most of the company look as though they wish they'd been left alone to get on with the *Saint Joan* they could have managed so much better. It is just possible that with the acid touch of a Sondheim or the fluid brilliance of a Bennett, *Seberg* could have been made to look a bit better than the recent *Marilyn* at the Adelphi.

1984

IN A RECESSION PEOPLE START to reach for their tap shoes and maybe even their tap shows: that at least was the received wisdom of Busby Berkeley in the Hollywood 1930s, and it is surely no coincidence that the *42nd Street* he started to work on all of fifty years ago should this year have won awards at Drury Lane, curious though it seemed to be offering such nominally new awards to a show which had neither a song nor many lines of dialogue written since the war. But this was a year of big old singalongs: sixteen of them were at one time running simultaneously in London, as if to prove that, with ticket prices at last breaching the £10 barrier and the American dollar making tourist theatre going the greatest bargain since the five-cent cigar, what people wanted was not just to come out of the stalls humming the hit song but to go into them humming it as well.

Admittedly the few musicals around were, with one glowing exception, something of a disappointment, though Andrew Lloyd Webber's courageous and

Jeff Shankley, Timothy West, Al Pacino and Ian McKellen

splendid championing of *The Hired Man* more than compensated for his *Starlight Express*, a show about rollerskate racing incidentally, in case anyone had formed the understandable impression from the extract seen on the televised awards ceremony that it was in fact a show about two gay black hairdressers falling in love. Elsewhere, however, this may well turn out to have been a year remembered more for its flops than its hits: after a decade or so in which we told ourselves smugly that marathon disasters only happened on Broadway, 1984 brought us three nights of *Top People*, the Danny La Rue *Hello Dolly*, *Mandragola*, *Peg*, *Blockheads*, *Big in Brazil*, *Seachange*, *Happiest Days of Your Life* and a musical of *The Importance* from which audiences exited (often before the interval) looking as though they had just been treated to a revival of Mel Brooks's *Springtime For Hitler*.

On the legit stage there were other and more curious disappointments: an Albert Finney double (*Biko* at Riverside and *Serjeant Musgrave* at the Old Vic) which delivered a lot less than it promised, a Royal Court still floundering around in search of a budget and a policy and at the year's end going back into Bondage with the early plays of Edward: if this was to have been heritage year, the early Osbornes would surely have been a better idea. Meanwhile the National veered from the depths of *Mandragola* to the heights of *Fool for Love*, the RSC still seemed unable to cope with anything in the seventy-five years that separate *Peter Pan* from *Golden Girls*, and the West End went on looking so far back over its shoulder that it remained imminently in danger of breaking its neck.

The best of the year almost invariably resulted not from any subsidised company policy or commercial enterprise but simply from individuals sticking to what they believed in and then making it happen: Glenda Jackson determinedly brought *Strange Interlude* back to life despite its five-hour sprawl, Sam Walters gave us a wonderful and shamefully under-rated look at Rodney Ackland's great *Dark River* at the Orange Tree in Richmond, Vivian Matalon brought another disgracefully ignored modern classic, *Morning's at Seven*, across the Atlantic to the Westminster, Wendy Toye gave us a first look at the classic Rodgers and Hart *Babes in Arms* performed suitably enough by drama students from LAMDA, Bill Bryden brought back *Golden Boy* to confirm the lasting greatness of Clifford Odets.

Away from London, the Royal Exchange in Manchester pulled off a powerful treble with the late Michael Elliott's *Moby Dick*, the Tom Courtenay–Julie Walters *Jumpers* and a summer season *Carousel*, while on the London fringe the Lyric, Hammersmith, seemed doomed to good plays denied an afterlife – notably Harwood's *Tramway Road* and Gray's *Common Pursuit*, either of which would surely have found a West End home in a year less desperate for tourist nostalgia.

A rich season at Stratford from *Henry V* to the Sher *Richard III* on the main stage, and a poor one at Chichester until they got to *Way of the World*. The Bush overtook Hampstead as the best London home for new work, thanks largely to Doug Lucie, while in the West End the survival of the appalling *Nerd* and the shaky *Trumpets and Raspberries* came as a sharp reminder of what a couple of hot TV comics (Rowan Atkinson and Griff Rhys Jones) could do to overcome thin reviews and thinner plays. That lesson seemed not to have been lost on the National either, where both Rik Mayall and Graeme Garden joined the company.

Watford developed an interesting line in failed snobbery-with-violence thrillers (*Raffles* and *On The Spot*), late-night cabaret pianists (Steve Ross and Peter Greenaway) made a surprising return to public favour, Michael Frayn did a brilliant rewrite of Chekhov (*Wild Honey*) and Tom Stoppard a disastrous one of Molnar (*Rough Crossing*). Al Pacino signed a lot of autographs after *American Buffalo*, Alan Ayckbourn continued to turn one mildly okay comedy into eight desperately overstretched variations (*Intimate Exchanges*), Wendy Hiller gave the dowager-of-the-year performance in *Aspern Papers*, Claudette Colbert made her first London starring appearance in more than half a century, Alec McCowen did a lot for Kipling, most of which was then undone by a *Jungle Book* of stunning boredom, and the year ended in a blaze of starry female turns.

Not only Glenda Jackson following the O'Neill with an Old Vic *Phedra*, but Judi Dench as a miscast *Mother Courage*, Joan Plowright and Maggie Smith in *Way of the World*, Nichola McAuliffe in the Wesker monologues, Hiller and Redgrave in *Aspern Papers*, Julie Walters in *Fool For Love* and Julie Covington in *Tom and Viv*, Sheila Gish in the Mermaid run of *Streetcar* and Makarova in *On Your Toes*. Male equivalents seemed to get somewhat scarcer, though Timothy West deserved some sort of versatility award (*Master Class*, *War At Home*, *Big in Brazil*), while the Michaels Williams and Kitchen turned in two of the great comic turns of the year in *Two Into One* and *Rough Crossing*.

But for my money four of the most impressive performances of the year came from Daniel Massey at the Barbican: in two main stage transfers from Stratford (*Measure for Measure* and *Twelfth Night*) and in two twentieth-century plays in the Pit below (Saroyan's *Time of Your Life* and Poliakoff's *Breaking the Silence*) he confirmed what I had long suspected, that he was the most impressively versatile if still under-rated leading actor of his generation.

The Record Breakers

Power plays have always made good box-office, and David Pownall's *Master Class* (at the Old Vic in a Leicester Haymarket production by Justin Greene) is no exception. We are in Moscow in 1948: a Musicians' Union conference has been summoned, not (as Western observers might expect) to discuss needle-time copyright repeat fees on Soviet Radio, but instead to consider the whole future of piano-bashing in an ideal Stalinist state. Tone-deaf Joe from Georgia therefore summons to the Kremlin two of the leading conference delegates, Prokofiev and Shostakovich, firstly to frighten the living daylights out of them and secondly to enlist their aid in the composition of a folk song cycle suitable for the new dawn.

It needs here to be established that we are not dealing with documentary truth: though there was indeed a Musicians' Union conference in Moscow in 1948, Prokofiev was already too ill to attend it and there is no evidence that Stalin invited any of the delegates round to his place for after-hours lessons in musical appreciation. But here, as in Robert David Macdonald's recent *Summit Conference* (about the meeting of the mistresses of Hitler and Mussolini), a dramatist has seen in an imaginary backstage confrontation a joky and intelligent way of highlighting recent political truths.

Thus we get to meet the cringing Shostakovich (David Bamber), the patrician, ailing Prokofiev (Peter Kelly), Stalin himself (Timothy West in another of his Madame Tussaud's gallery of from-the-life impressions) and a butch Soviet Marshal (Jonathan Adams) in a male four-handed conversation piece which rambles over a wide variety of arguments about the role of music in a police state. Essentially all we have here are two doomed composers being shouted at by two old soldiers; but Pownall's achievement lies in the subtlety of their differentiation.

Stalin is in no doubt about his role: 'I am the past; I make the present; I will supervise the future.' Music is just one item on an endless agenda of things to be dealt with on the long route to totalitarianism: it needs to be cleaned out, purified and given back to the people, preferably in the form of folk music and who better to guide it than a man who, as Stalin memorably says of himself, is 'more folk than any of you. I am the ultimate folk.' To establish his musical superiority, just as he has already established his political superiority, he has first to destroy the past and that is here easily done, in a stunning first act closing routine in which he ritually smashes an entire Prokofiev record collection across the back of a chair. Had the invention of the long-playing record in America come only a year or two earlier, Mr Pownall would have had no play.

So while Stalin is smashing the musical past, watched by the increasingly terrified Shostakovich, who, if asked, would, you feel, have been willing to set Red Square to music, Prokofiev alone has the arrogance and courage to start outlining the limits of the musical support that Stalin can reasonably expect from his composers. Already so ill, suggests Pownall, that he can afford not to fear death quite as greatly as Shostakovich, it is Prokofiev who with an infinitely weary kind of elegance measures up for the final battle as if aware already that both Peter and the Wolf might outlive even Communism itself. But what in the end is, I think, wrong with Pownall's play is its inability to decide whether it's in fact a comedy about a mad dictator trying to compose a folk opera with two professionals of widely differing musical training, or whether it's a drama about the role of the artist in a totalitarian state. As a result we get a good deal of both, and yet not enough of either to make for a totally enthralling evening: a slim musical joke has been blown up into a power play that is only sometimes about power; its fundamental seriousness, however, and the quality of its quartet playing does happily suggest that the new Vic is in the legitimate drama business as well as that of visiting musicals.

Back in Old Tennessee

In this column five months ago I suggested that we should not see a better *Streetcar Named Desire* than the one Alan Strachan was then directing at Greenwich and that it urgently deserved a West End transfer. I suppose it is debatable whether five months counts as urgency, or whether the Mermaid counts as West End, but I see no other reason to alter that original verdict. Strachan's *Streetcar*, though not much changed since its original first night, has in fact grown intensely so that Sheila Gish is now giving a great instead of a merely very good performance in surroundings that have also gathered confidence.

This immensely thoughtful, careful and loving revival comes, in the immediate aftermath of Williams's death, as a sharp reminder of his dramatic brilliance, one that was much needed considering how seldom the play has ever been revived in London and how hopelessly the property is now overhung with memories of Vivien Leigh and Marlon Brando playing Beauty and the Beast through that much-overrated Kazan film of 1951. Despite the comparisons that have elsewhere been made, it needs to be recalled that Brando was not Mr Williams's first choice for Stanley: he in fact wanted the infinitely more subtle and intelligent John Garfield, and it is towards that kind of performance, rather than Brando's, that Paul Herzberg's new Kowalski is pitched. Nor need Blanche be the simpering loony immortalised by Miss Leigh: Sheila Gish portrays her until the final crack-up in vastly more controlled neurosis, thereby making the ultimate reliance on the kindness of strangers leading her to an asylum all the more tragic.

Though carefully located in the New Orleans of 1947, with a brilliant split-level set and a haunting jazz background for the scene changes, this is still a production very much in the tradition of what Strachan has been doing at Greenwich over the last five years with Priestley and Rattigan and Coward: slow, studied revivals of contemporary classics that you always think you know only too well until you get there and find that you really hardly know them at all except by faulty memory or screen travesty.

And talking of the tricks that memory can play, the current revival of *Jumpers* at the Royal Exchange in Manchester also comes as something of a revelation. This was Tom Stoppard's first full-length play after the *Rosencrantz and Guildenstern* that made his name: it was seen originally at the Old Vic back in 1972, in a production starring Michael Hordern and Diana Rigg which most of my colleagues have compared more than favourably to the current and first major revival at Manchester, which stars Tom Courtenay and Julie Walters, two of our present Oscar nominees.

It is of course quite true that the production we have now (by Nicholas Hytner) is very different from the one we had twelve years ago: for one thing it is now in the round, and for another it is a great deal quicker. That does not, however, necessarily mean that it is any worse, and I for one am inclined to think (at the risk of getting into one of Mr Stoppard's own tortuous linguistic distinctions) that what we originally gained on the swings we have probably now not lost on the roundabouts. *Jumpers* is quite literally a play on words, a sort of dramatised Scrabble, where plot and characterisation take second place to a dazzlingly loony display of verbal pyrotechnics with which the playwright and his professorial leading character beat us into temporary submission. *Jumpers* is, in short (which it seldom is), the kind of play on which the image and reputation of Stoppard was founded, and which you have to see if only to judge how far he has moved in another and more human direction with *The Real Thing*.

Facts first: the play is focused on George, a lecturer in philosophy who appears to owe his job to a nominal similarity to George Moore the philosopher (as opposed, if you're still with me, to George Moore the novelist). He is married to Dottie, a fallen music-hall star who has certain difficulties in remembering the lyrics of well-known American songs and is inextricably involved with the vice-chancellor of her husband's university. Not that he's your ordinary kind of vice-chancellor: he's also the local coroner and the leader of a team of incredible liberal-radical jumping men who are available for such sinister tasks as removing the body of another academic acrobat who has been mysteriously shot while forming the base of a human pyramid at one of Dottie's parties.

A decade on from the moment in our history when moon landings and radical politics and relative philosophy looked briefly as though they might be going to mean something, *Jumpers* holds up wonderfully well as a vaudeville of the human mind at its most uncertain. A lot of the characters in the play only exist there for the sake of their names: the first British astronauts on the moon are therefore Scott and Oates, and it is Oates of course who gets accidentally detached from the landing craft and may therefore be hanging about in space for some time. Similarly Bones the policeman was previously an osteopath until being called Bones the Bones drove him to a new career in the CID. Yet these and other characters only exist as a baroque background for the play's central figure: George is the greatest linguistic acrobat of all the Jumpers, a walking thesaurus who starts his lectures with the word 'secondly' and gradually dismantles himself as he delves deeper and deeper into a semantic forest of impenetrable gloom.

But the real trouble here still starts from the interval: despite an agile performance from Tom Courtenay, who can stand on a tortoise better than any actor around, and despite the fact that Julie Walters is rather more convincing than was the even starrier Miss Rigg as a failed cabaret turn, act two still suggests that it has been tacked on to a one-act play for reasons to do with the bar trade. *Rosencrantz* apart, the one act form was then still what Stoppard knew best, and the first ninety minutes of *Jumpers* is one of the most brilliant linguistic turns in the business. But having piled on acrobats, jugged hares and the moral uncertainties of moon landings, the author suddenly seems to have discovered that he has not the faintest idea how to get us out of his own maze. It is true that I have no idea at all how *Jumpers* should end: but it is mildly alarming to find Mr Stoppard himself in apparently the same predicament.

Training for the Stage

If you can imagine what it must be like to be locked up for more than two hours in a roller-skating rink with a lot of acrobatic dancers while they prepare for the Eurovision Song Contest you will have some idea of the success, and also my dislike, of Andrew Lloyd Webber's *Starlight Express* (at the Apollo, Victoria). There is no doubt that what we have here is a major international moneymaker which will rival and possibly even improve on the track record of Webber's four previous musical hits, though where they had T. S. Eliot or Tim Rice or the Bible to help them along, this one has nothing but a lot of brilliant technical engineering. From the moment you enter the theatre and see the model trains running around the stalls you know you are in for an evening at Disneyland, and nobody here seems to be pretending that they've got a book or a plot or even a single idea about trains to be followed through.

Instead (thanks largely to the lighting of David Hersey and the settings of John Napier) what we get is a mindless spectacle of stunning stage management but no actual theatrical intensity of any kind. Roller-skating tracks have been built, at a cost of over a million pounds, around the perimeter of the theatre, thus allowing the cast to leave the stage periodically and set off on frantic chases around the building. But as these chases are necessarily often out of sight, video screens are solemnly lowered and you are invited to watch a hazily and inadequately photographed relay which stops the show dead in its tracks for upwards of five minutes at a time. *Starlight Express* is thus programmed, computerised and constructed with all the brilliance at Webber's financial disposal (a budget of somewhere over £2 million, to be recouped after a year's playing to the capacity houses they are certain to get) but it is as artistically dead as a landing strip.

Ironically, one ten-minute sequence in *Cats* entitled *Skimbleshanks* said all that needed to be said about humans pretending to be trains, and said it with more wit and intelligence than is to be found in the whole of this sprawling shambles. There is only some point in doing a whole show about trains if you have some point to make about them and, apart from mild regret at the passing of steam, it is clear that neither Webber nor even his agile lyricist, Richard Stilgoe, have any more to say about them than could neatly have been contained on one of the flyleaves of *Thomas The Tank Engine*.

There are only a certain number of times that a chorus can sing 'Freight is Great' before you start to think that the score has been written by, as well as for, roller skates, and a series of epic final choruses starting early in the evening and interrupted later only by the occasional chase round the building do not add up to a structure. Most of the best performances are given by the scenery, which lights up, moves around and generally has all the good parts: there's a lot for the eye here, one or two good songs for the ear, but for the mind absolutely nothing at all. A ton of scaffolding gets flown around, and there is, in the second half, during the title song, the most dazzling lighting effect I have ever seen in a theatre. But just occasionally, usually when Lon Satton is on stage as the old Deuteronomy figure, you realise what kind of show this could have become if it had been left to human beings.

Despite the involvement of Trevor Nunn as director, who has clearly achieved one or two moments of intelligent humanity, the overall impression of *Starlight Express* is of being invited by a millionaire to watch him play with some extremely expensive and ingenious but ultimately wasteful toys. If only the money and talent involved here had actually gone out and found a show, instead of a project that is one of the most mindless and moribund displays of energy since the marathon dances of the Depression, then *Starlight Express* might have been something to cheer.

1984

As it is, I just hope it will make enough money to allow Webber to get away from the electronics and back into the theatre where he belongs. The emperor is badly in need of a new tailor.

Design for Living

To have written a modern *Master Builder* and peopled it with characters from the cartoons of Marc and Posy is in itself no mean achievement: but what makes Michael Frayn's *Benefactors* at the Vaudeville the best (and also incidentally the best acted) new play in town is his realisation that in the South London architectural wars of the late 1960s there lay the basis for genuine debates about the way people live now – and how many of those have you heard in the West End lately?

Admittedly, the quartet who play this chamber piece seem at first almost too perfectly and neatly paired. On the right we have David and Jane (Oliver Cotton and Patricia Hodge), natural do-gooders as per the title: she forever helping neighbours in distress, he planning an idealist South London estate, a sort of postwar Welwyn Garden City that disintegrates before his very eyes. On the left we have Colin and Sheila, natural beneficiaries but also natural destroyers: she forever cadging

Benefactors Patricia Hodge *as Jane*, Brenda Blethyn *as Sheila*, Tim Pigott-Smith *as Colin* and Oliver Cotton *as David*

meals and husbands, he determined to tear down whatever David builds up for the sheer fun of the destruction. And through the many doors of Michael Annals's box set they appear and disappear like so many little weathermen, Jane popping out to indicate sun and Sheila forecasting the inevitable deluge which follows.

Like Frayn's *Clouds* rather than his *Noises Off*, this is a play about what people look for in life and then about what they find there; it's a play about the tyranny of the helpless, the inevitability of change and the fact that in the end we are no better at human planning than we are at town planning. *Benefactors* is perhaps the closest that Frayn has come on stage to his own journalism, but it remains for all that a marvellously comic and dramatic and truthful piece, and not only for those of us who happened to live on South London architect-planned estates in the late 1960s and for whom it resembles the drowning effect of having your entire past life flash before your waterlogged eyes.

As the architect devoted to new buildings who finishes the play being supported by a wife who has dedicated herself to the preservation of old ones, Oliver Cotton manages to sustain an amiable air of *Guardian* liberal bewilderment; as the wife who hates nothing more than her own willingness to be helpful on every possible occasion, even to the neighbour who may be about to steal her husband, Patricia Hodge has a kind of icy enchantment; as the lethally squatting neighbours Brenda Blethyn and Tim Pigott-Smith manage a perfect pairing of the kind of people who could set fire to themselves and still have you accused of their murder. It is true that in the last fifteen minutes Mr Frayn gets himself into his usual trouble with endings, which is essentially that he always seems to have mislaid them somewhere around the beginning of act two: it is high time the Codron management equipped him with an automatic play-finisher.

Apart from that, though, this is a human scaffolding of quite brilliant design and realisation: like Stoppard's *The Real Thing* and Pinter's *Betrayal*, it may well be another example of the word-playing English dramatists of the 1960s getting back to emotional basics, but it is the most literate explanation of how we got to here from there that I have heard in a very long time. It is also immaculately directed by Michael Blakemore, and a likely starter in just about every category of this year's awards. In short, go.

Vivat Rex

A rich and rare theatrical collector's piece at the Haymarket: Frederick Lonsdale's *Aren't We All?*, last seen in London a few months before his death in 1954, at which time it provoked a barrage of abuse from Tynan and others complaining about clapped out drawing-room comedies from the Cowardly 1920s. The problem with that objection (and it is one that has still not been fully appreciated by reviewers of the present revival) is that, although officially dated 1923, the play in fact goes back to 1908, when Lonsdale first wrote and staged it as *The Best People*. At that time the last act was, however, a bit dodgy, as they so often were with Lonsdale, and he put it back in the drawer for revision fifteen years later.

What we have here is, therefore, not a drawing-room comedy at all, but a 'problem' play from the era of Barker and Galsworthy and the young Somerset Maugham: a Woman With A Secret comes back from Egypt to find her husband in the arms of another woman. She too has been having a bit of a fling while abroad with a young Australian, but declines to confess this while accusing her husband of infidelity. Then, thanks to her conniving father-in-law, the young Australian turns up: so who should confess what to whom? Onto this admittedly fragile frame Lonsdale has grafted a vicar and his wife straight out of Wodehouse, a fancy-dress ball out of an early Ben Travers farce and tracts of dialogue which still sound as though they are awaiting revision and some heavy cutting.

The real 'problem' with Lonsdale's plays, and indeed his leading characters, is that not only did he attempt to make bricks without straw but he often couldn't remember what a brick was supposed to look like. And if Rex Harrison and about half his cast seemed to be having a little trouble with the dialogue on opening night, that was as nothing compared to the trouble that Lonsdale always had with it. Unable to plot like Pinero or joke like Wilde, he fell back time and again on a series of ramshackle character sketches in search of a frame, and the rhythms of his meandering speeches were essentially the rhythms of his favourite actors and house-party hostesses around World War I.

The new Clifford Williams production is therefore essentially an evening for stargazing: we have Claudette Colbert, a fantastically well-preserved octogenarian Franco-American movie star making her return to the West End after fifty-six years away (and of how many other actresses could that ever have been said?) dressed like a Christmas tree and turning in a performance of equally dazzling certainty as Lady Frinton. Then we have Rex Harrison, a master light comedian who for thirty years hasn't done a light comedy, turning the old Ronnie Squire role of Lord Grenham into a power-broker whose strongest suit is still the suit he stands so elegantly up in. Add to them Michael Gough and Madge Ryan as a wonderfully melancholic vicarage couple, and then Francis Matthews and Nicola Paget dealing with the play's curious morality, and what you get is a rococo museum piece of baroque fascination. Intermittently shaky though the opening-night performance may have been, I would still like every drama student in London to be shown the moment when Mr Harrison reads with some surprise of his own engagement in *The Times*.

To see timing like that nowadays you usually have to go to work in a watch factory.

Having, as she sharply reminds me, been about the only critic in the business to find the *Salonika* that made her name largely unwatchable, I once again find myself in disagreement with most of my colleagues over a play by Louise Page. This time it's *Golden Girls* at the RSC's Other Place in Stratford, a topically Olympic account of women training for the 100 metres relay which, with one or two honourable exceptions, has received a shamefully grudging press considering that it's far and away the best new play the RSC have done since *Good* and also the best thing I've ever seen in ten years at the Other Place.

Within the cramped confines of that Avonside Nissen hut, helped by the occasional strobe lighting and some gymnast weights, but precious little else, the director Barry Kyle has brilliantly evoked the sweat and the tension and the final burst of energy that this play is all about.

Far from a latterday *Chariots of Fire*, it's really about the impossibility of running clean or free in a world where sexism and racism and sponsorship and drugs have already taken their toll on a sporting ethic. Like the shows its title most recalls, *Top Girls* and the Broadway *Dreamgirls*, this is also a play about a team of women forming a female front line only to have it crack from within, and affords wonderful acting chances not only to Josette Simon as the starriest of the athletes and Jennifer Piercey as their doctor but also to Kenneth Branagh as the falling male track star and Polly James as the pushy sponsor. Again not since *Good* have the RSC been this good in a new play; performances at Stratford are few and far between this summer, but I have a feeling the play will be around on both sides of the Atlantic for a long time to come.

Meanwhile, on their other studio stage at the Barbican Pit, last year's Stratford company can now be seen in the London transfer of William Saroyan's *The Time of Your Life*, a vintage bit of Americana from 1939, which resembles nothing so much as the flip side of O'Neill's *Iceman Cometh* written in the same year. Again we are in a downbeat bar-room where drinkers are serving life sentences, only now the agony has been stripped away to reveal a kind of gently lyrical resignation. A guy looking like Dooley Wilson's uncle gets hired to play piano; another guy, less plausibly, gets hired as the joint's resident comic dancer. A cop gets shot in the closing moments, before which not a lot has happened except that over two mesmerising hours we have learnt to live with a hooker who wants it known she was once in burlesque (Zoe Wanamaker) and a mysteriously affluent central figure (Daniel Massey) whose marvellously rambling and shaggy charm perfectly captures the play's mood.

Saroyan wrote drama the way the *New Yorker* publishes short stories: great aimless tracts of prose meandering around a central theme of lost illusions, and in its own shambling way this is probably as good an epitaph for prewar American innocence as we shall ever get. Essentially it's about a lot of actors who happen never to have worked in theatres: but it takes, as one of them notes, a lot of rehearsing for a man to get to be himself and along the way we get to meet some memorably starry turns.

Gray Matter

Simon Gray's new play *The Common Pursuit* (at the Lyric, Hammersmith in a production by Harold Pinter) is the one about undergraduate dreams drifting into the corruption and disillusion of middle age. To point out that Kaufman and Hart and Sondheim did it a lot better in *Merrily We Roll Along*, or that whole chunks of Mr Gray's first act look like offcuts from one of Frederic Raphael's *Glittering Prizes*, is not to deny the arrival of real dramatic intensity towards the end of act two. By then, however, some of the cracks in the fabric have become dangerously wide.

From the very beginning it looks as though we have two quite different plays here: the first is a waspishly bitchy light comedy about the Oxbridge literary mafia in the 1960s and 1970s, complete with nostalgic references to Ken Tynan and wonderfully accurate jokes about *The Sunday Times* taking on other drama critics because the paper was impressed by their lack of qualifications. It is with this acid social commentary, in the best traditions of *Butley*, that most of the Lyric's starry cast (Ian Ogilvy, Simon Williams, Clive Francis leading) seem happiest and most at home. Underlying it, however, is an infinitely darker play about failure and marital betrayal and violent homosexual death which can only really work if we start to care deeply about the characters as people instead of prototypes of a certain literary aristocracy. And the trouble is that we don't: only Clive Francis as the doomed North Country poet-professor makes us believe that here is a man worth caring what happens to, and as a result we have a curiously broken-backed piece not helped by an unusually heavy-handed production by Pinter.

Curiously enough, a recent and marvellous and heartbreaking American movie called *The Big Chill* cut through this same postgraduate wilderness with vastly greater success, because it established its cast as people first and students and magazine editors only second. Doing it the other way around, Mr Gray runs up against precisely the social carelessness he is writing about, and the curious imbalance of his play has not been helped by the crucial miscasting, in the role of the editor, of the one actor on the stage actually lacking the star quality he would have required to keep all the other stars around him if the plot is to make much sense. Mr Gray is still the master of elegantly clenched despair and at Hammersmith you will hear some of the most carefully and acerbically crafted dialogue in town. What you won't see is a very strong play.

In a year that has been altogether marvellous for rare American treats (*Strange Interlude* at the Duke of York's, Saroyan's *Time of Your Life* at the Barbican) perhaps the rarest of all is Paul Osborn's *Morning's At Seven* at the Westminster. Set in a small Mid-Western town in 1922, premiered on Broadway in 1939 when it flopped, and revived there in 1980 when it became an award-winning success, this is essentially popcorn Chekhov: four sisters living in neighbouring houses deal with three husbands, a son and a surprisingly pregnant girlfriend across three acts of domestic drama all the more fascinating for having come from precisely the year when O'Neill and Saroyan were telling more poetic tales of bar-room losers.

For Mr Osborn's characters are not losers at all, nor are they much given to poetry: they are the backbone of America, the people Miller was soon to write about in *All My Sons*. Sure there are a few skeletons in the closets: one of the sisters may well have been off with one of her brothers-in-law, and another may well have driven her husband to the very brink of mental and physical decay. But these are what Thornton Wilder would have called Good People: if they drink it is with caution, if they go to the pictures it would doubtless be the paintings of Norman Rockwell or the movies of Frank Capra. Indeed, one of the greater mysteries of the piece is why Mr Osborn, a deeply neglected playwright who finished up in Hollywood doing journeyman screenplays, never made this one over for Jane Wyman.

But in fact it's a better script than that might suggest: Osborn's four sisters may lack some of the potency of Chekhov's three, but they are still a formidable team, wonderfully played here by Teresa Wright (the only Broadway survivor), Faith Brook, Margaret Tyzack and Doreen Mantle. In this country you feel they'd have formed themselves into a Bach Choir, or at least revolutionised the WI and made guest appearances in the plays of Dodie Smith and Enid Bagnold. Tough, occasionally bitchy, in total control of men they have reduced to gibbering wrecks or else forced into self-contained apartments within their own houses, they are a formidably funny and touching sorority and when, at the very end of the play, one of them (Margaret Tyzack) announces that she is leaving, though only in fact to move into the house across the street, it is still a heart-stopping moment.

Thirty years after its joyous opening at the Players, Sandy Wilson's *The Boy Friend* has been made over as a Broadway big-band show and put into the Old Vic for a summer season en route to Manchester and the West End. Curiously enough Mr Wilson himself, who deeply objected to the Ken Russell movie of *The Boy Friend*, has here left his name as production supervisor on a treatment which seems to me to make very similar mistakes in expanding what was essentially a very small show to a point dangerously near puncture. The director of this revival, Christopher Jewett, seems to have at least one eye on the current Broadway success of *My One and Only* in particular and tap-dance nostalgia in general: accordingly we get a sextet of extras draped across the back of Robin Don's cavernous sets, massed-band orchestrations and an awful lot of reprises.

Somebody seems to have forgotten that this was once a little tiny show whose entire score fitted neatly onto two sides of a ten-inch LP: it now looks like a minor musical from the Twenties instead of a pointed satire from the Fifties. I'd never realised before that the plot is actually Rattigan's *French Without Tears* in drag rather than anything closer to *The Girl Friend* or the Astaire/Gershwin stage shows of the time, nor had I ever realised quite how little happens in the last forty minutes. A staging of this extravagance inevitably makes that more obvious, and there's a lot of unnecessary campery going on all over the place, though Anna Quayle's Madame Dubonnet, stationed exactly halfway from Sarah Bernhardt to Bea Lillie, is a constant delight, as is the discovery of Linda-Mae Brewer, the most electric musical talent I've seen since Minnelli.

Genuine Guinness

Early in the rehearsal period for the new Chichester *Merchant of Venice* (Patrick Garland's last production as director of that non-operatic Glyndebourne festival) Sir Alec Guinness let it be known that he was hoping to give his Shylock in simple and unopinionated surroundings, and those are surely what he has got. Even the Pamela Howard setting is so no-nonsense functional that to indicate the change of scene from downtown Venice to up-country Belmont a centre-stage fountain is merely revolved a few feet to the left.

So far, so basic; this is an ideal Shakespeare for schools, commendably unencumbered with the rustic campery that strangled Garland's last Chichester Shakespeare, the appallingly twee 1983 *As You Like It*. Instead we get a clear, cool look at the text, intelligent readings of the usually interminable casket scenes and even a mercifully brisk couple of Gobbos. What we don't get, though, is much of an idea about why we are being asked to watch this *Merchant*, beyond the fact that a Guinness Shylock was undeniably a good and long overdue idea and Sir Alec happens to live close at hand. In the event, his is an oddly muted turn which, at any rate on the first night, resolutely refused to blaze into any kind of dramatic power while remaining consistently watchable. There was a moment at the very end, when he came off after the court scene and happened to descend a staircase right by where I was sitting, which showed how powerful his Shylock would have been had it been caught by a close-up camera: his eyes were ablaze with the injustice that had been done his tribe by

Venetian laws, but you'd not have noticed from more than a couple of feet away, and Chichester has some vast open spaces to fill.

There are also moments towards the end when it becomes clear that Mr Garland has indeed had a number of thoughts about the text: he suddenly lights up stone inscriptions at the back of the set which have been in shadow until they spell out the full historic arrogance of Venetian anti-semitism, and (again within minutes of the end) we suddenly get the feeling that Jessica (a hitherto subdued Leslee Udwin) is about to rebel at the ghastly double standards of Belmont. But by then it is really too late: a couple of hours have passed in a bland canter through the plot, and though Joanna McCallum makes a wonderfully statuesque Portia, there were still times when I had the distinct feeling that she was going to slap her thighs with a riding crop and announce that Dick Whittington would be Lord Mayor of London after all. This curious pantomime feeling also comes of having the Duke and some minor friends of Antonio cross-cast from the current Gershwin revival on that same stage: a certain gravitas is missing, and the gondolas seem full of chorus boys on some European tour.

None of that would much matter were Guinness able to pull his scenes into some kind of shape: but given a supporting cast often unversed in much Shakespeare, and his own determination not to go the Olivier route to a flamboyant defeat by Portia, we are left with an oddly unfocused kind of dutiful adequacy. Jane Carr is a bouncy and splendid Nerissa, and Frank Shelley brings a welcome moment of tribal dignity to the Tubal scene; for the rest, it is an evening of elegant neutrality perfectly suited to a Saturday matinee outing for some old Sussex ladies who happen to have an Israeli cousin staying the weekend.

Wild Chekhov

The only thing better than an old Chekhov play is a new Chekhov play, and that is essentially what we now have on the National's Lyttelton stage, where Michael Frayn has taken the seven-hour untitled manuscript that was found in a bank vault some sixteen years after the good Doctor's death in 1904, entitled it *Wild Honey* and whittled it into a totally new shape. The play itself is not exactly unknown: Rex Harrison did it at the Royal Court twenty years ago as *Platonov* and it has turned up elsewhere as *Don Juan in the Russian Manner*. But the advantage of a seven-hour manuscript is that you can find in it most of whatever you happen to be looking for, and Frayn was clearly looking for two things: a manic farce in the best traditions of his own *Noises Off* and, since this was a first play, some kind of guidelines to the later Chekhov.

Happily the seedlings for *The Cherry Orchard* are all here: the lovelorn country doctor, the loss of the estate to the new bourgeoisie, the manic student, the merchant bully and the drunken schoolmaster all point the way through the trees to the long hot summer party which somebody will one day start to call Chekhovian. But that day is not yet, and what we get in the meantime are all the signs of a young playwright trying out various comic sexual entanglements to see which ones are likely to stay the course.

True there are times when Frayn seems in his adaptation to be parodying Chekhov rather than simply translating him: lines like 'Silence – somewhere a fool is being born' and 'Sometimes I miss her after lunch – so it's love,' suggest an Oxbridge arts revue circa 1960 rather than the long-lost training ground of a master dramatist, but gradually it becomes clear that the intention is to restore the notion of Chekhov as a group writer from the very start. Because the play has more usually been called *Platonov*, it has been assumed to be about him: in fact, despite Ian McKellen's marvellously comic turn in that chaotic role of the schoolmaster forever falling over his own broken promises, this is now a tragi-farce about fourteen people, all of them hopelessly locked together in a series of increasingly disastrous extra-marital relationships.

Christopher Morahan has given *Wild Honey* a production of extreme confidence and spectacle (when did you last see a man going under a train on stage?), but he has managed also to give it moments of absolute tranquillity so that the final lurch into Feydeau bedhopping farce is made all the funnier by its social desperation – 'if you won't stay as my wife, stay as my nurse!' Sharing the moments with McKellen are Charlotte Cornwell as the landowning feminist Anna Petrovna, Brewster Mason as the old Colonel who could have been a General and Roger Lloyd Pack as a murderous but ultimately murdered local horse thief. Nobody could ever have accused the young Chekhov of dramatic inactivity: from murder to suicide by way of divorce, desertion and firework displays, *Wild Honey* would probably have worked best on first discovery if it had been handed over to D. W. Griffith for the Gish sisters, and the young John Barrymore.

Relative Values

Though he may lack the Scrabbled intellectual and verbal intensity of David Mamet, or indeed the more laid-back nostalgia of A. R. Gurney, there's a case to be made for Sam Shepard as the most dramatically powerful of current American dramatists; and there's no doubt that his *Fool For Love* (newly arrived at the Cottesloe in an English production by Peter Gill) is the best thing he's yet done. We are in a stark, low rent motel room on the edge of the Mojave Desert: two lovers (played with unusual transatlantic energy by Julie Walters and Ian Charleson), unable to live either apart or together, are tearing the living daylights out of each other both sexually and emotionally. In the corner, half-hidden by the darkness, sits an old man. He is the girl's father. Unfortunately, he is also the man's father.

If you can imagine Thornton Wilder's *Our Town* rewritten as a case history of downtown Incestville Nebraska, you will have some idea of what is going on here: a mythic study of impossible lust in which the family that preys together stays together. But I am giving nothing away: the revelation of incest, which any lesser dramatist might have saved for a shocking final curtain, here informs and energises the one-act piece from the very start. It is precisely because we know they are related that this affair has its awful and gripping fascination, and from the outset they know it too.

Eddie has trekked two thousand miles in search of May after she has abandoned him yet again in an ongoing series of semi-marital disasters; neither character has much in the way of a job, or a life, or a purpose beyond this all-consuming illicit love for each other. Yet there is something both epic and mythic about the intensity of their affair, and the way it can be conveyed on a bleak studio stage across ninety uninterrupted minutes. Here, as in his current movie *Paris Texas*, Shepard seems concerned to throw small people up against huge landscapes and problems: though we never leave the motel room, we are left in no doubt that the desert is out there waiting for Eddie and May, and there is throughout the quality of Greek tragedy, of domestic disaster written in the heavens.

What saves *Fool For Love* from being merely a bus-and-truck roadshow of Albee's *Virginia Woolf* (with incest replacing the mythical child as the Awful Secret) is primarily Shepard's ability to give two desert rats an immediate but haunting pedigree, so we feel we have known them and their shared father for years; there is also the dramatic courage of giving us not just the central couple and the old man as a kind of anti-narrator but also an appalled onlooker and an unseen but all too audible offstage heiress who provides a final conflagration. These two are there to suggest that some sort of other life might be possible for May and Eddie; we, of course, know that they are in fact locked together with father (Tom Watson in yet another rich performance) for some kind of hellish eternity. Marlboro Country is never going to look quite the same again.

Train of Events

In a crumbling, animal-infested railway carriage at the back of the Moscow shunting yards sometime in 1924, a Jewish inventor of considerable and starry eccentricity is about to perfect the talking picture some five years ahead of the Warner Brothers. The idea itself has a certain fascination, leading as it presumably would have done to a musical remake of *Potemkin*, not to mention an all-Soviet *Jazz Singer*. But Stephen

1984

Poliakoff's new play *Breaking the Silence* (in a marvellous RSC production by Ron Daniels at the Barbican Pit) is not in fact another trip down the might have been byways of history; instead it is based on the true story of his own grandfather who, due to a little local difficulty involving Lenin's death and its effect on railway employment prospects, then had to flee in his socks across the border without his invention.

In the end the Poliakoffs didn't do too badly (the son took to inventing hospital bleepers and the grandson to being one of the best playwrights of his generation), but it is never quite clear why the grandfather had this terrible vision of himself as a mad old man trying to convince English bus queues that he was the true inventor of cinematic sound instead of pressing on to California, like so many of his fellow exiles, and turning the dream into a reality. Partly that is because the playwright has no interest in his family once they reach Britain, and partly it is because he doesn't have much interest in cinematic sound. The silence that is being broken here is not really that of the cinema at all: rather is it the silence of the inventor's wife who, in his hour of need at the border, at last finds her voice and saves his life.

To that extent this is, therefore, also a play about female liberation and about the shift in family power structures that came with Communism; it's also a play about a son in revolt against his father, but so hugely mesmeric

Breaking the Silence Daniel Massey *as Nikolai Pesiakoff*, Gemma Jones *as Eugenia Pesiakoff* and Jason Lake *as Master Alexander*

is Daniel Massey as the manic inventor that in the end we really can only care about him and wonder how long it will be before one of the best and still most under-rated actors of his generation gets to play the Diaghilev for which this performance would seem to be a last rehearsal.

Admittedly Poliakoff has here written a better part than a play: a man of Tsarist wealth and influence suddenly turned into a minor Soviet bureaucrat ('I am not the right person to watch telephone poles being erected') is a funny idea, and if you add to that the touching notion of a man already removed from reality now also condemned to live in a railway carriage which may take off at any moment for Siberia or worse, you end up with an epic study in human destabilisation. It may seem odd that a man who has never yet managed to boil a kettle can invent talking pictures, and still odder that in act two the play lurches into a Soviet re-run of *Pygmalion* with Massey trying to enlist the aid of his maid (Juliet Stevenson) in a cultural project unlikely to do her much good. Jason Lake is, however, touching as the gawky rebel son, and Gemma Jones wonderfully manages the transition from aristocratic wife to freedom organiser, but this remains Mr Massey's evening and not for the first time this year he is giving one of the finest performances in the whole history of the RSC.

1985

Theories based on any single year's play-going are bound to be a little suspect, but if 1985 established anything in the London theatre it was surely the return of the actor to a centre-stage position of full strength. From Ian McKellen and Edward Petherbridge running the first actors' company within the National, through Antony Sher and Anthony Hopkins giving the two most honoured star performances of the year in *Richard III* and *Pravda*, to players like Simon Callow and Steven Berkoff establishing that Charles Laughton and Bransby Williams did not die in vain, this was a twelvemonth in which acting in the grand manner made a welcome return from the outer boundaries of unfashionability.

Colm Wilkinson, Anthony Hopkins, Antony Sher, Michael Gambon, Vanessa Redgrave and Jonathan Pryce

These swings of the pendulum were not of course entirely accidental: a decade or more of a directors' and writers' theatre, in which the company ethic was the only one that appeared generally respectable, had left a very real hunger for blazing star turns, and I suspect that we have not seen the last of them. In the theatre as in politics, Victorian values were again bankable: how else to explain a West End full of *The Scarlet Pimpernel* and *Mrs Warren's Profession* and *Camille* and *Les Misérables*, let alone a Stratford full of *Nicholas Nickleby*?

The irony here was, of course, that in the name of those Victorian values, notably self-sufficiency and chronic tight-fistedness, the Government through the Arts Council was waging an unprecedented war on subsidised companies at a time when the supposedly commercial West End was in fact being kept alive by those companies. In 1985 the Royal Shakespeare Company at the Barbican sent *Waste* to the Lyric, *Breaking the Silence* to the Mermaid and, most gloriously, *Les Misérables* to the Palace, while from Stratford they sent *Camille* to the Comedy. In the same year the National Theatre's Cottesloe stage (the very same stage that was actually closed for six months because of reduced government subsidy in real terms) sent *Fool For Love* and *The Mysteries* into the West End. At the end of this year, the Olivier awards, which were specifically designed to honour commercial theatre achievement in London, gave almost all their leading nominations to performances and scripts which had, in fact, opened in the subsidised sector.

Brave talk of a restoration in the fortunes of the West End needed to be considered in the light of what was actually playing there: outside of *Les Misérables* (shamefully under-rated by most of my colleagues, but happily recognised by American critics as the musical of the decade, which it undoubtedly was) this was the year of *Mutiny*, of *Adrian Mole*, and of the still worse rundown of *Guys and Dolls* to a tacky shadow of its once great National revival. It was a year of pop-star necrophilia (*Lennon*, *Are You Lonesome Tonight?*, *Judy*) and of variable attempts to turn classic Hollywood movies into stage shows (*Gigi*, *42nd Street*, *Singin' in the Rain*). Some of these, like the Lloyd Webber trio, were holdovers from previous seasons; but in the search for an honourable new musical, at least one awards committee was forced back on to the revival of *Me and My Girl*, while another chose the Presley obituary. That the two best musicals of recent times, *Hired Man* and *Les Misérables*, should have opened to a mixed press while a roller disco like *Starlight* wheeled on for ever was perhaps some indication of the problems that would face the theatrical composers of the next decade – if there were many left out there beyond Rice and Lloyd Webber.

One encouraging musical note of this year, however, was the rebirth of cabaret: David Kernan at the Warehouse came up with a joyous celebration of Jerome Kern (which went on to Broadway) in which Elisabeth Welch gave a performance of *Smoke Gets in Your Eyes* which ought to have qualified for every theatrical award

1985

of the year, and as long as there was a piano in the restaurant of the Ritz it looked as though the minor classics of Rodgers and Hart would be heard as clearly as the nightingales in Berkeley Square all of fifty years before.

Away from the orchestra, this was an uncharacteristically lacklustre twenty-fifth anniversary year at Stratford, where only the closing *Othello* with Ben Kingsley and David Suchet seemed worthy of a Barbican transfer for the winter. Even there, however, a major opportunity was missed: not since Burton and Neville alternated Othello and Iago at the Vic in the middle 1950s had there been an English stage production in which the two central players were so evidently capable of each other's roles. Instead of leaving Kingsley as Othello and Suchet as Iago, it would surely have made sense also to try them the other way around?

At the National, this was the year of *Pravda* and McKellen: *Pravda* because it established (for the first time since David Hare's earlier *Plenty* there) that the South Bank could occasionally find major new plays on contemporary themes, and McKellen because he established for the first time since Olivier a company there run by actors rather than directors. Anthony Hopkins's return (as the wonderfully evil press baron in *Pravda*) to stage greatness after an uneasy Hollywood decade was also a cause for some celebration, and the news that he was to go on to a National *Lear* suggested that he was back to stay. It would need a psychiatrist rather than a drama critic to note that the two most applauded performances of the year (his in *Pravda* and Sher's in *Richard III*) were by actors playing larger than life Fascist villains who endear themselves to audiences by destroying all liberal opposition for several hundred miles in every direction.

While strong male performances (not only these but Michael Gambon in Ayckbourn's *Chorus of Disapproval* and Colm Wilkinson in the aforementioned *Misérables*) came from within the subsidised battlements, with only Jonathan Pryce turning in a West End performance of classic stature (in *The Seagull*), strong female turns seemed to thrive away from the National or the RSC. This was the year of the Glenda Jackson *Phedra* at the Aldwych, the Vanessa Redgrave Chekhov season at the Queen's, and still more notably of Janet Suzman as *Vassa* at Greenwich.

National Treasure

Though not, as some of my colleagues would have you believe, the greatest Shakespearian thing ever to have happened at the National (does nobody now recall the Olivier *Othello*, nor yet the Miller *Merchant*?), there's no doubt that the new Ian McKellen *Coriolanus* is far and away the best Shakespearian thing to have happened there in Peter Hall's time. Sir Peter is, of course, no stranger to the play: he first made his name with it at Stratford a quarter of a century ago, in a production which ended with Olivier hanging by his heels twenty feet above the stage, an image of sudden death so powerful and so eternally haunting that a few random gunshots at the end of the present production seem, even after all that time, something of an anti-climax.

It also has to be said of the present production that Ian McKellen, classically magnificent as ever, still lacks something of the sexual charisma brought to the role by Alan Howard in the last RSC revival five years ago, and that the thrill of the first two hours is oddly lacking in the final and most difficult hour, so that the audience leaves at the interval on a high which is just not there at the close. Yet these are minor complaints about a major achievement: Hall has, in launching the second-phase National of five separate companies, mercifully abandoned the masks and the operatic

Coriolanus Ian McKellen *as Caius Martius Coriolanus*

excesses of his recent work and gone right back to what he did best at Stratford all those years ago, complete with the sandpit from *Troilus*, which now forms the central arena.

Around it are ranged members of the audience, who double as the crowd, forming at one and the same time a mob, now threatening, now docile, and a forum of worthy senators. Into their midst comes McKellen, dressed at first like Edward VIII about to demand popular support in return for precisely nothing but arrogance and a sense of the blood royal. Half a play later, he turns up outside the gates of Antium in a trenchcoat looking like a Warner Brothers detective out for vengeance down the mean streets of an enemy city. Both those images work well enough, as do countless others: Hall's production is a feast for the eyes and ears with both a set (John Bury) and a level of verse-speaking that at last bring the National up to Barbican standards in Shakespeare, and not before time. McKellen makes the play's Fascism both attractive and easily understandable; but Hall's achievement has also been to give us in David Ryall's senior tribune and in Greg Hicks' surprisingly young Aufidius rivals of considerable subtlety and power, while bringing us back Irene Worth as a Volumnia of classical Greek strength and tragedy.

The result is a political thriller of spectacular and splendid tension, one which overcomes all the usual problems of modern dress and audience walkabouts to bring this great play back into focus as a timeless masterpiece about power and public relations.

The Stately Home of England

When they come, as surely they will in some American university drama department, to write a thesis on the social significance of the post-war stage comedies of William Douglas Home, they are going to have a lot of explaining to do. In the first place, here is a dramatist who has written about three of the best and a dozen of the worst drawing-room comedies I have ever seen without apparently being aware of the difference. In the second place, here is the brother of a former Tory Prime Minister, and the uncle of the present editor of *The Times*, much of whose autobiographical and theatrical writing looks, in Thatcherite times, like that of a revolutionary socialist.

He has, of course, a long history of being unexpected: a wartime prisoner of conscience for refusing to obey the barbaric bombing orders of his own side, he went on to write (in *Chiltern Hundreds* and later *Reluctant Debutante* and *Secretary Bird*) a trio of comedies which will, I believe, survive with the best of Rattigan and Lonsdale and even Coward. He is probably the only dramatist this century to have played the leading role in one of his own scripts entirely in drag, and I have always believed him to be a vastly more ambiguous and intelligent writer than his houseparty image would ever allow.

The trouble is that, though there is no better recorder of stately homes in social and political decay, Mr Douglas Home has outlived most of his own best players. People like A. E. Matthews and Ronald Squire and David Tomlinson and Wilfrid Hyde-White just don't exist around the West End any more, so that when his latest work (*After the Ball is Over* now at the Old Vic) hits the stage like a lead balloon, it is largely because neither of its principal players, the otherwise admirable Sir Anthony Quayle and Maxine Audley, are what you would call light comedians. True, we do also get Patrick Cargill as the butler, but years of television sitcoms have, alas, turned him into the paperback version of Mr Hyde-White. The genuine eccentrics just aren't available for eight shows a week, and without them the author has a distinct staff shortage both above and below stairs.

It is considerably to the credit of Maria Aitken as director that she has managed to stop the play lurching to a halt more than about half a dozen times, since a creaky farce about aristocratic wife-swapping and the end of fox-hunting really cannot sustain the classical grandeur of Quayle, nor a supporting cast who seem to have been recruited from small ads in *Horse and Hound*. But how much better had the Compass company gone back to one of the vintage and stately Homes that still work in regional reps up and down the country; then maybe I could have proved my point about the author as the last great chronicler of the upper classes in sexual and social disorder.

Back at the Royal Court a year after it first opened there, Michael Hastings's *Tom and Viv* is holding up very well; it remains a spare, elegant and enthralling account of the wasteland of T. S. Eliot's first marriage to the sexually and mentally crippled Vivienne Haigh Wood. Here still is the play with everything: Bloomsbury, Roaring Twenties, British aristocracy in loony decay, feminism, young Jamesian American come to London in search of fame and fortune before going on to write *Cats* or at any rate the inspiration thereof.

But Hastings has brilliantly avoided most of the more obvious pitfalls: nobody here is much afraid of Virginia Woolf, and we never even get to see Viv pouring her hot chocolate through the Fabers' mailbox in that great twentieth-century gesture of publishing discontent. We don't even get the famous Edith Sitwell quote about Eliot going mad and promptly certifying his wife. Instead we get this touching play about a young anglophile religious poet coming from America to Europe in search of sex, fame and revelation, and finding himself caught up in the attic cobwebs of an old English family stifling in a lost world of dust and suppressed lunacy.

Edward Herrmann now plays Tom, more convincingly American than

1985

Tom Wilkinson originally, but also faintly smoother, as if rehearsing for the television part-work on Eliot's life; but this is still Julie Covington's evening and she makes of the increasingly dotty Viv a rare theatrical feast. In her gradual decline to the mental home is mirrored the frenzy of an unfulfilled life: though the play brings us up to 1947 with medical explanations of her hormonal imbalance, that is merely the postscript to a tragedy of the 1920s. What Mr Hastings has written is a family chronicle, and though the father has been recast rather weakly, Margaret Tyzack and David Haig are still happily on hand to play Viv's mother and brother in all their landed and clenched eccentricity. The result is a carefully documented and stylishly staged (by Max Stafford-Clark) clash of transatlantic culture and temperament.

Paper Tiger

In that broad-scale new plays with large casts and about contemporary themes are an increasingly endangered species we ought to welcome *Pravda* on the National's Olivier stage with open arms. David Hare as director and co-author has come up with a blazingly theatrical event, at the centre of which Anthony Hopkins gives the scenery-chewing performance of his career. As a production, *Pravda* works wonderfully; as a play, I am not so sure. On one level it would appear to be the tabloid version of Stoppard's *Night and Day*, another look at the curious willingness of the British (and for that matter American, though nobody gets on to that) journalist to shackle himself to a proprietor and a political line he really doesn't much care for.

But where Stoppard was prepared to stage a reasoned Shavian debate about Fleet Street ('I'm all for the freedom of the press, it's just the newspapers I can't stand') Hare and his co-writer Howard Brenton have gone for what they call 'a comedy of excess', in which a series of quickfire sketches from Fleet Street life are presumably meant to work towards an indictment of modern journalism. About halfway through an inventive but diffuse evening, the authors seem however to have realised that their central character, the wonderfully evil proprietor, is actually more intriguing and more dramatic and more fun than anything they have to say about the people and the papers he has purchased. Just as Richard III overshadows and obliterates all the history that is supposed to be going on around him on stage, so Le Roux runs away with this play in what appears to be his Japanese sauna rather than the street of shame.

In recalling most of the major Fleet Street events of the past decade (the takeovers by foreign proprietors, sackings of ethical editors, wars over Bingo and union chaos) and trying to cobble them together into one two-act play through which a coherent pattern of political and social awfulness will be seen to emerge, the authors have I think taken on rather more than even their broad canvas can encompass. Moreover Le Roux occupies so much of their time and attention that his various opponents, even in such strong performances as those of Tim McInnerny as the young editor on the make and Basil Henson as the old one on the way out, become mere shadows for Hopkins to box out of existence. There is just no context here, nor is there much of a debate on why it is that the British press is so often inclined to censor itself in case nobody else remembers to; for all that, *Pravda* remains a savagely bitchy and often wildly funny evening which should be shown to anyone planning to buy a paper, whether from a newsvendor or the proprietor.

Of the four operatic and musical productions I have seen of Stephen Sondheim's *Sweeney Todd* in London and New York over the last five years, the chamber version that has just opened at the new Half Moon theatre in Stepney Green is far and away the most exciting and best conceived. It is directed by Christopher Bond, on whose original stage adaptation of the melodrama Sondheim based his musical, and what Mr Bond has now done is to pull *Sweeney* away from the vast open spaces of Drury Lane, away from the operatic excesses of City Centre, and back to where it belongs as an East London cut-throat caper. The more I see of scaled down Sondheim, the more I begin to think that his original

Pravda Tim McInnerny *as Andrew May*, Anthony Hopkins *as Lambert Le Roux* and Billy Nighy *as Eaton Sylvester*

producer Hal Prince was perhaps unwise to surround him with huge sets and Broadway budgets: *Sweeney* works so wonderfully at the Half Moon precisely because nobody in the audience is more than a few feet away from the barber's chair or the stench of Mrs Lovett's human pies, and never has this great score been sung with such intelligence and clarity and love as here by a cast of only ten and an orchestra of five. We even get the Judge's song cut at Drury Lane in the show's British premiere, and a tale of blood and murder and fire comes up looking fresh and stunningly powerful, nowhere more than in the ending, which Bond has drastically reshaped to return it to its Victorian theatrical origins. If we get a better musical production than this in the rest of 1985, we shall be more than lucky.

One of the many problems facing non-company theatres in London is how best to cope with the over-familiar classics. Thirty years ago, when John Clements was staging starry short seasons of West End Chekhov, the new Charles Sturridge *Seagull* (at the Lyric, Hammersmith, from the Oxford Playhouse) would not have looked either inadequate or out of place. But now that we have become accustomed to companies like the RSC or the Manchester Royal Exchange giving such scripts the benefit of long rehearsal periods and (often enough) casts who have been together for months rather than weeks, expectations are inevitably inclined to be rather higher.

This *Seagull* has all the vices and a few of the virtues of a BBC television Play of the Month, and not just because it is directed by a man who made his name on the small screen with *Brideshead*. It is starrily cast, but with actors working in totally different and often conflicting conventions, so that the meeting in Act Three between Trigorin and Arkadina as played by John Hurt and Samantha Eggar is in fact the clash between screen acting styles of the British 1980s and those of the Hollywood 1960s.

In the Rain of King Henry V

At the Barbican, this is proving to be a remarkable season for laying at last the ghosts of Olivier's greatest hits: after the Sher *Richard III* comes the Kenneth Branagh *Henry V*, again a radical rethink of a play which for nearly half a century had been trapped within the memory of the stage and screen presence of our greatest living actor. Sher uses the cacodemon's crutches to propel himself out of Olivier's shadow as Richard; as Henry, Branagh simply uses the changing patriotic perceptions of modern British history.

The Olivier *Henry V*, the one we all remember on film, came at a D-Day time when we needed all the jingoism we could get: the Branagh *Henry V* comes at a post-Falkland time when we have the luxury of no immediately discernible threat of invasion. Adrian Noble's rainsoaked production (water actually pours down on it from the grid in the height of battle) therefore takes an altogether soggier view of the call to arms. What will it actually mean for men in the field? Is the prize in fact worth fighting for and, if so, up to what exact cost? Until that final and quite literally miraculous discovery on the battlefield that God has indeed been fighting on his side and saved virtually all his lives, Branagh's Henry remains in some doubt about the wisdom of going once more into that bloody breach, and his doubts are what inform much of the rest of an intelligently low-keyed reconsideration of a play that is, in fact, a great deal darker than Olivier's Technicolor allowed.

With Ian McDiarmid's unusually mocking, cynical, intelligent Chorus to set the tone, we follow Henry's education in violent death from Scroop to Bardolph, so that by the time he coaxes his 'poor starved band' into battle against the gold-clad French, he seems to have aged even faster than Falstaff. This is not a *Henry V* of easy patriotism, but it is as careful and finely balanced a Shakespearian production as I have seen.

Turning towards Mecca, theatregoers might like to note that for the first time since 1939 the Lyceum has been restored to drama from dance: Bill Bryden's three *Mystery* plays have moved there from their original home on the other end of Waterloo Bridge at the National, and can be seen on all the Saturdays of this summer as a one-day-long treat from eleven in the morning until ten at night. The only difficulty with these marathons is that of course they conjure up memories of such others as *The Greeks*, *Nicholas Nickleby* and *Wars of the Roses*, all at the Aldwych over the last fifteen years or so. And by those exacting standards, what we have here is indeed a little thin. Tony Harrison's version of the street theatre that started out in 1453 Coventry does not have any of the subtle commentary that he brought to *Phaedra Britannica*, and deprived of much depth of character or plot, the cast are often reduced to those helpless grins you see on the faces of Morris Dancers, grins which manage simultaneously to regret the boredom but emphasise the traditionalism involved in their proceedings.

Yet these *Mysteries* are an event, and one which should be shown to thousands of schoolchildren: they offer a potted history of the Bible from the creation through to the damnation by way of Adam, Eve, Noah, Lucifer, Herod & Son and all the regulars in the first great theatrical soap-opera of all time. Bryden has had one or two really bright ideas, like a team of tumbling acrobats to build the ark and a huge Big Wheel for hell, but circus notions run a little thin elsewhere and the cast at the Lyceum is by no means as distinguished as once it was at the National. Yet this remains a spectacular in the finest old tradition of the Lyceum, and if you don't fancy joining the uneasy cocktail-party atmosphere of the on-stage audience, the management have kindly supplied seats around the gallery for those of us who have never wanted to be folk dancers or unpaid extras.

At Greenwich, following on from his Sheila Gish *Streetcar*, Alan Strachan has another immensely powerful Tennessee Williams revival: *The Glass Menagerie* was the play that first established Williams on Broadway all of forty years ago, but it has seldom been given major revivals over here and comes up now as a fascinating explanation of where he came from both as a writer and as a man. His mother was always understandably keen to deny that she was the ageing, overblown Southern belle who has crippled her son emotionally just as surely as her daughter had been crippled physically, but in giving the narrator his own initials and many of his own escapist aspirations, there's not too much doubt that the author wanted us planted deep in old Tennessee.

Yet what Strachan has brilliantly recognised is that this is not just a fey slice of deep Southern autobiography: it is also a resolutely black comedy about a dragon mother draining the blood of her own offspring, and Constance Cummings gives one of the most haunting performances of her career as the dread Amanda. Gerard Murphy's Tom is also the best I've seen: still with tricks in his pocket and things up his sleeve, but resilient rather than resigned to his poetic fate, fighting all that Southern comfort rather than drowning in it. Toria Fuller as the Blanched daughter and Michael J. Shannon as the gentleman caller complete a cast which richly deserves to stay together and prey together in a four-hander of ruthless and relentless emotional power.

Up from the Pit

While we await this autumn's musical staging by Trevor Nunn of *Les Misérables*, which has already one of the best French scores I've heard since the demise of Edith Piaf, the main argument against the Barbican is that in its opening three years there the RSC has singularly failed to generate the kind of new-production excitement that once existed for them at the Aldwych. True enough, if you consider only the main stage, where Stratford transfers have provided almost all the glory; but if you venture below ground into that claustrophobic 200-seat Pit you will usually find some of the strongest new shows in town, two of which have now ventured up for air into a West End that is dramatically improved by their presence.

At the Lyric on Shaftesbury Avenue, John Barton's adaptation and production of Harley Granville Barker's great political melodrama *Waste* is to be seen with only minor cast changes, though the loss of Maria Aitken as Trebell's sister is admittedly a sad one. But at the centre here we still have Daniel Massey as the doomed politician and Judi Dench as the woman who brings about his ruin in what is essentially the play that got the British theatre across the bridge from Wilde to Shaw at the turn of this century. Barker managed to combine the wit of Wilde with the dialectic of Shaw and then to add a cynical detachment of his own, which makes one regret all the more his decision to spend the last fifty years of his life writing Shakespearian footnotes for students instead of great plays for audiences.

Waste manages to be at the same time a debate on the disestablishment of the Church and a tragedy about a wasted career and two if not three aborted lives; it is also a play of breathtaking cynicism and bitchy intelligence about the unchanging machinery of cabinet government in this country, and it affords wonderful parts not only for Masscy and Dench but also for Charles Kay as a silky prince of the lay church and Tony Church as a time-serving Prime Minister-elect. Decades ahead of its time in subtlety, sophistication and sexuality, *Waste* is also the most savage indictment in town of the class and country from which it comes.

At the Old Vic, a revival of *The Corn is Green* to mark the eightieth birthday of its author Emlyn Williams, never quite recovers from the curious central casting of Deborah Kerr as Miss Moffat, the English schoolteacher loosely based on the one who in real life got Williams away from the Welsh valleys and on the road to an Oxford education. This is a role which has atracted all the craggy, battleaxe *grandes dames* of the English and American theatre from Sybil Thorndike through Ethel Barrymore and Bette Davis to Katharine Hepburn, and Miss Kerr is anything but one of them. To a part which demands rage and energy and power, she brings a kind of gracious condescension: instead of opening a pit-boy's eyes to the wonders of education she appears at best to be opening a Welsh fête in the style of minor visiting royalty, and the pity of it is that an otherwise extremely intelligent and powerful production is overshadowed by her insecurity in the role.

The only truly new play of the week is in fact a semi-documentary staging of *In the Belly of the Beast* which the Wisdom Bridge company from Chicago have brought briefly to the Lyric Hammersmith Studio. The Beast in question is the American long-term prison system and the other beast in the Belly of it is Jack Henry Abbott, the killer who achieved a kind of media fame a couple of years back through a literate correspondence with Norman Mailer which came to an abrupt halt when Abbott, out on parole, killed a waiter in New York. Out of this ghoulish material the director, Robert Falls, has carved an immensely powerful three-character drama which intercuts Abbott's trial on his last murder charge with his experiences across twenty-four years of prison in a life only thirteen years longer than that. But this is not in fact a plea for Abbott: in William Petersen's superb performance we are left with no illusion about the man's guilt, merely the question whether a lifetime of prison does in fact reduce man to such animal status that he kills to survive.

Key Largo

Not the least of the many achievements of Harold Pinter in his new Haymarket production of *Sweet Bird of Youth* has been to give us for the first time, live and in person, Alexandra del Largo, the Princess Kosmonopolis herself. In the gallery of Tennessee Williams's great, doomed and ravaged heroines, hers has always been a rather shadowy figure. Geraldine Page played her on screen and Broadway as a muted has-been, and over here the play has memorably been seen only once, at Watford, where intriguingly enough she was played by the late Mrs Pinter.

But now, in Lauren Bacall's memorably extravagant star turn, we get an even mix of Lady Macbeth and the Lady of the Camellias; indeed to hear Miss Bacall's throaty litany of exiled cities suitable for a falling film star is alone worth the price of a ticket. There is, however, a lot more here than a blazingly good central performance: *Sweet Bird of Youth* was Williams's most outspoken attack on the Southern Discomfort which had always been at the heart of his writing, and what Pinter has seen is a play about the castration not just of men but of careers and ideals and nations.

Sure, it starts a little slowly with the two visitors (to the London stage and the small Gulf hometown where the play is set), Lauren Bacall and Michael Beck, edging their way hesitantly into a duologue so full of pauses that for a fearful moment we seem to be in Pinter rather than Williams territory. But then it is, oddly enough, as the English take over (in above-average American accents) that the play races into life. James Grout's big-daddy Boss is a gargantuan villain surrounded by suitably seedy henchmen; with them, and Williams's wonderfully prodigal use of two dozen supporting players, we are off and running into a tale of political corruption and sexual agony, so that by the time the Princess and her blond gigolo are back, they too are playing at twice the speed of their first encounter.

Borrowing from Hart Crane, Williams once called his *Bird* 'a relentless caper for all those who step the legend of their youth into the noon' and that is precisely the mood that Pinter and his company keep alive through this sprawling saga of insides out, so that even the usual embarrassment of Chance Wayne's final speech to the audience is avoided. Lauren Bacall's non-musical London debut has also become the best company treat in town: the poisoned treacle of Williams's prose has seldom been better poured or more lovingly matured.

A new *Duchess of Malfi* marks the much-heralded arrival at the National Theatre of a new acting company led by Ian McKellen and Edward

Petherbridge, but is, in fact, mainly notable for bringing to the South Bank and not before time the considerable and often exotic talents of the Glasgow Citizens' director and designer, Philip Prowse. Indeed, one of the main indictments of a closed shop directing policy at the RSC and an unadventurous trawling by the National has been that Mr Prowse is so seldom to be found south of the border with Scotland. When he is, as last year at Greenwich or now at the National, the result is never less than mesmeric; indeed he is so far ahead of his contemporaries in theatrical flamboyance and designer flair that you would, I reckon, have to go back to Orson Welles at the Mercury to find a young stage artist of comparable power.

That doesn't of course mean you have to like or agree with everything he does: in fact, his cavernous decaying church setting for this new *Malfi* leads to moments of startling inaudibility, and his casting of some very strong stage figures (Sheila Hancock, Roy Kinnear, Hugh Lloyd and Selina Cadell) in relatively minor roles is apt to unbalance the central quartet. Edward Petherbridge is an increasingly camp Cardinal and Ian McKellen a darkly sneaky Bosola, but Jonathan Hyde has yet to come to terms with the Duke in darkness and Eleanor Bron, surrounded by a rentacrowd mob of loonies for the mad scene, manages to make 'I am Duchess of Malfi still' sound like a programme note, rather than a cry of survival under appalling pressure. Here too is a performance which has yet to come into its own, but in a rich, decadent, sinister, shadowy, ritual staging there is the constant sense of brooding, atmospheric evil and of religion in decay, which essentially has to be what this political melodrama is all about. The first night at the National last week said a lot more about Mr Prowse than about whatever plans McKellen and Petherbridge may have for their new team, but they are to be hugely congratulated for getting him there and allowing his unique classical vision to pervade the Lyttelton for the first time.

Given that we now have old musicals playing at roughly one in every three mainstream theatres in town, it is perhaps not surprising that Broadway stocks are becoming somewhat depleted. We therefore now have no less than three old American singalongs in the West End which were never meant to be stage shows at all: *42nd Street, Singin' in the Rain* and *Seven Brides for Seven Brothers.*

The *Seven Brides* that just opened at the Old Vic is, however, an altogether English attempt to get that score in front of a stage audience. It started out at the Theatre Royal in York fifteen months ago and is now, after a long tour, in London for the summer, presumably to catch nostalgic tourists with vague memories of beautiful hides being blessed in the great outdoors. But the problem here is that a film musical never comes together the way that a stage musical does: *Seven Brides* has a patched together score with the old movie hits and a few innocuous new numbers added for the theatre, yet never quite manages to overcome its camera origins. It never had much of a plot (what there is appears to be a parody of *The Sabine Women* known as *Sobbin' Women*, in which seven farmers kidnap seven brides), but it did have a great soaring sense of what the wide screen and a good choreographer could do for a camera. What we now have is an air of vague provincial jollity as an English rep company try to remember how *Oklahoma* was done; it has an endearing and almost amateur quality of teenagers at a camp concert determined to do the show right here. But when Garland and Rooney did that, they had the vast technical and musical resources of MGM behind them, which brings us back to the central problem of trying to do big screen musicals on a small stage.

Chorus Lines

A Chorus of Disapproval (on the National's Olivier stage) is very nearly Alan Ayckbourn's fortieth play, counting the one-acters and the minimusicals, and, although its original Scarborough strength has been somewhat diluted by the vast and unsuitably open spaces of the Olivier, it is in my view far and away the most successful of his more recent and bleak journeys into mid-life crisis. The chorus of the title is that of an amateur operatic society currently engaged on a production of John Gay's *The Beggar's Opera*. Into their midst comes the quintessential Ayckbourn Man: a widower, recently bereaved ('Accident?' asks a well-meaning neighbour. 'No,' he replies. 'Intentional, then?') and hoping to rebuild his life in a small town where the only action seems to be on stage with the local amateurs.

Ayckbourn's intriguing achievement here has been to build a central figure who is almost totally invisible: beyond the sketchiest details of his job and recent marital loss, we know nothing about him and are not intended to. He exists purely in the eyes of others, and Bob Peck's wonderfully vacuous performance allows the author to make his usual points about the unthinking cruelty of a supposedly neighbourly society vastly more coherently and powerfully than usual. By giving us only very occasional glimpses of the actual *Beggar's Opera* production, Ayckbourn also neatly sidesteps any comparison with the backstage chaos of *Noises Off*: this is not a play about amateur actors, but about a group of people who happen to be doing some amateur acting as a welcome respite from the awfulness of their own marital and professional lives.

True, there are towards the end occasional indications that Ayckbourn had perhaps intended something altogether more ambitious; the *Beggar's Opera* itself is clearly meant to find modern echoes among the people who are performing it, and the mythical town of Pendon is not short of lascivious wives, corrupt aldermen or likely lads on the make. But the play is actually at its most ponderous and least successful when it attempts historical and musical bridges of that kind; where it works best is in the sketches from urban marital life in which Michael Gambon (as the fraught producer wishing his cast were professionals so he could sack them) and Gemma Craven (as the randy husband-swapping local siren) are able to outline whole areas of semi-detached uneasiness.

As a comedy of appalling manners, this *Chorus* works well enough; but beneath the surface, visible in such moments as the one where Gambon suddenly unleashes a stream of pent-up rhetoric about the anti-intellectual bias of his neighbours ('Tell them you're interested in the arts and you get messages of sympathy') is, I suspect, a lot of home truth about Ayckbourn and Scarborough.

Though it was still surfacing in the occasional amateur dramatic society of the 1950s, *The Scarlet Pimpernel*, now to be seen at Chichester, has effectively come back to us after almost a century away. The stage version in which Fred Terry toured the length and breadth of Britain for so many years was the last of the great Victorian swashbucklers, and it was overtaken and outdated by the Leslie Howard film of 1934. A decade later, Howard updated his *Pimpernel* to World War II, and by the time Korda tried to get it back to the guillotine (in a catastrophic David Niven remake of 1950) audiences were patently not seeking him here, there or anywhere. Nobody even bothered to do it over as a musical.

It is therefore considerably to the credit of the producer John Gale, his adapter Beverly Cross and his star Donald Sinden, and above all his director Nicholas Hytner, that eighty years on they have managed to reconstruct Baroness Orczy's ramshackle tumbril and turn it into a rare theatrical treat of rediscovery. The *Pimpernel* was never much of a script, partly because scene-shifting problems meant that a play almost entirely about rescuing people from under the guillotine had to be set almost entirely at an English country house party three hundred miles away. But what it does have going for it is Orczy's own exotically foreign view of the great English virtues, which is precisely why Leslie Howard (himself Hungarian) was so much better in the title role than the all too English Niven.

Orczy's *Pimpernel* had remarkably little to do with the French eighteenth century: he was a creature of The Breed, one of those snobbery-with-violence heroes more usually found in Buchan and Sapper and Dornford Yates and Rider Haggard. He was the perfect English gentleman, useful at a dance and invaluable in a shipwreck, whose exploits just happened to be set back a couple of hundred years, but whose heart belonged in the English country house, where most of the play is set.

On to this already complex historical timeshift we then get the superimposition of Donald Sinden, carrying as usual around the stage like a huge invisible trunk all the memories of Victorian showmanship which Terry, too, must have brought to this role. Thus we have a play about the French Revolution acted in Lyceum melodrama fashion by modern actors playing characters from turn-of-the-century country house parties. It would be a brave man who tried to direct that lot into any sort of coherence and Mr Hytner has wisely settled for the Coliseum style of a manic comic opera in the course of which guillotined heads get kicked around by visiting rugger teams and there is a great deal of camping about, not least from Mr Sinden, who spends much of the first act trying to work out whether his Lord Foppington from *The Relapse* can be cobbled together with his Harcourt Courtly from *London Assurance* to give us an altogether new historical hybrid, loosely stationed somewhere halfway from the Restoration to Lady Bracknell. Having decided that this will indeed be possible and that, since people are losing their heads, we may as well have a bit of the Ugly Duchess from *Alice* as well, Sinden then proceeds to romp through a joyous farrago in which his only real competition comes from Charles Kay, who has already given one of the two best supporting performances of the year in *Waste* and is here giving us the other one.

Danny Girl

When they come to write the history of the modern American theatre, they are going to have a problem with Wallace Shawn. A writer of rambling conversation pieces like *My Dinner With André*, he fits into no convenient theory of the new drama and indeed seems to cobble together his scripts on a curious axis of old movies and late-night radio phone-ins peopled by philosophic insomniac cranks. His latest play, written for the London/New York exchange scheme now operated by the Royal Court and Joe Papp's Public Theatre, is *Aunt Dan and Lemon*. Watching a preview, it seemed to me that Max Stafford-Clark's immensely strong production, while failing to bridge one or two severe cracks in the structure, yet comes as further proof that the shows which travel from the Court to the Public (as this one soon will) are still a lot stronger than the ones that come in the opposite direction.

True, *Aunt Dan* starts somewhere in mid-Atlantic: Mr Shawn is of course American, but writing here of English experience and for an Anglo-American-Australian cast led by the Oscar-winning Linda Hunt. He himself has also taken over from John Heard in rehearsal four of the male roles, making the whole affair as much of an evening with Wally as was his *Dinner With André*. Essentially we again have here a debate between two characters: where the one in *André* was about the difference between achievers and non-achievers, the one in *Aunt Dan* is about the morality of power and the rights of the individual to determine governmental behaviour. Central to this, and to the play, is a prolonged argument about whether Dr Henry Kissinger was (as they used to ask in *1066 and All That*) on balance A Good Thing or A Bad Thing.

This is the kind of argument that you can still hear at American dinner parties and find in the columns of small circulation magazines occasionally financed by the CIA, but it tends to lack a certain drama. Action is not, however, a main interest of Shawn's; instead he writes eccentric, languid, stream of consciousness monologues, some running upwards of ten minutes each, all of which then gradually overlap into exotic character studies. Aunt Danielle herself, as played by Linda Hunt, is a kind of academic guru who teaches Leonora, otherwise known as Lemon, secrets of the universe while failing to do anything about an apparently Lesbian attachment to her. Her Open University lectures on ethics are occasionally interrupted by other characters, mostly involved in a weird sub-plot about the murder of a gangster, and it is vastly to the credit of both Linda Hunt as Aunt Dan and Kathryn Pogson as Lemon that they manage to retain our interest, while working their way through sub-clauses that would be the envy of Kissinger himself.

Not only does Mr Shawn belong to no recognisable school of drama, but the one he is building for himself is still evidently under construction and inclined to fall apart around the edges. Yet, for all that, there is something deeply compelling about his courage in assuming that an audience wishes to eavesdrop on a debate rather than attend a spectacle or a coherent plot. And when he himself appears on stage, a Puckish, balding innocent abroad stationed somewhere halfway from Andy Hardy to Woody Allen, you begin to believe that perhaps there might be something happening here after all, though I suspect he has yet to work out quite what it is.

The Singer and The Song

Time has not been especially kind to Harvey Fierstein's *Torch Song Trilogy*: in the eight years since he started writing these three interlinked but self-contained plays about a New York drag queen who ends up adopting a fifteen-year-old schoolboy to the understandable horror of his own Jewish mother, perceptions of Manhattan gaiety have radically altered. In the light or rather darkness of Aids, the first play has become a period piece and the other two (as I thought when I first wrote about them reviewing from America two years ago) could still do with thirty-minute cuts, pulling this down to a three rather than four hour evening.

But there's still no doubt that we have at the Albery a remarkably bitchy,

1985

waspish and acerbically funny triptych on the nature of homosexuality. When we first meet Arnold, the Rita Hayworth of Coney Island, it is in a series of raunchy monologues about his misadventures in gay bars. By the time *The International Stud* gives way to *Fugue in a Nursery*, the second play, we have lurched into a domestic quartet faintly reminiscent of Albee's *Virginia Woolf* and made up of Arnold, his male lover newly married, the lover's wife and Arnold's new boyfriend. As these four re-group into ever changing bisexual power struggles, we then move on five years to the moment when Arnold's quintessentially straight mother has to face up to her son's irredeemable need to be a wife and mother himself. This last play is, in effect, a Neil Simon farce about gays tumbling out of closets, and Miriam Karlin plays it superlatively; but the evening belongs to Antony Sher, off his *Richard III* sticks and on to altogether different crutches. This is another epic bravura turn, and if I have any reservation about Robert Allan Ackerman's thoughtful production it is only that when, in New York, the author himself played Arnold, he seemed to be taking part in a lengthy documentary about his own life. What we have now is an actor giving a very strong performance, and that inevitably makes the whole tortured and tortuous affair a little further removed from its audience than once it was.

The 1985 Stratford season draws to a close with an immensely impressive *Othello*. Ben Kingsley (he who was *Gandhi*) may lack Olivier's animal theatricality in the role, just as he lacks Robeson's deep gravel voice, but he is far and away the most intelligent and believable Moor of recent years, and around him, Terry Hands has constructed a black box production of precisely the high confidence and assured style that the RSC has most lacked in Warwickshire this year.

This is an unusually graceful and mystic Othello; indeed, when Kingsley assures the Venetians that he is rude in his speech, one is left to reflect that they are a great deal ruder, and there is a marvellous moment when one of the Senators applauds him for being 'far more fair than black', only to receive a look of regal disdain from the Moor. Both Kingsley and Niamh Cusack, as Desdemona, glitter through the evening in a stunning array of jewelled tents, while David Suchet prowls around the edge of their bed as a bisexual Iago of equal intelligence and power.

Uneasily poised somewhere between a celebration of her songs and a clinical report from her psychiatrist, Terry Wale's *Judy* at the Bristol Old Vic is a Garland biomusical in urgent need of some more work before it reaches London in December. Despite the recent catastrophes that were *Jean Seberg* at the National and *Marilyn* at the Adelphi, superstar disaster stories are still potent at the box office: the West End already has Elvis Presley and is soon to get John Lennon or reasonable facsimiles thereof, and no singer of recent times was more constantly mocked by her own material than Garland. Having spectacularly failed to be born in a trunk or get happy, she also failed ever to find the end of the rainbow, so that her private life became a series of alcoholic falls into the arms of ever more unsuitable husbands. But her songs came from dozens of composers and were only ever given coherence and greatness by her singing of them, and a show about the corrosive nature of stardom still needs a star. Lesley Mackie in the title role is a tiny and talented actress who looks for much of the evening as if she'd have been just as happy playing Mickey Rooney.

The brilliance of Pam Gems's *Piaf* was in avoiding any impersonation of the great Edith or any attempt to explain her on-stage talent; the problem with *Judy* is that its book drifts through all the backstage clichés of pushy mothers and pushier drug dealers while also trying to explain and recreate the public stardom of the lady memorably described by her studio boss and Svengali, Louis B. Mayer, as a chubby hunchback who sang like a little old woman. Those of us lucky enough to have seen Garland, even at the start of her steep cabaret decline, knew that Mayer was wrong and that we were in the presence of a curiously blazing and unrepeatable talent. But two decades later that talent cannot be recaptured by a sketchy backstage peep through the curtain. Scripted like a TV movie and briskly directed in the same convention by John David, *Judy* makes occasional attempts to get us back to an Oz where the wicked witch of the West turns out to be Garland's own mother, but ideas like that need to be aborted early in rehearsal or else followed through with rather more confidence than is yet evident here.

Victor Victorious

We have the musical of the year, if not the half-decade, and it is at the Barbican. Not since Sondheim's *Sweeney Todd* back in 1979 has there been a score which soared out from the pit with the blazing theatricality of *Les Misérables*, and to those of my tabloid colleagues already in print with feeble and fainthearted objections to the gloom of Hugo's epic pageant of French life at the beginning of the last century, I have but this to say: remember the demon barber. *Sweeney*, too, we were once told, was too dark, too savage, too downbeat a theme for a musical. Six years on, that show has won more awards and has been acclaimed in more opera houses than almost any other in the entire history of the American musical. *Les Misérables*, in a brilliantly intelligent RSC staging by Trevor Nunn and John Caird, will achieve a similar kind of long-term success and anyone who fails to understand the reason for that should be locked in a cupboard with nothing but the soundtracks of *Starlight Express* and *Mutiny* for company.

The greatness of *Les Misérables* is that it starts out, like *Sweeney* and *Peter Grimes* and for that matter *Rigoletto*, to redefine the limits of music theatre.

1985

Like them it is through-sung, and like them it tackles universal themes of social and domestic happiness in terms of individual despair. The show first opened five years ago in a sports arena on the outskirts of Paris; the tape of that production is one I have played almost daily for the last few months, and it seems to me to consist largely of all the marching songs Edith Piaf never got around to singing. There is an energy and an operatic intensity here which exists in the work of no British composer past or present: the sense of a nation's history being channelled through trumpets and drums and guitars and violins and cellos. Claude-Michel Schonberg's score sounds even better at the Barbican than it does on record, while Alain Boublil's lyrics have been filtered through the translations of two ex-London drama critics, James Fenton (who did the recent and superb *Rigoletto* translation at the Coliseum) and Herbert Kretzmer (who wrote most of Aznavour's English hits as well as a couple of West End musicals back in the 1960s).

Nobody here is trying to make some quick money in the charts, and nobody believes that a couple of songs can make a show; this score has maybe fifty numbers, all of which fit like jigsaw pieces into a huge revolutionary pattern. There are songs of love, and war, and death and restoration; there are patter songs, arias, duets and chorus numbers of dazzling inventiveness and variety. For this is not the French *Oliver!* or even the musical *Nicholas Nickleby*, though it owes a certain debt to both. Rather is it a brilliantly guided tour of the twelve-hundred page eternity that is Hugo's text, and indeed there is no way that in three orchestral hours we can ask for more than that.

That now traditional RSC walkdown is here, as is a *Third Man* chase through the sewers and an autumnal ending worthy of *Cyrano*; there are even occasional lurches into lovable orphan echoes of *Annie*, and of course the result is episodic, fragmentary and evocative of other shows; just as John Napier's set (which itself looks like a tribute to Sean Kenny) is made up of yet another rich and rare collection of old treasures – chairs, tables, cartwheels, water barrels – so the whole production reflects what Nunn has learned from *Nickleby* and *Cats* and his Shakespeare musicals.

There is, of course, a central dilemma: though *Les Misérables* has one of the greatest books of all time to draw on, it has no book of its own. What it has is a score, and beyond it some thin and sketchy characterisations, but no chance of any plot development that cannot come through song. Again like *Sweeney*, the show exists in the most dangerous area of the stage musical in that it is not about glamour or success, but instead about failure and hatred. And yet, as that score surges through the theatre, you are made aware time and again of how well it works in English: anyone who ever heard Piaf sing in translation knows how quickly she sounded impossible, and the Kretzmer triumph has been to set these lyrics into an acceptable framework somewhere at the boundaries of Dickens and Brecht.

Les Misérables is everything the musical theatre ought to be doing, and within the inevitable limitations of its pageant there are some striking performances. The central casting here is strongly *Evita*-based, since we get Colm Wilkinson from that original recording as Jean Valjean and Patti Lupone from the Broadway premiere as the doomed Fantine. But we also get some very strong RSC classical support from Roger Allam as Javert, plunging into the swollen Seine, and from Alun Armstrong as the evil Thénadier whose *Master of the Game* is one of the most instantly accessible of the numbers.

Iron Curtain Calls

If, one of these cold winter nights, you wish to see some irons being pulled spectacularly from a dramatist's fire, hasten to the Queen's Theatre: seldom, in the twenty years or so since we moved away from an actors' theatre and Celia Johnson ceased being called upon to haul the minor comedies of William Douglas Home into some semblance of a triumph, can a star actress have been called upon for the artificial respiration job which Maggie Smith is currently giving Ronald Harwood's new play *Interpreters*.

Topically enough, we are in and around the Foreign Office during a multinational conference; Miss Smith and a wildly miscast Edward Fox are respectively the British and Russian interpreters at a debate to arrange the precise catering and political plans for a forthcoming state visit to Britain by the Russian President. But it rapidly becomes clear that Mr Harwood's interests here are anything but political: instead he wishes to tell us a very old-fashioned kind of multilingual love story, of precisely the kind that used to obsess Peter Ustinov in the long lost days of his *Romanoff and Juliet* and *Love of Four Colonels*.

Thus we get Mr Fox abandoning all the clenched and stiff-upper-lipped English reserve which he can present better than most, and giving us instead an uneasy impression of a manic Soviet lover who only has to hear the sound of running water to be away in pursuit of all the female interpreters buried within the United Nations. A decade before the play opens, he and Miss Smith have had a brief and tempestuous romance; now brought together again by the impending state visit, they are left to rekindle an affair which may have to entail his defection.

Like Tom Stoppard in an infinitely stronger play, Mr Harwood seems intent on making us understand that love is the real thing, and that it is very often impossible. The idea of a doomed love affair between interpreters ought perhaps to have offered him and us whole linguistic and

1985

geographic and national areas of romantic and sexual exploration, but instead it becomes all too clear by about the interval that this play has nothing much to tell us beyond the fact that a man can behave badly in more than one language. We do, in all fairness, get to meet along the way one or two other interesting characters, including an old Russian grandmother (Doreen Mantle) trailing clouds of the Ballets Russes and a couple of men from East and West ministries (Jeffry Wickham and John Moffatt) so perfectly typecast that they seem to have stepped straight from an Ealing Comedy of the early 1950s.

But because Mr Harwood has so little for them to do except reinforce national prejudice and prove the character acting art to be still just about alive, it is left to Maggie Smith alone to rescue a remarkably shaky evening. She does it with a vengeance: whether realising in midconference that her stockinged foot is halfway up the leg not of her faithless Soviet lover but of his appalling boss, or turning the last scene into a haunting cry of loneliness and rejection, hers is one of the most remarkably moving performances in town. This is a play about the language of love and about the moment in a relationship when the lies become more important than the truth; but it remains a desperately fragile and stilted script, and nothing that the director Peter Yates can do to move his characters around Farrah's unusually cumbersome set is inclined to persuade me that without Miss Smith there would be anything here at all. With her and because of her, there is in fact something very special: few plays of recent times can have started so unsteadily or proved at the last so undeniably touching in the acceptance of loneliness as a way of life.

In a good week for starry female turns, the enterprising Greenwich Theatre is offering the British premiere of Maxim Gorky's *Vassa* with Janet Suzman as the title character, a formidable shipowner who runs her business and her family as if in rehearsal for some pre-Russian Revolutionary episode of *Dynasty*. *Vassa* has recently and marvellously been filmed in the Soviet Union: but seeing it now for the first time on stage, in the director Helena Kaut-Howson's omnibus edition of the 1910 and 1936 Gorky rewrites, one realises that here essentially is the play that gets us from Chekhov to Strindberg. Vassa's abominable family, her childmolesting husband and her drunken brother and even her light-fingered secretary, are clearly seen by Gorky as some sort of metaphor for the bourgeoisie in terminal decay; against them he sets up a revolutionary daughter-in-law (Amanda Boxer) prepared to sacrifice even her child for the cause of a better world. But in a theatre, unlike a political tract, the star gets all the best lines and there is no real contest here: we stay with Vassa just as we stay with Hedda Gabler, hoping that she'll win through in the end because, however murderous she may be of people or ideas or revolutions, she is still a hell of a lot more interesting than anything or anyone going on around her. *Vassa* thus becomes a play not about the collapse of one social order or the birth of another, but instead about a matriarch desperately intent on survival whatever the order, and prowling around the cage that is her office and her home Miss Suzman has found one of the great unplayed roles for an actress on her way from Hedda to a dowager Borgia.

An Inspector Palls

The Inspector paused on his way out of the stalls bar. 'I think it's a thriller,' he said. 'And it's been dead a long time. Maybe since *Sleuth*. Maybe only since the last revival of *Deathtrap*. These things are difficult to pin down forensically. I blame Roald Dahl myself.'

There was a long silence while he tried to read the eyewitness account he had scribbled on the margins of his programme in the sudden darkness of the first night. 'Unusual for the Haymarket,' he noticed. 'Usual procedure there is to get very old American film stars making personal appearances in minor classics. Not often you get a death, let alone two, maybe three. Not all on stage at any rate. Once or twice perhaps in the dress circle over the years. Haymarket matinée audiences aren't getting any younger. Mind you, they have now built this new-fangled steambath in the middle of the set. That should keep them warm, at least if they've bought tickets near the front.'

Back at the old station typewriter, the Inspector considered the facts in front of him. Start at the very beginning. Tuesday night, late November, very cold, forecast of snow on the car radio. Usual beat, seven o'clock start, West End central. Report to Haymarket. About 300 potential witnesses, well-dressed mob, could be relatives or friends of the victim, investors even. Names and addresses may have to be taken later. Nothing suspicious yet, give or take an agent's hairpiece in the dress circle and a tuxedo in the stalls that seems to have had several previous owners. Check out the ice-creams. Think there used to be more nuts in the vanilla. Unsure of new EEC regulations on this. Routine briefing in programme lists title, *Fatal Attraction*. Some joker must want trouble in tomorrow's reviews. Stars Susannah York, Denis Quilley. No trouble there. Cast list also names four other characters, but this could be trap. In *Sleuth* they printed the names of three mythical characters and one of our most promising lads actually reviewed them. Transferred to the television previewing branch in Sidcup before you could say Shaffer.

Programme briefing also gives location: 'The action of the play takes place over three days in late October in the living-room of Blair Griffin's remote Nantucket beach house.' Thoughtful of them to give us that up front. Save a lot of time with the AA Book later, unless of course

1985

Nantucket is another of the female victims. Difficult to be sure, what with the steam pouring out of the bath and the bodies pouring into it. Probably not supposed to say that in the report. Better concentrate on the dialogue. Quite good, that. Not often you get jokes about Salvador Dali in a thriller. Hero a policeman, too, and writes his own bestsellers instead of lousy post-mortem reports on this collapsing station typewriter.

The Inspector paused again, this time to consider his life and career in the force. Forty-four this week, hair beginning to recede, he'd taken the drama beat twenty years ago because it seemed better than fixing traffic lights. Now he wasn't so sure. Night work, it was, often meeting undesirables in dark attics off Shepherd's Bush Green or Islington. Sometimes worse. Sometimes they did plays in Glasgow. Once he'd been beaten up in a pub by a suspect who hadn't cared for one of his reports. Female dramatists can turn very nasty after a few lagers. Mind you, times have changed a bit, not that you'd notice down the Haymarket. But when the Inspector started, back in the 1960s, different world. Friendly neighbourhood critics still able to walk the streets at night without armed escort, sometimes even invited in for a drink with Noël Coward around Christmas. More plays around then, too, leastways more plays he hadn't already seen 500 flaming times. And sometimes, you won't believe this, sometimes they actually put on a musical with new songs in it.

He'd always known, of course, the mistake. The mistake was not to take Films division when that was on offer. Foreign travel, Cannes, Venice, South America even; Meryl Streep on the expenses, no questions asked, films even get shown for inspection in the mornings. Strictly no night work at non-overtime rates. Maybe even California to follow up leads. No snow on the radio there.

The Inspector shivered and returned reluctantly to his Haymarket programme notes. Curtain goes up, read the first one. He liked to have these things in writing. Could save a lot of awkward questions later. Artist divorcing actress. Steam coming out of bath. Susannah York greatest living waif since Peter Pan. Quilley cop seems to have drifted in from remake of *Jaws*. Has female cop with him. Wish I had female cop with me. Plant pot falls off ledge. Heroine says, 'I'm having rather a bad day,' after second body in or near bath. Think this joke. Not often you get to see a play starring a whirlpool bath, even in Haymarket. Possible to suggest, in West End still besieged by moribund *Mousetrap* and deadly *Business of Murder*, that this *Fatal Attraction* is best thriller in town. On the other hand, if I do say that in the report they will doubtless quote me on the bloody posters, and then I shall regret it because, although this is the best thriller in town, it ought not to be; it just happens to be a lousy decade for thrillers. End of notes.

Samuel Beckett would have had an entire trilogy out of that lot, not just

OUR THEATRES IN THE EIGHTIES

a drama report. The Inspector typed it up and took it through to his senior officer. 'This it? A week on full pay, entirely alone in the Drama division, and you manage to see one half-way OK thriller down the Haymarket? What else?' The Inspector thought for a minute. 'Saw a *Royal Variety Show* at Drury Lane,' he said. 'On television too, this weekend. Nothing suspicious there. Not unless you count Alice Faye and Don Ameche in person. Not a lot else. I find I think a lot about J. B. Priestley. *An Inspector Calls* and all that. Notions of reality. Am I really here? Does a Bernard Slade thriller down the Haymarket actually represent the state of the art 2,000 years on from Aristotle? Maybe 3,000, I never did the Greek exam. I have started writing books. That never hurt Wambaugh. He was an Inspector too once. Mind you, he never had to do the Haymarket beat.'

1986

A YEAR WHICH GAVE us the Swan at Stratford, *Les Liaisons Dangereuses* and a regional Stephen Sondheim festival (*Anyone Can Whistle* at Cheltenham, *A Funny Thing Happened on the Way to the Forum* at Chichester and *Pacific Overtures* in Manchester) cannot be altogether bad, though there was something oddly lacklustre about 1986. It was the year of the Cork Report, highlighting the constant financial headaches still routinely given to arts organisations all over the country by a deep governmental unwillingness to commit money far enough ahead or in sufficient quantities, and a year in which the punitive Standstill Grant was more evident than ever before.

All the more credit, therefore, to a director like Peter James at the Lyric,

Yonadab Alan Bates *as Yonadab*, Leigh Lawson *as Amnon*, Patrick Stewart *as David* and Wendy Morgan *as Tamar*

Hammersmith, who, despite financial constraint, brought in Nuria Espert for the triumphant Plowright *House of Bernarda Alba* and allowed Simon Callow to give Maggie Smith her head in an infinitely theatrical *Infernal Machine*.

This was also the year that saw Simon Curtis's immensely powerful staging at the Royal Court of Jim Cartwright's *Road*, and when Frank McGuinness made his name with *Observe the Sons of Ulster Marching Towards the Somme*. The Barbican Pit ran a duet of new plays (Arthur Miller's *Archbishop's Ceiling* and Richard Nelson's *Principia Scriptoriae*) which dealt with the fate of the writer in a repressive regime, a double which Alan Bennett then converted into a treble with *Kafka's Dick* at the Royal Court.

Lloyd Webber's hit of the year was *Phantom of the Opera*, though this was also the year of *Chess* and *La Cage Aux Folles*. Away from London Nicholas Hytner established himself at the Manchester Royal Exchange with *As You Like It* and *Edward II*, while London was lucky enough to see Derek Jacobi as the tortured, gay Alan Turing in *Breaking The Code*, Albert Finney with Steppenwolf in the explosive American *Orphans*, and Vanessa Redgrave in a production of *Ghosts* which confirmed the Young Vic under David Thacker as one of the most consistently impressive playhouses in town.

It was a year when we lost both Alan Jay Lerner and Siobhan McKenna, when considerable anxiety was expressed in print about the earnings of Sir Peter Hall and Trevor Nunn, and when the playwright Willy Russell ought to have won some sort of award for conspicuous on-stage courage after stepping in drag into the leading role of his one-woman show *Shirley Valentine* at Liverpool after the actress cast for the role fell suddenly ill.

1986

Hampton's Court

These are admittedly very early days, but if the RSC in 1986 manage to come up with another production of the stylish, ultra-confident brilliance which hallmarks the Christopher Hampton translation of *Les Liaisons Dangereuses* that opens their new year in the Barbican Pit, then it will prove, even by their current standards, a vintage time. What Mr Hampton and his director Howard Davies have done is as close to the impossible as any conjuror's rabbit: they have taken the 400 pages of Choderlos de Laclos's epistolary novel, in which no two characters ever meet, and turned them into the most sensuously sexual theatrical encounter in years.

Admittedly there has always been a great plot here, albeit one best suited to a French film-maker of the Renoir school of art. We are in France in 1792: the Marquise de Merteuil, played with acid elegance by Lindsay Duncan, is persuading her former lover the Vicomte de Valmont, played in elegant decay by Alan Rickman, to seduce a fifteen-year-old schoolgirl in order to settle a batch of old sexual and social scores.

From that apparently simple beginning ('Love and revenge,' she tells the Vicomte sweetly, 'two of your favourites'), there develops a plot that would not have disappointed Machiavelli or Oscar Wilde; indeed it might have been written by them in partnership. 'If this book burns,' said Baudelaire once, 'it is in the manner of ice,' and that is precisely the feeling Mr Hampton has managed to dramatise: that Barbican basement has never felt so electric or so chilly, despite the rumpled bedsheets which make it look as though the whole area has recently been the site of a linen sale for lust-ridden bargain shoppers.

The result is a brittle, bitchy, waspishly funny and, at the last, genuinely tragic close-encounter grouping. Admittedly the shadow of the guillotine (outlined in Mr Hampton's script, but converted on stage into the roll of the tumbril) was nowhere in the original letters, and it could be argued that you might as well add the Sarajevo gunshot to a revival of *The Importance of Being Earnest*, if you wish to underline the nature of a society in terminal incestuous decline; but that lurch into familiar history only occupies the closing seconds of a play which otherwise exists totally within its own frame of reference. Where the book had to keep all its characters apart, so that they could go on writing to each other, the stage version brings them together for a series of overlapping duologues, which Mr Hampton has written in his best *Philanthropist* style of semi-detached cruelty. And nowhere is that better expressed than in the character of the Vicomte, destroyed at the last by the love he has always managed to convert into lust, but given along the way to some of the most silky evil manoeuvres since the screen retirement of the late George Sanders. Whether writing letters on the back of his naked mistress to yet another wife he has hopes of seducing, or merely receiving his due as the best seducer in town ('He has a way of putting things,' says the schoolgirl after a spectacularly well stage-managed rape), Alan Rickman is silkily splendid until the moment when the bed is pulled from under him in what might well have been the first great act of French feminist revenge.

The message of these *Liaisons* is that all sex is political and social and economic. But, in taking that quite literally as read, and moving beyond the letters to form a dialogue which is often a lot closer to Simon Gray or Noël Coward in its acid despair and sharp jokiness, Mr Hampton has come up with a marvellously funny bedchamber drama in which random one-liners ('Clothes don't suit her') sparkle through a wilderness of hatred and betrayal and ultimate death.

Everything that *La Ronde* always failed to be is, in fact, achieved here: lovers meeting, parting, raping, regretting and forever circling each other in a tense gavotte. But what is perhaps most remarkable is the intensity of the company style: from Fiona Shaw in cascadingly gracious form as the schoolgirl's mother, right through to Juliet Stevenson as the doomed Presidente, there is no better grouping (or indeed groping) in town, and by the time we leave them to the scaffold, with two already dead, one a nun and one retired to Malta, the French Revolution itself seems something of an anti-climax.

Bible Belting

It will not come as news to admirers of Peter Shaffer that his plays across the twenty years from *Royal Hunt of the Sun* through *Equus* and the less familiar *Shrivings* to *Amadeus* and now (on the National's open Olivier stage) *Yonadab* have principally concerned twin heroes, one of whom has God in him and can't recognise it and the other of whom hasn't but can. In *Yonadab*, the two are half-brothers, Amnon and Absalom, though their stardom is in this play usurped by the title figure, a voyeurist gossip who has all of Salieri's obsessions with his social and artistic superiors but, alas, not even any of his talent except when it comes to chatting up the audience.

But in abandoning Mozart and Salieri for the Book of Samuel and a justifiably minor footnote therein, Mr Shaffer and his National director, Peter Hall, have given up none of their love for ritual pageantry. Instead of a Viennese opera converted into a murder mystery, what we get here, however, is little more than the non-musical version of *Joseph and the Amazing Technicolor Dreamcoat*.

Behind a gauze curtain that is often left mercifully closed, minor biblical functionaries cavort around in vaguely choreographic fashion, while in front of it Alan Bates, as the all-seeing narrator of the title, tries with increasing urgency to retain our interest for all of three hours in a

1986

story which even the Book of Samuel wisely reduced to a few paragraphs. The tale of Tamar and how she was raped by her half-brother is of some interest as a prelude to the war of succession of the rival sons of King David, and if (as in *Equus*) Mr Shaffer had been able to come up with some altogether unexpected and amazing explanation of an apparently familiar happening, then the re-telling might have been of some interest. He seems here, though, not to be much concerned with biblical details; instead, it is Yonadab (attached forever to the tree of his own unattachment just as surely as Absalom is, in the evening's one closing moment of good drama, caught by his hair in other branches) who is required to retain our fascination if only with increasingly uneasy Old Testament jokes. But precisely because he is so deeply uninvolved in the proceedings, like a redundant vicar required to make sense of events he can neither halt nor control, Yonadab is totally unable to command in us the interest that alone could move the play along. Alan Bates achieves a finely bitchy irritation ('Come along,' he exhorts Amnon at the end of one characteristically turgid scene, 'there are other people to be stoned in this city besides you'), but it alone cannot stop the evening fast becoming either a parody or a re-run of all the previous debates about God and Man in all the other Shaffer plays. Wendy Morgan manages a final moment of feminist revenge, Leigh Lawson and Anthony Head are well contrasted as the half-brothers, and Patrick Stewart would doubtless be a fine King of Judah and Israel if Mr Shaffer had written the part in any coherent detail.

Better news, however, on the National's Cottesloe stage, where the Ian McKellen acting company is making its final appearance after an all too short year in Mike Alfreds's new production of *The Cherry Orchard*. As is well enough known from his work with Shared Experience, Mr Alfreds sets character and text but no precise moves: different audiences on different nights are therefore liable to find actors in totally different areas of the stage during the same scenes, and while in the past some Shared Experience players have found this a considerable challenge, the McKellen company is now in such peak condition (having worked the last few months on all National stages in everything from *Duchess of Malfi* to *Real Inspector Hound*) that they have no trouble at all with a characteristically intelligent production.

This *Cherry Orchard* is neither valedictory tragedy nor bleak farce: when Firs (Hugh Lloyd) is left locked up to die in the house at the end of Act Four, it is not some symbolic passing of the old guard, but merely another accident in a house that has always been full of them. An immensely strong female troupe (Sheila Hancock, Eleanor Bron, Selina Cadell, Julie Legrand) do most of the rest of the night's work, though Edward Petherbridge as a wonderfully semi-detached Gayev and Ian McKellen himself as the triumphant peasant purchaser of the orchard both give performances that are sharp reminders of how much the National will have lost if their company is indeed allowed to disband at Easter.

Briefly to the Royal Court from Newcastle has come the first British production of David Mamet's *Edmond* (first seen in Chicago in 1982). A brief 80-minute new morality tale of the New York streets, it takes the form of blackout sketches written in a kind of staccato poetry, like Feiffer cartoons printed in blood and acid. On one level, what we have here is a digest of all those Charles Bronson anti-mugger movies filtered at last through a literate typewriter; on another, we have (as in Wally Shawn's recent *Aunt Dan*) a debate about preconditioning; and on still a third we just have the story of a guy in midlife crisis who leaves his family, gets into a few fights and ends up in prison as a killer. But what makes Mamet, along with Sam Shepard, the most exciting writer to have come out of America in the last twenty years is his ability to work on all those levels simultaneously: Mr Mamet writes his plays the way war photographers shoot battles.

High Spirits

As Noël Coward was forever pointing out to over-eager amateur dramatic societies, his plays only read as though they might be easy to stage; when you come to rehearse them, you discover they are treacherous, fiendishly difficult to time right, and hedged around with misleading memories of previous productions. *Private Lives*, arguably the most touching play ever written about two people unable to live either with or without each other, is generally remembered for clenched cigarette-holders and jokes about the flatness of Norfolk. Similarly *Blithe Spirit* now all too often means a memory of Margaret Rutherford shaking her chins at Rex Harrison in one of David Lean's earliest movies.

Written and first produced in 1941, when jokes about sudden death were highly topical and audiences must have wanted to laugh through the bombing of London at the idea of tangible ghosts, since people went on going to the first production for 2,000 nights, *Blithe Spirit* emerges now at the Vaudeville in an altogether different and intriguing new light. In the past this play has always been dominated either by Madame Arcati, who seemed to belong to Miss Rutherford the way that Lady Bracknell always belonged to Edith Evans, or else, as in the 1976 Pinter production at the National, to an immensely starry Elvira, in which ghostly role Maria Aitken was the last of a stylish high-comedy line that stretched back through the Kays Hammond and Kendall to Judy Campbell in the 1940s.

But what the director Peter Farago has opened up at the Vaudeville is the possibility that this was always meant to be an even four-handed play,

1986

in which the characters of Charles Condomine and his second wife Ruth are no less important than those of Arcati and Elvira. Indeed, for the first time, we now have in Jane Asher a Ruth who is able to challenge Elvira on her own supernatural territory, a wife no less starry or glamorous and able at the last to join her predecessor in a deadly double-act, from which we know, despite the evidence of the final curtain, that their surviving husband is never really going to escape nor ever really wishes to.

Having thus turned *Blithe Spirit* into a quartet, Mr Farago is able to get four performances of equal strength and interest out of his principal players: if it is Jane Asher who explains for the first time how Charles could have married someone like Ruth after someone like Elvira, it is Joanna Lumley who explains the original waspish fascination of Elvira herself. Trapped between them as the astral bigamist, Simon Cadell gives Charles precisely the right kind of weary semi-detachment that comes of living with two noisy and sexy women for just too long to preserve any real independence, while Marcia Warren makes of Madame Arcati a hand-crafted, home-knitted village eccentric deeply convinced of her own thoroughly shaky spiritual powers.

This impressive company seems to have understood that Coward never really works unless he is played for real instead of for laughs, but that there

Blithe Spirit Joanna Lumley *as Elvira*, Marcia Warren *as Madame Arcati*, Simon Cadell *as Charles* and Jane Asher *as Ruth*

is still a difference between real seriousness and reverent solemnity. A serious comedy about ghosts, therefore, becomes hilarious with the realisation that death doesn't really change anything very much, if you can indeed come back after it and be just as awful as you were before, and if there is a fifth star of this *Blithe Spirit*, then it is surely Carl Toms's ultimately explosive set. It's also good to hear again the background score of Richard Addinsell, though what will keep this production happily at the Vaudeville for many months to come is not the best conversation ever devised about Budleigh Salterton, nor yet the memory of Elvira expiring while laughing helplessly at a BBC music programme. What will keep it there is the simple fact that an eminently well-made comedy has been given a production of rock-solid craftsmanship and tremendous affection.

Blunt Weapons

The postwar political history of Britain comes neatly strangled in old school and college ties: the point has been made by Alan Bennett in two plays about Guy Burgess in exile (*The Old Country* and *An Englishman Abroad*) and one by Julian Mitchell about Guy Burgess at Eton (*Another Country*). Now we have a fourth: at Greenwich – which is also where *Another Country* was first seen – they have another chilly winner in Robin Chapman's *One of Us*, which neatly fills in another part of the treachery jigsaw by giving us a glimpse of Burgess at the time of his disappearance through the Iron Curtain with Maclean in May 1951.

Mr Chapman also introduces us to the third-man figure of Anthony Blunt, but his play is in essence about neither Burgess nor Maclean nor Blunt. It is about the fourth man in that curious Comintern complex, the Welsh journalist and academic, Goronwy Rees, who managed, like Blunt, to spend most of the rest of his life in British Establishment jobs (estates bursar at All Souls, principal of the University of Wales) rather than a small flat in the wrong area of downtown Moscow. But Rees was not technically a traitor. True, he did once agree to join Burgess in working for the Comintern, but he never actually got round to doing anything specific on Soviet behalf, and by the time we meet him in the play he has long since decided that treachery is not for him. He is also married, and far removed to a riverside house in Sonning from the world of 'celebrated Marxist queens' like Blunt and Burgess. 1951 is a long way from 1936. Rees has decided that on balance even America under Senator McCarthy is preferable to Russia under Joseph Stalin, and when, therefore, Guy reappears on his doorstep bearing gifts for the children and anti-America discussion documents, he receives a somewhat chilly welcome.

In Ian Ogilvy's splendidly starry first-act turn, Burgess is still seen as the flamboyant alcoholic gay or, as Rees defines his discussion document, 'overheated, abstract and opinionated'. And it is clear that Burgess wants something more than a weekend by the Thames in the village where his parents conceived him, 'while in the bar below their bedroom, dry martinis mixed themselves'. What Burgess now wants is nothing less than the silence of Rees. He has decided, though we do not discover this until long after his departure from Rees's idyllic riverside English country garden, to go over the wall with Maclean and he wishes now to be sure that in leaving an old lover (Blunt) behind, he is not exposing him to unnecessary risks resulting from what Rees knows about their shared past. But, by the interval, Burgess is gone and we are left with Mr and Mrs Rees to face a quite different dilemma: who, precisely, is Rees to betray and to whom? If he keeps silent about all that he knows, he betrays his marriage to a wife who knows only that treachery is unforgivable and that homosexuality may be just about as nasty. If he tells all, he betrays men with whom he once shared a kind of hazy pre-war ideal about freedom; indeed, at the very end of Alan Strachan's marvellously tense production, Blunt himself arrives on stage in a superbly sinister performance by David Horovitch to remind Rees of his 'loyalties'.

We are, of course, once again back at Morgan Forster and his line about having the courage to betray your country rather than your friends, but it is not quite as simple as that: Rees himself has technically committed no crime, and because he had no idea that Burgess was going over the wall, there was precious little he could have done to stop him. After the event, the most Rees could have achieved would have been the exposure of Blunt, and we now know that the security services were already about to do a deal with him in return for information anyway. So Rees is left forever on the sidelines: Mr Nobody Changes Trains Again, as Guy Burgess unerringly damns him in the Isherwood title. So he is the play's one of us; but one what? A traitor who just never got around to doing anything about it? A man who sacrificed his greatest friend to his own marriage? An Establishment figure who knew that, if he sat on the fence long enough, people would get used to seeing him there? As he himself says in a wonderful moment of Welsh–English logic about the nature of his spiritual treachery, 'I was asked and I didn't quite say no.' On the other hand, he didn't quite say yes either, and through the series of long duologues that make up his play Mr Chapman examines precisely that borderline. In the two central roles, Anthony Andrews and Jenny Quayle as Mr and Mrs Rees give the performances of their careers thus far.

Elsewhere this week, two strong plays that seem to have been moved to the wrong addresses: Doug Lucie's *Progress* was, when first seen at the Bush a couple of years ago, a splendidly acerbic conversation piece about a trio of gays: a tabloid hack of hilarious awfulness, an unreconstructed chauvinist pig who beats up his bride, and a TV researcher married to a now-Lesbian women's leader. All are sharing a North London commune, where the vodka gets thrown into eyes as often as glasses, and Lucie is, as usual, writing here with a powerful mix of insight and loathing about enclosed groups of the socially privileged. In his ever-darkening world, Mr Lucie writes of people who find themselves impossible and their friends worse, and he remains our best war correspondent in the political battle of the sexes. But what we have lost (in a starry new production at the Lyric, Hammersmith, starring Mike Gwilym and Diana Quick) is some of the original intensity of that hothouse premiere at the Bush: in short, a faint lack of *Progress*.

Similarly Stephen MacDonald's *Not About Heroes*, a touching account of the World War I friendship between the poets Wilfrid Owen and Siegfried Sassoon, looked very strong in the intimate confines of the King's Head last year, but now is over-extended on the National's Cottesloe stage. Essentially a *Journey's End* away from the trenches, it remains a clenched and ineffably English love story about two men who couldn't face their own passions or the death that was inevitably to claim one of them a week before the Armistice.

Philadelphia Story

The current powerhouse of the American theatre is located in Chicago, where the Steppenwolf company (now in their tenth year) under John Malkovich and others have been responsible for most of what was best not only in Mid-Western drama but also in transfers to off-Broadway. The news of their exchange deal with the Hampstead Theatre is therefore doubly welcome: alongside the Royal Court's similar arrangement with Joe Papp's Public Theatre in New York, it means that we now have direct access to two of the best companies in the United States and with them, of course, come their new plays. Not only Larry Kramer's *The Normal Heart* in to the Court (of which more next week) but at Hampstead Lyle Kessler's *Orphans* in a Steppenwolf production which now adds Albert Finney to the original staging.

The play itself is at times almost alarmingly close to an American rerun of *The Caretaker*, which may well be why the Finney character is even christened Harold. In this case he is a sinister gangster heavy who, drunk in a bar one night, gets forcibly adopted by two Philadelphia brothers thinking to make a fast buck from his wallet. Kevin Anderson and Jeff Fahey from Steppenwolf are the brothers who make up the rest of the cast, and the first fascination of the Hampstead evening is the contrast between them and Finney. While he remains somehow oddly un-American, a Lee J. Cobb from the north of England rather than the Mid-West, these two young American athletes literally throw themselves around him on

1986

Hampstead's small stage, one of them finally aroused to such a frenzy of illiterate rage that he hurls himself up against the back wall of the set with so much ferocity that he is flung back against almost into the audience. You don't get acting like that in North London very often. The play may well be Pennsylvania Pinter, and concerned only with a role-reversal power game in which the kidnappers finally become the kidnapped, but the style of Gary Sinise's production is unmissably intriguing.

At Wyndham's, Robin Ray's *Café Puccini* has been unjustifiably torn apart by many of my colleagues for failing to achieve what it never sets out to do. This is neither an opera nor a play, so to worry about a lack of vocal authority or drama is needless; what we have here instead is an amiable cabaret derived from Ray's earlier stage work on such latterday composers as Sondheim and Lehrer. True, this one is more ambitious than either *Tomfoolery* or the Ned Sherrin *Sondheim* in that it does attempt, and often very successfully, to tell the story of Puccini's uneasy life within the framework of his greatest hits. Certainly the first half of the evening sounds like an unusually jovial Radio 3 documentary, but when in the second half we move into the darkness of Puccini's tortured marriage and the awful affair of a maid driven to suicide by a wife who on this one occasion had misjudged her husband's infidelities, it becomes clear that we do in fact have the beginnings of a play at last, and a very strong one at that.

No cabaret format will, however, allow such a transition, and one comes here almost to resent the musical interruptions that were so welcome before the interval; yet to have given us in barely two hours the best of Puccini's music and an instant guide to his life and loves is no mean achievement, and Mr Ray has been lucky in the casting. Nichola McAuliffe does a wonderful double as wife and mother, Lewis Fiander is a suitably bemused Puccini watching his life unfold around the cabaret tables, and William Blezard leads a superbly jaded six-man band.

On the National's Olivier stage, Peter Wood's *The Threepenny Opera* opens with a funeral parade – brilliantly choreographed by the star of the National's *Guys and Dolls*, David Toguri – worthy of New Orleans, and then proceeds to go rapidly downhill. Nobody here seems to have decided quite what period they are in (though the coronation of Queen Victoria would be the most likely bet) or whether they are celebrating a classic musical or engaged in a vicious satire about capitalist corruption. Certainly, having the show sponsored by Citicorp and Citibank may have added to the confusion, but every possible style from pantomime to Mafia movie is briefly invoked here, while all we are really left with are those great songs. Nobody can sing them the way Lenya once did, but Tim Curry as Macheath does a nice line in Soho spivs, while Sally Dexter, one of the National's rare discoveries, does a terrific *Barbara Song*. Robert

David Macdonald's new translation is brisk and spare, Michael Bryant does a hunchbacked Jake that looks like something from a left-over tour of *Treasure Island*, and the rest of the show looks like a guest night in Highgate Cemetery.

Aids Memoir

Far and away the best of the three or four plays about Aids that have thus far surfaced on either side of the Atlantic is Larry Kramer's *The Normal Heart*, now in a British premiere at the Royal Court. A great cry of dramatic and journalistic rage at the way the plague-panic has been handled by and in New York City, it indicts Mayor Koch, President Reagan, the *New York Times* and sundry other public monuments for coming too little too late to the rescue of a gay community that has already been decimated.

Taking its title from an Auden poem which also includes the line 'All I have is a voice to undo the folded lie', *The Normal Heart* is at least in part autobiographical: like the hero of his play, Mr Kramer was also expelled from a Gay Men's Health Crisis organisation for shouting too loudly in political and social frustration about what he sees as a fundamentally anti-gay establishment in the USA. 'Who cares if a faggot dies?' is one of the central questions of the script, and rather than pussyfooting around this truly terrible subject (as does the infinitely more clenched *As Is*) Mr Kramer's play comes to grips with the politics of health. 'If this epidemic were happening to Jews instead of Gays,' says another character after yet another attempt to get proper medical funding has failed, 'there'd be a hospital already built,' and it is that sense of rage and despair which gives this play its tremendous emotional energy.

Whereas Arthur Miller when he wished to attack McCarthyism went back 300 years to find a parallel in the witch hunts of Salem for *The Crucible*, Kramer stays firmly in the present, comparing the treatment of dying gays in New York in the Eighties with that of dying Jews in Germany in the 1930s. But some of the nervous intensity which characterised *The Normal Heart* off-Broadway, in particular that of Joel Grey in the central role, has been diluted by a London production which casts Martin Sheen (making his English stage debut) in the title role. Mr Sheen is a player of considerable charisma, but an oddly laid-back Californian quality which ill-suits the chippy, downtrodden Manhattan rebel he is asked to play, while in substituting vague English newspaper headlines for the roll-call of the dead that appeared on the back of the New York set, the director David Hayman and his designer Geoff Rose have lost some of the specific New York documentary quality of the original tragedy.

For all that, *The Normal Heart* is still a melodrama of Shavian strength,

1986

and Frances Tomelty as the paralysed doctor, Richard Kane as the straight brother and John Terry as the acceptably butch gay, who fronts up the organisation which expels its founder and chief fighter in the name of middle American prejudice, all give performances of considerable intelligence. There is one other line from that Auden poem which runs unspoken all through this unmissable evening: 'We must love one another, or die.'

A serious and strong new play in a commercial London theatre almost invariably now means one presented there by Michael Codron, and with *Made in Bangkok* (at the Aldwych) that most distinguished and distinctive of managements now introduces West End audiences to a playwright in the best ironic tradition of Peter Nichols and Michael Frayn. What we have here is, in fact, a tragi-comedy strongly reminiscent of Frayn's *Clouds*, and not only because in the central role Felicity Kendal is giving a performance ten years more mature but otherwise not so greatly different from the one she gave there. Again we are concerned with a group of tourists in a foreign land of which we and they know all too little, but this time the group is of salesmen in Thailand rather than journalists in South America. As its title might suggest, *Made in Bangkok* is about trade and sex: of the five British we follow from airport to factory to brothel only Miss Kendal, as the wife of a sadistic British factory executive, has not come East to exploit the natives either physically or commercially. Apart from her husband, the group is made up of a gay Hong Kong dentist (Peter McEnery) and a couple of textile men, one of whom (Benjamin Whitrow) is attempting to get the other (Christopher Fulford) into so much sexual trouble that he will no longer be in a fit state to marry his daughter.

The best new English play since *Benefactors*, this is another bound for a long London and Broadway life; it asks all the right questions about human exploitation, while managing also to be a bittersweet comedy about impossible sexual differences. One scene alone, played by Miss Kendal and Mr Whitrow in two of the best performances to be found anywhere in town, will tell you all you ever need to know about married people in love with married people to whom they happen not to be married, while the rest of Michael Blakemore's production is a triumph of touchy international uneasiness.

Cliffhanger

'Greetings,' says the disembodied head of Laurence Olivier, emerging uneasily from an extraterrestrial egg suspended several feet above the stage of the Dominion Theatre at the start of the new Cliff Richard rock musical *Time*; 'I am Akash. All your questions will be answered.' Unfortunately they are not. My questions would include how does the greatest actor of our century come to be entering his eightieth year involved, even if only in facsimile, with what may well prove to be one of the worst musicals of this century, and I have not forgotten *Troubadour* nor *Thomas and the King* nor yet *Springtime for Hitler*.

One hopes that Akash is getting a lot of the cash for his retirement, since a reputed £4 million has gone into this catastrophic cosmic extravaganza. What has not gone into it is any kind of script, though several people are now reported to be fighting over who had the original idea. Since there is no discernible original idea here, this could be quite a long battle.

Considering all that Cliff Richard has been doing for heaven these last twenty years, somebody up there might have bothered to find him a writer. Or a plot. Or a composer. Or a cast. What they have found him instead is a designer: the star of *Time* is the only star to have emerged from the British musical in the Eighties, John Napier, who has turned the Dominion into a planetarium where under a constant blaze of laser lights twenty tons of scenery rises to the rafters like a spaceship. This is not just a set: this is a feat of mechanical engineering which, when it works, makes all humans and certainly those involved here totally unnecessary. True, it doesn't always work: Lord Olivier's nostrils have a weird habit of moving off in different directions during some of his longer speeches, most of which he appears to be reading off some celestial Autocue machine with an understandable mixture of irritation and amazement that he should have been asked to get his Shakespearian lips around such platitudinous garbage as 'To know me you must truly know yourself' and 'Go forth with love.' The temptation to go forth with hate into the night after about twenty minutes of blinding laser-lighting and a deafening rock score that seems to have been fed through a synthesiser at the wrong speed is considerable. But that Napier set does command attention, if only in the hope that it will finally rise up and demolish all its occupants before setting off across the auditorium in search of Dave Clark, who takes no fewer than seven programme credits, most heralded by the dread words 'devised' and 'created', which signal the absence of an actual author.

Students of the Cliff Richard career who have followed him through the youthful promise of *The Young Ones* to the classic middle period movies like *Summer Holiday* and *Wonderful Life* and then the full dramatic intensity of *Two A Penny* and *Take Me High* may not be entirely surprised to find him here making his legit debut in the role of yet another pop singer, this one apparently summoned into outer space to defend the Earth against Time Lords who wish to blow it up, presumably on the grounds that any planet capable of creating a musical like this one would look better in smithereens. Accordingly, Cliff and a female backing group are

1986

airlifted into the kind of celestial courtroom you may recall from a David Niven film of the 1940s called *A Matter of Life and Death*: here, three judges uneasily perched on forklift trucks are required to sit very still while Cliff sings at them about the fundamental virtues of life on earth. Sometimes the whole stage gets covered in fog, which at least saves you having to watch the choreography; at others Sir Laurence pops out of his egg to utter another cliché about Time being of the essence, which on this occasion it patently is not. Like the old moral rearmament musicals at the Westminster, this one would seem to be trying to tell us that the world would be a better place if we could all be jolly nice to each other and plant a few trees maybe, but for three hours in the theatre this is not quite enough, which may well be why the lighting designer Andrew Bridge has given the judges a natty line in neon collars.

Until you have seen an actor sitting on a forklift truck forty feet above the stage, wondering whether his neon collar is about to explode and meanwhile having to watch, eight times a week, a film of Laurence Olivier doubtless earning more than he is while managing to stay at home every night, you have not appreciated the full terror of being a supporting player in modern British musicals. But if *Time* lasts, and I have a sinking feeling that it just might since Cliff's pop fans of the early Sixties presumably had their brains rotted by *Summer Holiday* anyway and can now afford the £15 it will cost them to watch these flashing lights, it will come after *Mutiny* and *Starlight Express* as ultimate proof that West End audiences now really do prefer musicals that resemble a mindless *son et lumière* staged at Disneyland. Napier's set here does all of the acting and most of the singing and dancing; if they could just find a way of getting all the other actors like Olivier into mechanical replica (and don't think the Disney people haven't already achieved just that in California and Florida) then there would be no need for any human involvement on stage of any kind. Not that there is a lot here anyway: a grotesque and profligate spectacular has been laboriously erected to mask a truly appalling failure of dramatic imagination or intensity, and the sooner the audience too is allowed to send in mechanical replicas of themselves to fill the stalls, then the sooner this entire ghastly mechanical mish-mash can be shipped off in a *Time* capsule on permanent orbit.

Stratford Swan

There's a new Swan on the banks of the Avon at Stratford, and it puts the heart back into a building that for sixty years has always seemed lopsided. When the great fire of 1926 destroyed the original Memorial Theatre, the present, functional and hideous red brick structure was put up at the side of it, leaving the original space as only a rehearsal or store room. Thanks now to a massive donation by an anonymous American benefactor that space has been turned by Michael Reardon (the Stratford architect who also brilliantly turned Hammersmith's Riverside space from a television studio back to theatre) into a 400-seat wooden playhouse, which rises in steep balconies of pine from an apron stage around which the audience is wrapped like a horseshoe.

Visually, acoustically and theatrically this is the most exciting dramatic space to have opened up in my playgoing lifetime: there is an intimacy and a resonance here which has been achieved by none of the studio spaces of the Barbican or National, and if you can imagine a modern Globe carved out of a timber loft, you will have some idea of the magic of this new and joyous Swan. I only wish I could be equally enthusiastic about its choice of opening production.

The RSC policy at the Swan is clear and admirable enough: while the Royal Shakespeare Theatre, with which it shares a back wall, will continue to do mainstream Bard, leaving the Other Place to more experimental work, the Swan will explore the rarely or never seen work of Shakespeare's contemporaries, the plays that influenced him, the plays he influenced and those he may even have helped to write. Whole areas of Elizabethan and Jacobean writing are thus available to Stratford's directors for the first time: Beaumont and Fletcher, Massinger, Ben Jonson, Chapman, Marlowe, Dekker, Middleton, Webster, Tourneur, Heywood and Ford, all ripe for revisiting precisely because they now have a natural home at the Swan. True, it was wise to avoid so obvious an opening as *The Duchess of Malfi* or *The White Devil* or *The Changeling*. But with *The Shoemaker's Holiday* and *The Broken Heart* and *The Chances* and half a hundred other neglected classics out there, it does seem almost perverse to lead off with *The Two Noble Kinsmen*. Originally reckoned to be by Beaumont and Fletcher, now thought to be Shakespeare and Fletcher, it is either way a bizarre plundering of Chaucer's *Knight's Tale*, which offers neither dramatist at anywhere near their best.

Perhaps aware of this and of the remarkable resemblance the Swan stage bears to a Japanese kabuki platform, Barry Kyle's production is a weird and wondrous mix of oriental and rustic styles which looks at times as though Kurosawa had been asked to rethink *A Midsummer Night's Dream*. In that the script is anyway a grab-bag of conflicting conventions and left-over scenes from better plays, and that what was needed was an opener which would show off the theatre, this is an amiable start. But the test will come with a play which grabs our hearts and minds rather than our academic curiosity. Here, neither Hugh Quarshie nor Gerard Murphy can persuade us that it much matters what happens to the kinsmen in their romantic or military pursuits, though Imogen Stubbs as a local gaoler's daughter plays a mad scene on an imaginary boat with such haunting and luminous brilliance that she promises to be the Ophelia of her generation and the RSC's most intriguing discovery since Anton Lesser half a decade ago.

At the London Palladium, *La Cage Aux Folles* is, after *Mame* and *Hello Dolly!*, another of Jerry Herman's shows about big women on even bigger staircases, the difference being that in this case the women are mostly men. What was once a small, gay, French art-house movie, about a nightclub singer having to pretend to be the wife of the man he lives with in order not to shock the prospective in-laws of the man's son, has now become a baroque blow-up of *Charley's Aunt* hedged around with some of the longest, slowest costume parades in recent West End history.

The fact that the show works rather better in London than when I saw it (admittedly late into the run) on Broadway is largely a tribute to Denis Quilley, who manages to bring to the old Gene Barry role a sharper sense of timing and an edgy classical distinction; but this has always been George Hearn's evening and his *I Am What I Am* is essentially the torch song of *Torch Song Trilogy*. The author of both the *Trilogy* and *La Cage* is Harvey Fierstein, but in making his gay philosophy that men are wonderful mothers acceptable to a musical audience of more conservative habits, both the director Arthur Laurents and Mr Herman have gone for a softer option. *La Cage* is thus heavy on sets and costumes, light on plot or characterisation and dominated by the classic *Gypsy* device of a star having a breakdown during the big number.

At Chichester, Ronald Eyre has an intelligent and massively underrated revival of Enid Bagnold's *The Chalk Garden*, and before you think this is the summer-stock playhouse at its most reactionary, I would remind you that here was a play hailed in 1956 by Ken Tynan as 'the finest artificial comedy to have flowed from an English pen since Congreve'. He was wrong, of course. What we have instead is essentially Agatha Christie by way of J. M. Barrie: an arch and whimsical mix of murder mystery and childhood fantasy. But no play which starts 'Maitland, where are my teeth?' can be all bad, and *The Chalk Garden* has over the last thirty years attracted to it the talents of Edith Evans, Peggy Ashcroft, Gladys Cooper, Sybil Thorndike and Judith Anderson because it offers two splendid parts for sharply contrasted actresses, one a grande dame in need of dental repair and the other a tight-lipped governess who may also be a killer.

What saves *The Chalk Garden* from being a better class of *Mousetrap* is Bagnold's rich, heightened prose and her evident desire to turn an uneventful if true story into the best of Maugham. She wrote every line as if engraving on glass, and though neither time nor the wide open spaces of the Chichester stage have been kind to her hothouse plant, it is good to see Googie Withers and Dorothy Tutin driving an eccentric vintage car safely home.

Endgame

In the theatre as in chess, and indeed in *Chess*, the timing is all and it is therefore more than a little hard on Tim Rice and Abba that their first partnership should have hit the West End at the end of a time in which critics and audiences alike have been clobbered with more musicals than they would normally get to see in half a decade. From the greatness of *Les Misérables* through the gaiety of *La Cage Aux Folles* to the technological wastelands of *Mutiny* and *Time* and *Starlight Express*, the hills of Shaftesbury Avenue have been unusually alive with the sound of musicals new and old, and as a result the critical response to one of the most important homegrown scores and shows of the Eighties has been distinctly muted.

Perhaps we already knew it too well; the trouble with pre-selling scores on disc is that for almost two years now the hits of *Chess* have been on every turntable and most radio stations. How dynamic or revolutionary would *Oklahoma!* have sounded in 1943 if the first-night audience had been able to go into the theatre whistling the title song?

The other central problem is that *Chess* still has no book. In abandoning the idea of a librettist, Rice has also effectively abandoned the idea of a strong plot, so we have characters and songs and even a few ideas about chess as a metaphor for East-West relations, and yet no overall shape to a show which is precisely about the plotting of pawns in an international power game.

But what matters at the Prince Edward is the way that Trevor Nunn, taking over the production from Michael Bennett only eight weeks before its first night, has hauled it into a remarkably coherent dramatic shape. From its opening parody of *White Horse Inn* right through to a long Chorale conclusion, this is a staging of considerable intelligence and invention, played out on a brilliantly engineered chessboard, which can tilt and light and travel in all directions, but is mercifully never allowed star billing.

Around it are ranged banks of video screens to give us everything from newsreels of Hungary 1956 (the heroine lost her father there) through to news flashes of the latest Soviet or American scores in the all-important tournament, but even here, Nunn has managed to keep his actors far enough away from the technology so that they remain in control of the stage throughout. He has also managed to bring Elaine Paige far from her frozen and static Eva Peron so that, playing the secretary and aide to the bully-brat American champion (at least until she falls in love with his rather more butch Russian opponent), she at last gives a performance of dramatic as well as musical distinction.

The best of the rest of the score is sung by Murray Head and Tommy Korberg as the rival players, though Richard Lyndon and Paul Wilson have a British embassy duet which comes as a sharp reminder that Rice

1986

is the wittiest lyricist we've had here since Coward, while John Turner has a wonderful parody of a Russian drinking song, which Nunn has rightly staged as a left-over scene from *Three Sisters*. Molly Molloy's choreography veers from parodies of *Sound of Music* and *King and I* to highlights from Bob Fosse and Larry Fuller, but it too manages to use the chess metaphor with considerable variation, while the only thing wrong with Robin Wagner's set is that, in the Temple of the Reclining Buddha, the Buddha seems not to be reclining at all.

Doomsday Chic

Precious few theatrical fortune-tellers could have predicted that Harold Pinter, darkest and most distinguished of dramatists, would become the George Cukor of the 1980s, but in his productions last year of Lauren Bacall in *Sweet Bird of Youth* and now of Faye Dunaway in *Circe and Bravo* at Hampstead, there can be no doubt that he has developed precisely Cukor's talent for drawing immensely strong performances from hugely starry ladies in often shaky scripts.

Miss Dunaway's European stage debut comes, and not before time, in a play by Donald Freed, set at Camp David during what would appear to be some kind of nuclear alert. She has been taken there under house arrest by the only other character we ever get to meet, a monosyllabic security guard played with dark glasses and a barely suppressed anxiety complex by Stephen Jenn, and is being held captive for the simple reason that she is married to the President and talks too much, especially in times of crisis, to journalists from the *New York Times*.

Mr Freed is a dramatist and screenwriter whose track record would suggest a considerable interest in the conspiracy theories of recent American history, but as his title indicates, he wants us now to see something Greek and mythological in what could otherwise have been just another post-Watergate thriller. Yet for those of us who had enough trouble just relating the Kennedys to Camelot, the idea of a First Lady acquiring Greek grandeur is usually allied to another Onassis marriage rather than anything more classical, and that essentially is the central problem with Mr Freed's otherwise intriguing play.

For as long as it stays rooted in Camp David, *Circe and Bravo* has a lot to say about the intolerable sexual and social lives of most First Ladies and about the desire of a woman, at the centre of power but unable to wield it personally, at least to achieve some satisfaction as an informer. This, known doubtless as the Martha Mitchell Syndrome, is what Miss Dunaway manages best: prowling in a white bathrobe around her Presidential prison, a designer bunker complete with every modern convenience except the vodka she most needs, the Louisiana beauty queen who made a good political marriage is coruscatingly funny about White Houses past and present, and then very moving in a lament about how the American military heroes of World War II turned into the butchers of Vietnam.

In these sequences, and in those which involve a Pinteresque power game with her security guard, by the end of which it is she who is guarding him, *Circe and Bravo* is an unmissable dramatic near-monologue which establishes Miss Dunaway as a formidably powerful player in the best traditions of Bacall and even the Joan Crawford she once played on film. It is when the play lurches into poetic childhood memories of the deep South or the First Lady's mythomania problem that it proves irretrievable even by such powerhouse playing, and its final collapse comes as the declaration of nuclear war itself is made to seem almost an anti-climax to the First Lady's personality problems. Yet, time and again, Miss Dunaway drags an overblown, verbose and semi-static play into raw life by the sheer force of her own stardom, and though tickets at Hampstead are now the hottest in town, you would be well advised to catch up with a blazing star trek when it makes what will, I suspect, be a rapid transfer to a larger West End and then Broadway house.

Talking of blazing stars, for thirty years now John Osborne's *The Entertainer* has been overshadowed on stage and screen by the memory of Olivier as Archie Rice, dead behind the eyes, telling us not to clap too loudly in a very old building or asking us where we were playing tomorrow night so he could come see us on account of what a lovely audience we had been. Others who have attempted the most demanding role written for an English actor in the 1950s have almost always been specialist comedians like Max Wall or Jimmy Logan, so it is considerably to the credit of Peter Bowles that he should be the first straight man to tackle it in a West End revival now to be seen at the Shaftesbury.

The surprise and the success of Robin Lefevre's production is that it takes us away from false memories of the first production and back to the play itself. If you recalled *The Entertainer* the way I did, as a play about England seen as a dying vaudeville act, or as a play about Suez and national pride, or even as a play about the impossibility of being Max Miller any more, look again. What we have now at the Shaftesbury is nothing less than the English *Long Day's Journey Into Night*, a vast rambling family tragedy about death and failure and despair within which the front-cloth vaudeville numbers that were so central to the Olivier production come as little more than occasional musical interludes. The role that brought Olivier the greatest non-classical success of his career is thus now returned to the bosom of its appalling family: alongside Mr Bowles as Archie we have Frank Middlemass as the old-trouper father, Sylvia Syms as the long-suffering wife, Joanne Pearce as the militant daughter and Paul Mooney as the surviving son.

Certainly the music-hall origins are still powerful, as is Osborne's great last act salute to Max Miller; but the easy equation between England and a run-down pier show now seems only part of a more complex social tapestry that is to do with families and nostalgia and inevitably the potency of cheap music. Within the ornately tacky and wonderfully suitable surroundings of the Shaftesbury, Mr Bowles splendidly manages Archie's mix of fear and hatred and self-loathing, that inability ever to decide whether he hates his audiences more than they hate him. But this is now a company play in which, while Archie roars out his life in four-letter words, the rest of his family try to come to terms with their own declining roles in a fast-declining nation. In that sense *The Entertainer* is a rancid *Cavalcade*, held together and given lasting fascination by Osborne's realisation that it is the family which preys together that stays together.

Shaken and Stirred

Few plays in the postwar history of the British theatre have risen or fallen further in critical esteem than *The Cocktail Party*, reckoned in 1949 to be the greatest achievement of a shortlived movement in verse drama, yet generally now welcomed back with all the enthusiasm normally reserved for a dead duck. Yet why should it have been chosen this summer by John Dexter to launch a remarkable new acting company at the Phoenix led by half-a-dozen players who would be the envy of any subsidised stage in this country? First perhaps because of what we now know of Eliot's own marital agonies, which would seem to be reflected here. Secondly because it gives Alec McCowen the chance to play the Uninvited Guest and therefore to return with Dexter to the world of high intellectual chic they first explored across another psychiatric couch in Shaffer's *Equus* a decade or more ago. And thirdly because whatever my colleagues would have you believe, this is still a play of rich and rare fascination.

Though it would be hard to imagine a better production of *The Cocktail Party* than the present one, it remains a thoroughly curious attempt to consider religious principles through the reflection of a cocktail shaker. Eliot appears here to have taken stock of every successful West End dramatist of the interwar years, from Priestley through Coward to Barrie, and to have borrowed from them all before setting off down his own mystic and spiritual path. Just as Robert Eddison, in a wonderfully craggy and strange performance as one of the Guardians who watch over the destiny of the central characters, is an eccentric cook forever trying to pour more ingredients into an already overstocked pot, so Eliot seems at different times to be writing everything from a religious thriller to a black comedy of marital despair.

As his play opens, Lavinia Chamberlayne (an acidly elegant Sheila Allen) has just walked out on her husband, leaving him to host the cocktail party at which her disappearance is the main source of conversation. The husband (Simon Ward going stylishly to pieces) is a wealthy barrister, and as we soon discover both have been involved in extramarital affairs, we are by the end of the first act already well out of the missing-wife mystery and into an apparent divorce drama set against the Cowardly framework of Brien Vahey's art deco set. Already we seem to have had a complete survey of West End themes and attitudes in mid-century, but it is not until we get into Harcourt-Reilly's consulting room for the second act that we discover the full extent of Eliot's vastly darker and more ambitious design. Having won over an audience who did not expect to have to face eternal truths along Shaftesbury Avenue forty years ago, *The Cocktail Party* turns from a glossy if mysterious drawing-room drama into a religious and psychoanalytical exploration of guilt and martyrdom and atonement.

The psychiatrist, who is also one of the Guardians, puts the Chamberlayne marriage back together again by removing their illusions about the nature of love and teaching them instead to live with the bickering reality of each other's limitations. But for Chamberlayne's mistress, Celia Coplestone (Sheila Gish in a performance which dominates even this starry evening by its intense intellectual and spiritual energy), an altogether higher and more terrible fate has been reserved: she is to die a martyr's death by crucifixion.

At this point the play has clearly taken off, via the higher church, for the realms of mythology and it is a tremendous tribute to Alec McCowen and this production that it remains rooted in a kind of reality: during the series of duologues with his patients which makes up the second act, our interest in him and them is never allowed even momentarily to weaken. *The Cocktail Party* is worth another look precisely because it is such a curious mixture of heavenly and earthly considerations: Rachel Kempson, in a welcome return to the stage as the third Guardian, manages to combine cascading social uneasiness with sudden alarming glimpses of the infinite, and therefore gets as close as anyone to the heart of the matter. Nervous breakdowns, it would appear, cannot be solved by psychiatrists alone, but if the psychiatrist happens to be of another world, then Eliot's three-hour debate on the nature of guilt and retribution need know no boundaries at all. What Dexter has done here is also to underline the humour and the narrative drive of a script which could all too easily get lost along one of its own detours, and to give us a feast of the best character acting in town. If he manages to hold this new company together, it could well prove to be the best hope the West End has of pulling itself away from an almost exclusive diet of old farces and even older musicals.

At Hampstead, *Observe the Sons of Ulster Marching Towards the Somme* is the story of eight Ulster volunteers going towards their death in World War I. Written by a Catholic dramatist (Frank McGuinness) who seems to find the poetry of theatre as natural as breathing, where Eliot found it as difficult as whistling under water, this is to some extent the Irish *Journey's End*, but what makes it so consistently moving and intriguing is the connection that McGuinness has seen between death in the trenches and the death of Irish peace. These soldiers are not really fighting Germans: instead they are still fighting out their own past, re-enacting the Battle of the Boyne on each other's shoulders and never forgetting that a war only really makes sense when it is a war about the future of Ireland or possibly its past.

Michael Attenborough's production achieves a strong sense of character separation among the bakers and millers and lapsed priests and Belfast thugs who make up the volunteer force, and their obsessive desire to keep the soil of Ulster under their feet rather than the mud of France is what gives the play its central energy. We meet the men as ghosts, summoned back by the only one who survived (John Rogan) and it is he as a young man (John Bowe) who is the focus for what McGuinness has to say about the nature of Ulstermen: that their courage on the Somme was both blood lust and death wish.

Miller's Time Piece

Much rewritten since a brief off-Broadway run five years ago, and drastically revised in production after a Birmingham outing more recently, Arthur Miller's *The American Clock* now reaches the stage of the Cottesloe in a National production by Peter Wood of considerable emotional and documentary power. Acknowledging a debt to Studs Terkel and his *Hard Times* chronicle of the Depression, Miller and Wood have here opened up a play that once looked like a minor Clifford Odets family tragedy, and turned it into a social history somewhere between Dennis Potter's *Pennies From Heaven* and Coward's *Cavalcade*.

Yet the single central idea remains intact: to turn back the American clock to the 1930s and find out why it was that a period of Depression and despair did not lead to any kind of national revolution but instead, by the time Hoover had given way to Roosevelt, to a renewed faith in a country that from any objective point of view should have crumbled into anarchy or frozen into totalitarianism on European principles.

Writing in short, fragmentary scenes intercut with twenty-five songs from the inevitable *Life is Just a Bowl of Cherries* through the best of the Gershwins to *We're in the Money*, all sung by actors who know they are not there to be singers, Miller starts at Black Thursday in 1929 and traces the effects of the Wall Street Crash on two families. One, the Baums, could have been an early outline for the Lomans: a middle-class family fallen on hard times, for whom poverty now means the loss of a beloved piano and the need to board up their windows to keep the mortgage man away. Michael Bryant, as the salesman no longer able to live even on a smile and a shoeshine, Sara Kestelman, as the wistful musical wife, and Neil Daglish, as the son who (in a direct echo of Miller's own childhood experience) manages to get all his money out of a bank just before it closes, buy a bicycle with it and then have the bicycle stolen within a matter of days, all achieve here a family unit that holds an otherwise sketchy evening together.

Whether faking a family row so that the son can qualify for a rent cheque, or looking uneasily across at their cousin Sydney determined like Yip Harburg to keep the brightest songs coming out of the darkest times, the Baums remain at the Brooklyn edge of the tapestry. The other family we get to know, the Taylors of Iowa, are having to defend their own farms from knock-down auctions by holding the local sheriff hostage. Life may be tougher out there, but the collapse of the Market still means the collapse of the old morality: if twelve executives dealing in tobacco can make more money than the 30,000 farmers who grew it, then something in the States has gone very rotten indeed.

Yet this is no *Grapes of Wrath*, and Miller's view of the decade that shaped him as a writer and a man is an oddly complex one. He has in *The American Clock* no nostalgia for an appalling time, nor does he bathe the farm-auction scenes in the current Hollywood glow of poverty recalled in affluence; and yet he is suggesting here that the Depression was America's last 'real' time, before the movies and the images and the myths were allowed to take over. No other event except the Civil War touched every family so deeply, and those who lived through the 1930s as breadwinners could never quite get away from the feeling that the bread might one day be taken out of their mouths again.

It is the incidental moments that make this production one of the most impressive in the recent and admittedly patchy history of the National: the President of General Motors seeing his job in terms of a flashy song-and-dance routine from a Fred Astaire movie, neighbours recalling silent streets suddenly full of the cries of babies as parents returned to live with grandparents, a street vendor going under a subway train while financiers go out of sixty-floor skyscrapers.

What is most bleak about the ticking of this clock is Miller's realisation that, in America, the economy only really started to come right with the rearmament for World War II, so that the paper-money debts of the fathers were repaid with the lives of their sons in battle. But not everyone crashed; indeed the play's narrator (Barrie Ingham) learns in the opening scene to keep his dollars in his shoes and is therefore able to walk on them

1986

around the cardboard shanties that were set up along the Hudson, wondering gently why anyone ever believed in banks.

A whole generation was allowed to wither in the prime of life, but *The American Clock* still has two faces: Miller remains torn between horror at the waste and a realisation that, even at the time of their greatest defeat, the failed financiers and the bankrupt farmers knew something about the truth of America that has now been lost for ever, in which case that history may well be doomed to repeat itself – and not as farce. By consciously setting his play in a style which seems almost to parody Odets and the social-conscience dramas of the middle Thirties, he is also commenting on the theatre of that time. Wood's company, most playing three and four roles, is immensely strengthened by the arrival of Marsha Hunt as a politicised prostitute, David Schofield as the dancing tycoon and Paul Curran as the financier going off to die broke in a bowling alley.

A Fright at the Opera

The plot of Andrew Lloyd Webber's *Phantom of the Opera* is essentially simple enough: ghost gets girl, ghost loses girl. But the show that he and Charles Hart, the lyricist, and Hal Prince, the director, and Gillian Lynne, the choreographer, have built around the old Gaston Leroux melodrama (much filmed but seldom staged) is a marvellous celebration; it has found at Her Majesty's the perfect home. How delighted Beerbohm Tree, the theatre's builder and first manager, a man not above sticking live rabbits through the scenery of Shakespearian pastorals to hold his audiences' attention, would have been by the gasps from the stalls as a chandelier rises to the roof of the theatre only to come crashing down again later, or as the stage is magically transformed into candlelit underground lakes or Parisian rooftops. The whole of this *Phantom* is in fact a tribute to the old Victorian theatrical values, almost as though Lloyd Webber wants to reassure us that, after the chilly mechanics of the roller disco that is *Starlight Express*, he is still capable of returning us to a world of lyrical romanticism somewhere halfway from Ivor Novello back to Puccini.

This must, in fact, be the first musical ever to star a chandelier; nothing else in the production is quite so dramatically effective or well lit, though as the Phantom Michael Crawford manages to be here, there and everywhere around the set, wreaking murder and mayhem on those who dare thwart his plans to make a star of his beloved Christine. Sarah Brightman has exactly the right kind of wide-eyed innocence for this role, but neither she nor Steve Barton as the Vicomte who also loves her has been given any but the most minimal characterisation. In stripping away the minor themes and strands of Gaston Leroux's 1911 chiller, the production becomes a simple spectacular which could almost as well have been derived from *Beauty and the Beast*. But there are some marvellously tricky moments here, and if the Phantom is made out to be no more than a crazed subterranean organist, nevertheless Michael Crawford yet manages to create a literally haunting figure in a half-mask.

Elsewhere, a week of Shaw and Ibsen in rarely seen revivals: to the Barbican comes *Misalliance* while, at the Young Vic, Vanessa Redgrave is Mrs Alving in an immensely impressive in-the-round *Ghosts*. By cutting away much of the Victorian drapery which usually surrounds the cupboard where Ibsen rattles all the skeletons of the Alving inheritance, the director David Thacker gives us a cool and sparse but crystal-clear production dominated by Miss Redgrave, but powerfully played also by Tom Wilkinson as the wretched time-serving Pastor Manders and Adrian Dunbar as the doomed, syphilitic Osvald.

Away from the proscenium arch there is now the chance to see the play at close quarters, and what emerges is the sheer narrative power of the melodramatic storyline: a soap-opera of modern American television might even think twice about a burning orphanage, an illegitimate daughter unknowingly attempting to seduce her half-brother, and a mercy killing all within one episode. But what is so strong here is the sense of the past in the present: all the characters are haunted by the ghosts of the title and of their own pasts, as well as the ghostly orthodoxy of a society that was still refusing to allow the honesty of youth to disturb the treacherous compromises of middle age. Not that Victorian England was any better at accepting what one critic called 'this loathsome sore unbandaged'.

But the play now seems to be less about incest or venereal disease or euthanasia, more about the social pressures on Manders and Mrs Alving to conform to a world which, like Osvald, was rotting from within. Vanessa Redgrave wonderfully conjures up a woman who, though intellectually emancipated, has devoted herself to suppressing the truth about her late husband's affairs above and below stairs. But now, with Osvald back from Paris, and the Pastor over to celebrate the new orphanage, all manner of home truths are about to emerge. Tom Wilkinson offers a pale Manders, forever tying himself in knots of social and sexual unease in his efforts to stay inside the body of current public opinion, while Osvald seems to know from the very outset that he has come home only to die. Thacker's production steers the company safely around the rocks of melodrama and leaves us with a sharp impression of the play's modernity in psychological debate.

On the main Barbican stage, *Misalliance* is a debate of an altogether less dramatic kind, despite the arrival in mid-play of a light aircraft which comes crashing spectacularly into the garden pavilion, where a neat array of Shavian stereotypes has been lined up for an otherwise uneventful three-hour dialogue on democracy, marriage, inherited wealth, parents, children, education, colonial government, the class structure and whatever other topics crop up along the way. But John Caird the director has managed with the help of a strong cast to keep the conversation piece from talking itself into the ground, and Jane Lapotaire as the Polish adventuress down from the skies is a figure of considerable fascination. What we essentially have here are nine characters in search of a plot and, though none emerges, there is a kind of delight in what could well have been the first play destined solely for the wireless.

Meanwhile, down in the Barbican Pit, Richard Nelson's *Principia Scriptoriae* is a drama from off-Broadway about two young writers thrown into gaol by the right-wing regime of some unnamed Latin American country only to meet again fifteen years later on opposite sides of a conference table negotiating the freedom of a poet gaoled by the country's now leftist government. Across the back of Bob Crawley's set are flashed one-line homilies about the writer's craft ('Choose Your Setting Carefully'; 'Always Like Your Characters'), which are in bleak contrast or ironic counterpoint to the events taking place beneath them. Anton Lesser as the American and Sean Baker as the local man are nicely contrasted in David Jones's production, one which also points up the sharp mix of satire and sympathy in Richard Nelson's writing about the relationship between a writer and real life.

Enigma Variations

Alan Turing was the man who fathered the modern computer and cracked the German Enigma code during the war, thereby winning Churchill's acclaim as one of the principal architects of allied victory. He was also the man who, a decade later, took his own life with a poisoned apple after the police had charged him with homosexuality, and it is on Turing's biography that Hugh Whitemore has now built his play, *Breaking the Code* (at the Haymarket). Clearly there is a social code as well as a secret one being broken here, and by building his play as for television, with a lot of fragmentary flashbacks and rapid changes of time and place, Whitemore has achieved a stage documentary of compelling interest and power.

Derek Jacobi plays Turing across almost thirty years. We meet him as a Sherborne schoolboy already in love with a classmate, we meet him as the war-time codebreaker at Bletchley, and as the Manchester University professor intent on building an electronic brain that can think for itself. We meet him lecturing to his old school and under police interrogation; we meet him in Manchester pubs and Greek hotels picking up young men, and we meet him with his mother who is unable to understand either his science or his own sexuality.

As in his last stage play *Pack of Lies*, based on the Kroger spy case, Whitemore is concerned with the gap between private and public codes of morality; but this is more of a one-man show, with Jacobi never off the stage and the figures around him all very shadowy in the darkness of Liz da Costa's huge steely set, one built to resemble the inside of some vast machine which occasionally opens itself up to daylight.

But this is Jacobi's evening and he gives what I would guess will be an award-winning performance as the crumpled, stammering visionary mathematician unable to deal with his own private life, but desperately intent on the creation of a machine that can deal with the numbers which became his only true friends. Around him are ranged Michael Gough as the senior Bletchley code-breaker, Isobel Dean as Turing's mother, Joanna David as the scientist who wants to marry him and Dave Hill as the policeman whose interrogation gives the play its framework; all do what they can with sketchily written characters, existing only to bring out the various aspects of Turing's complex nature. Yet this is not a crusading piece; Whitemore leaves us to our own conclusions about the kind of man who could crack everything but his own nature, and in the jigsaw of his play are most of the clues we need, while Clifford Williams's production is suitably brisk and spare.

Breaking the Code Derek Jacobi *as Alan Turing*

1986

Carrie On

A couple of years ago it was the bright idea of Keith Waterhouse to create a diary for Carrie Pooter, since that of her husband Charles had been for almost a century the best-selling *Diary of a Nobody*. What we have now, on stage at the Garrick as *Mr and Mrs Nobody*, is the dramatisation by Waterhouse of his own book and the original classic by George and Weedon Grossmith, bound together into a double diary of considerable charm and tremendous loyalty to the mood of the original.

Michael Williams and Judi Dench are the Pooters in Ned Sherrin's agile production, one which keeps its only two speaking characters up and about Julia Trevelyan Oman's marvellously cluttered Victorian parlour setting, thereby neatly avoiding the potential danger of the play becoming a static recital from two desks. Instead of that, we get a sharp insight into life at The Laurels, Brickfield Terrace, Holloway, a residence rather too close to the railway line for Carrie's liking. Indeed, Carrie has a number of complaints that were only ever hinted at in her husband's original diary: we also now learn of her romantic, but unrequited, passion for a Mr Darwitts of the local stationery shop, and of her determination to acquire an ice-safe before the year is out. In Judi Dench's wonderful mix of dutiful wife and scathing domestic commentator, and in Michael Williams's bearded, pompous and yet oddly endearing husband, we get a perfectly matched pair of performances, totally at home in their own parlour and venturing out only for such social functions as the Lord Mayor's banquet and a trip to a nearby theatre, both of which end in predictable disaster of one kind or another.

The invisible other characters include their son, Lupin (whose fiancée's hair is, notes Carrie sharply, 'no stranger to the automatic curlers'), and Pooter's two friends, Cummings and Gowing, who are also not quite what Mrs Pooter might have hoped for in regular visitors. That she is more socially aware and ambitious than her benign husband is one of the play's constant themes; another is the difference between her reality and his daydreaming: 'I could always dine at my club,' muses Pooter. 'You'd have to join one first,' retorts his loving but sharp-tongued wife. All in all theirs is the best double-act in town; if you have cherished the book, this will come as a pleasant reminder of it, and if you haven't, then the Waterhouse variant is the best possible introduction to the world of the Pooters.

1987

A YEAR OF CURIOUSLY MIXED FORTUNES for plays and players: two of the best fringe theatres in town burned to the ground, four adjacent playhouses on Shaftesbury Avenue went simultaneously, if only briefly, dark, and the Arts Council decided to do remarkably little about the recommendations of the Cork Report on our national theatrical future. As against that, all theatres, bar the Tricycle, were open again by Christmas, three others in the West End came back to life from long years of disuse, and the Arts Council did manage, at the year's end, to announce an overall funding increase of seventeen per cent.

Nothing is ever quite as bad as it looks in the theatre, nor quite as good either:

Lettice and Lovage Maggie Smith *as Lettice Douffet* and Margaret Tyzack *as Lotte Schoen*

the Royal Shakespeare Company got saved by £1 million or so from Royal Insurance, and, although actors had not yet been told to wear the RI logo on their Shakespearian breastplates, the time might not be far off. It was already on all their posters and programmes.

In a spirit of Thatcherite free enterprise, Kenneth Branagh set up his own classical company with City funding and a Royal blessing from Prince Charles, thereby begging one of the most important of all backstage questions. If the future meant private rather than public funding, there might be no trouble in getting sponsorship for the RSC or the National or even a golden boy like Branagh, but what about the experimental company with a dangerous new play that stockholders might not consider suitable for a night out with wives or clients? How many City firms would, even before the crash, have been willing to invest in what was unquestionably the play of the year, Caryl Churchill's *Serious Money*, which just happened to be about the total corruption of the City itself?

Presumably the perfect show for 1987 would have been an Andrew Lloyd Webber musical called *Hats* and featuring Mrs Thatcher on a forklift truck surrounded by a roller-skating chorus of indigent arts administrators; the trouble was that Barry Humphries had already more or less done that. The other trouble was that crises in the arts generally, and the theatre particularly, were only ever dependent on how you juggle the figures. You could for instance have looked around the West End at the time, seen more hit musicals playing there than ever before (many with second casts, since the first had gone off to make another fortune on Broadway with the same songs) and wondered what on earth the problem was. You could have looked at the RSC, operating on a total of nine Stratford and London stages, or the National working on another four as they moved into the handover year from Peter Hall to Richard Eyre, or the Royal Court and Hampstead in vintage form, and wondered what on earth anyone had to worry about.

Looking around a little more closely: how many serious new plays had actually opened in the West End rather than simply transferred there from a subsidised or fringe address? By my reckoning there were less than half a dozen in nearly fifty theatres; the rest of the non-transfer total was made up by musicals, farces and thrillers, so that the commercial theatre was now in real danger of following Broadway into the twilight of a museum existence.

Equally, in the subsidised sector there were indications that risks were now generally confined to studio stages: who'd have thought, even five years earlier, that the RSC would have had four major musicals in production (*Les Misérables*, *Wizard of Oz*, *Kiss Me Kate* and the then forthcoming *Carrie*), or that a decade of control by directors would have ended in a return to the blazing star power of such actors as Antony Sher at Stratford and Anthony Hopkins at the National?

1987

There were changes, too, around the fringe: the three best theatres of the outer London ring, Hammersmith, Greenwich and Hampstead, all found themselves under some form of threat from local councils no longer sure where their own money was coming from, while around the country the pattern was much the same, with Glasgow and Manchester and Leicester becoming increasingly isolated centres of excellence.

Back on the up side, the glories of the year were easy to list: Michael Gambon in Ayckbourn's definitive revival of *A View From The Bridge*, Julia McKenzie in *Follies*, Thelma Holt's World Theatre Season at the National, Judi Dench's Cleopatra there, the ENO's *Pacific Overtures* at the Coliseum, a brilliant treble at the Royal Court (*Serious Money*, *The Emperor* and *Lie of the Mind*) and Maggie Smith in Shaffer's subversive comedy *Lettice and Lovage*.

Lullaby of Broadstairs

At a time when virtually all other London musicals are about either scenery or nostalgia, the magic of Stephen Sondheim's *Follies* (at the Shaftesbury) is that it takes both those elements to pieces and puts them under a spotlight of considerable cynical doubt. First written more than twenty years ago, and originally staged on Broadway by Hal Prince and Michael Bennett in a 1971 production which had as its inspiration a press photograph of an ancient Gloria Swanson standing amid the bulldozed rubble of the theatre where she had first been seen, *Follies* is a broken-backed and still oddly unfinished account of a group of ex-Ziegfeld girls coming together after thirty years for a reunion in the ruins of their old home.

For London, on a scaffolding set by Maria Bjornson which often threatens to be more eventful than the plot, the director Mike Ockrent has had to find some local equivalents to the original American mix of ancient Broadway and Hollywood legends: thus we get Leonard Sachs as a master of ceremonies from *The Good Old Days*, Adele Leigh from the Vienna Woods, Pearl Carr and Teddy Johnson from seaside singalongs and Maria Charles from *The Boy Friend*. We also get the splendid Margaret Courtenay belting out the first big hit of the evening, though here not so much a Broadway as a Broadstairs Baby, and that essential Englishness remains something of a problem.

So too does the fact that, although Sondheim has written four new songs for this London premiere, most seem to belong in *Company* rather than replacing some strong originals here, while none solves the surviving difficulty of the second half, which is that James Goldman's plot still runs out at the interval. Up to there, what we have is architecturally and musically a fascinating folly about the schizoid nature of nostalgia: if you can imagine a spectacular cobbled together on a wet afternoon by Proust and Pirandello with a little help from the Berlins, Irving and Isaiah, you'll have some idea of the scale on which it has been conceived. Old ladies are shadowed on stage by the ghostly dancers they once were, while an admittedly banal central tale about two of the chorus girls having married husbands destined for each other is surrounded on all sides by one of the most brilliant scores that even Sondheim has ever devised, one which manages to recall three entire generations of Broadway musicals while simultaneously celebrating and parodying the very essence of big band shows.

The central casting now features Daniel Massey and Diana Rigg as the wealthily clenched upmarket couple, with David Healy and Julia McKenzie as the rather better written pair from the back of beyond, and the new conclusion allows them to avoid nervous collapse while staying within those very rocky marriages, despite the reminder of how they once were meant to be cross-partnered. All four take to Bob Avian's musical staging (in the cases of Massey and Rigg, for the first time in classical years) with a kind of edgy confidence, and four decades on from *Annie Get Your Gun* Dolores Gray does the great hymn to greasepainted survival *I'm Still Here,* though it's only Rigg's acid *Could I Leave You?* and McKenzie's heartbreaking *Losing My Mind* that reach the pitch of the recent concert performance.

The rest of a company of forty get to stand around a lot, and three hours on we are left once again with the realisation that even when, as in this case, a Sondheim score has after much revision yet failed to find a perfect theatrical framework, it is still musically and lyrically one of the most richly rewarding treats in town.

Beset by a £1 million deficit, the Royal Shakespeare Company are commendably determined not to let it show from the front: within the last few days they have opened major new productions on two stages in London and one in Stratford, which bring their total up to almost fifty in nine theatres during the current season. Clearly they are going for broke, and just as clearly, if they do go broke, it will be said that they catastrophically over-extended from their original Stratford base in an attempt to be all things theatrical to all people in a manner that might have been envied by Barnum and Bailey themselves, let alone such lesser impresarios as Florenz Ziegfeld or Joe Papp.

The present RSC openings give some idea of the range of their ambitions and also suggest some of the problems that come with them. At Stratford there's *The Jew of Malta* on the Swan stage, which is a constant delight, but begs to be efficiently cross-cast with the Antony Sher *Merchant of Venice*, a programming double that has somehow been largely fluffed. At the Mermaid, there's a staging of *They Shoot Horses Don't They?* which would look vastly stronger if so much of the present company's big-band strength had not disappeared into *Les Misérables* and *Kiss Me Kate* elsewhere in London, leaving apparently precious little for this their third major musical in less than two years. And on the Barbican main stage, there's a new Jean Genet season starting with *The Balcony* in what looks like a daft gesture of academic, economic and anti-populist defiance: neither the play nor, I would guess, the understandably limited number of Genet addicts have a hope of fully occupying that cavernous space for too long.

Terry Hands first directed *The Balcony* for the RSC at the Aldwych fifteen years ago, and his reasons for returning to it are not made clear by an over-long, over-dressed and over-stated revival, which comes as little more than a turgid reminder that this is the kind of play you teach rather than try to act. A sprawling sub-erotic fantasy about the occupants of a brothel in a city under siege, it is largely concerned with the more obvious connections between sex and power, along with the fact that even a house of ill repute, or perhaps especially a house of ill repute, can usefully be turned into a working model of the world around it.

Genet himself once said that he wanted all the characters played by Grock; what he has got at the Barbican instead is an uneasy assembly of middle-range character actors led by Dilys Laye and Joe Melia in a huge set and a great many unwieldy costumes, suddenly aware that what they are trying to put across is not a play at all but an intellectual thesis remarkably lacking in dramatic coherence or emotional power.

They Shoot Horses Don't They? works somewhat better, though it too suffers from the undercasting that is now increasingly evident as the company continues to sub-divide itself. Horace McCoy's novel (dramatised by Ray Herman) of the dance marathons in 1930s America needs a couple of blazing star turns from the appalling master of ceremonies and at least one of the dancers, played by Gig Young and Jane Fonda in a film still much better known than the book; but if, as at the Mermaid, it fails to get them, we are left with little to focus upon. There also seems to be a strange uncertainty in Ron Daniels's production about whether we are into showbiz nostalgia or social realism: when the dancers, ever more exhausted by weeks and then months of shuffling around a ballroom at the end of a California pier, are invited on to the bandstand to sing us ironical period songs of escapist optimism, they do so with all the energy of people just back from a long holiday.

McCoy's novel was about a mercy killing and the unacceptable face of mass entertainment in a Depression; it was about the ghoulish audiences and the corrupt managers as well as the destitute hopefuls who danced on, in literally blistering pain, towards the elusive dream of a place in the Hollywood sun. The show at the Mermaid (admirably choreographed by David Toguri) tries in fragmentary flashbacks to deal with all of that, but ends up falling between the cracks in the pier bandstand: a musical documentary drama is at the last fatally uncertain where to point its own spotlights, and neither Imelda Staunton as the unlucky Gloria nor Henry Goodman as the marathon manager can attract our attention for long enough to give the production its true roots. An American sweat of desperate ambition and murderous failure has again been replaced by the sweeter English smell of amateur night at a local church hall.

Sher Madness

Stratford's new main stage *Twelfth Night*, directed by Bill Alexander, has one of those sets (here by Kit Surrey) that do most of the acting before the players have a chance to take up residence. 'Which country, friend, is

1987

this?' 'Illyria, lady,' is thus an odd opening exchange, since we are clearly in downtown Paxos or on some neighbouring Greek island where you constantly expect to find Zorba setting up a dancing academy for the tourists. A hugely picturesque, sunbaked and white-walled little square, with its own functional water pump and a candlelit shrine to Olivia's dead brother, might not appear to be the most likely location for this traditionally chilly play, and its permanence means that we cannot actually move with Feste from Orsino's court to Olivia's mansion or Malvolio's gaol; in order for anything to happen or anyone to meet, the cast have instead to assemble around the pump. But once you make that geographic leap, and get acclimatised to the heat, there emerge certain distinct advantages.

First of all, Antony Sher can play Malvolio looking like Groucho Marx dressed as a Greek none-too-orthodox priest, with black fez and pointed beard in a performance which allows for a reversal of the usual character development; this steward starts effectively mad, pursuing Viola around the square with Olivia's ring like a manic travelling salesman, and only becomes increasingly and alarmingly sane as he is incarcerated in a prison for lunatics. Yet, although he is single-mindedly taking on all the great Olivier roles in his time with the RSC, first Richard III and in this season a Shylock as well, Sher seems to recognise that he is not a natural or leading comedian: when the going gets tough, he neatly replaces Malvolio somewhere down the cast list in what then becomes a company play about mutual deceit.

The rest of the casting is equally offbeat: a thin and distinctly unjovial Sir Toby Belch from Roger Allam, an unusually meek Olivia from Deborah Findlay and a Viola from Harriet Walter who looks as though she would far rather be leading a troupe of Girl Guides on an archaeological dig around the island than sorting out the complex romantic obsessions of Orsino and Olivia while disguised as her own missing twin brother. Orsino himself (Donald Sumpter) is an aged, melancholic loner, outclassed even in this specialist category by David Bradley's superb Aguecheek, a man of such total exhaustion under a burning sun that he can barely drag himself to the end of a sentence, let alone the beginning of a duel. Add to them a Maria (Pippa Guard) who, instead of the usual chubby housekeeper, is far and away the most sexily glamorous character on stage, and it becomes clear that Mr Alexander wishes us to consider the play not only in a new setting but also peopled by eccentrics we have never really met before.

The result is a kind of holiday romp shot through with dark and scary moments when the sun suddenly goes behind a cloud and it gets unexpectedly chilly. There is no attempt to pretend that, even when all the partners do get sorted out into their correct sexes and couplings, the general happiness will last for much longer than the average summer romance, and we are left alone with Feste singing of the wind and the rain presumably somewhere well away from the offices of the local tourist board.

When Turgenev first published his *Fathers and Sons* in 1862, it seemed satisfactorily to irritate almost everyone: conservative readers were appalled by an apparently sympathetic portrait of Bazarov, literature's first great nihilist, while radicals felt that far too much kindness had been lavished on the old aristocratic family with whom he goes to spend a few languid months in the country. Those less politically concerned are usually now able to recall the novel, often with difficulty, for one scene towards the end where the rich widow who has refused Bazarov's love nevertheless kisses him once she discovers that he is dying after heroically working his way through a typhoid epidemic, a moment of melodramatic self-sacrifice which Brian Friel bravely ignores altogether in the gently moving play he has carved out of the book for a Michael Rudman production on the National's Lyttelton stage.

Friel is an intelligent and intriguing choice for this task: his adaptation of *Three Sisters* and above all his writing about the roots of the current Irish troubles in *Translations* suggest a playwright wonderfully able to set domestic drama in the forefront of social upheaval, and what we have now is the realisation that, despite its apparently neat arrangement of political and intellectual opposites, *Fathers and Sons* is really about the way that the natural order of the world starts with a strict ordering of the generations. Nothing is so important, not even the future of Russia, as the fact that one of the fathers of the title is to marry again on the same day as his own son, while the other is forced to bury his own heir. History has thus been disturbed around the samovar, and it is only a matter of time before that disturbance starts to spread.

The sons are, in fact, fellow-students: Bazarov (Robert Glenister in a state of clenched though unspecific social indignation) has come to stay for a summer with the family of Arkady (a wistful Ralph Fiennes) only to find himself in a pre-Chekhovian household, where Alec McCowen, as the father, is clearly in training for Vanya, while Richard Pasco (as the decaying dandy uncle who once spent ten years unsuccessfully pursuing a Princess across Europe) is getting closer day by day to Gayev in *The Cherry Orchard*. But the immediate contrast between the sons, one rabid for social change, while the other is about to inherit an admittedly fast disintegrating estate, gets soon confused by Bazarov's hopeless love for the wealthy widow and by his inability to come to terms even with his own ideologically acceptable parents (Robin Bailey and Barbara Jefford in gloomy isolation), so that in the end the typhoid epidemic simply offers him an irrelevant kind of martyrdom as a way out of social and filial confusion.

1987

A Chekhovian search for happiness and a new Russia is already here, but filtered through Turgenev's more realistic familiar vision of a world where relative values are determined by second marriages and mad old aunts (Joyce Grant as a memorable mix of Madame Arcati and Lady Bracknell) and sudden death rather than the forces of the outside world. Beyond a duel instigated by the Pasco character known as *beau de cologne*, and the final typhoid death, this is a play in which not a lot happens apart from the confirmation of various characters in their own isolation across barriers of family differences, but at a time when the Minister against the Arts and other members of the new Government seem to be again asking themselves why we need a subsidised state theatre, Rudman's production provides a perfect answer: because nowhere else in the world will you find ensemble acting of this calibre, even if it is occasionally walled in behind Carl Toms's oddly Canadian timber setting. Just try telling a commercial sponsor that you'd like a cast of sixteen, including some of the most highly respected character actors in the land, plus a small orchestra, to turn a largely forgotten Turgenev novel into an evening of classical distinction maybe twice a week in repertoire for six months on the South Bank and see how long it takes him to write the cheque. I would guess about a decade.

Talking of high finance, to Wyndham's from the Royal Court has come Caryl Churchill's *Serious Money*, a scabrous comedy of Big Bang dealings which does for the City roughly what *Pravda* did for Fleet Street and will doubtless pick up most of the year's new play awards before going on to Broadway while being quoted on the Tokyo Stock Exchange. A frenetically brilliant production by Max Stafford-Clark is choreographed like a ballet of corrupt trading, in which a central cast of eight double and redouble increasingly shady fixers of rubber futures and criminal pasts; the revelations of Guinness and the Boesky scandal may have increased its relevance, but essentially (like the Restoration comedy it echoes at the outset) this is just another everyday story of greed, corruption and all else that has made the world of international high finance so highly regarded by right-thinking investors everywhere. Or at any rate those still in profit.

Porgy and a Mess

A brace of five-hour stage epics this week, one of which is the greatest glory of the summer and the other is *The Wandering Jew* at the National. There is actually nothing wrong with this new Mike Alfreds production on the Lyttelton stage that a few songs and maybe a textual cut of about three hours couldn't solve, and it might even have worked on its present scale had it been conceived in the spirit of *Nicholas Nickleby* or *Les Misérables*; but in the first production for his National ensemble, Alfreds has denied us anything so enjoyably theatrical as those, and come up instead with the kind of desiccated dramatised reading of random moments from a long lost text which might just about survive on Radio 3 across several dull weekends.

The first problem is that text itself: *The Wandering Jew* turns out not to be the old melodrama with which Matheson Lang used to barnstorm the countryside, but instead the vastly more complex Eugène Sue partwork, published across an eternity of Parisian newsprint during the middle 1840s. On the evidence of this dramatisation by Michelene Wandor and Alfreds himself, Sue seems to have lacked the strong grasp of plot and character that have made Dickens and Victor Hugo so eminently stageworthy; instead, what he had was an obsession with the Jesuits, whom he saw as a clerical Mafia out to deny the descendants of the Jew their rightful inheritance.

The second problem is that, despite the everlasting nature of the production, we never have long enough to know or care about any character before we are whisked off into yet another subplot of religious or financial intrigue. Only in the last hour or two does Philip Voss, as the snake-like evil genius Rodin, rise above the rabble and fix us with his glittering sense of criminal purpose. By then our main hope is that he will kill all the others as yet unclaimed by cholera, inherit the fortune and let us go home to a good book.

Sixteen other actors led by Sian Thomas and Mark Rylance and Paola Dionisotti do their best to double and redouble all the other inhabitants of this fragmented and shambling saga of missing letters and mysterious tokens and Indian princes and Siberian orphans and corrupt priests, but, stripped of its social tracts and part-work philosophy, all we are left with is a turgid and tangled plot which grinds on relentlessly from tedium to inconsequence by way of total coincidence. By the time the inheritance finally goes up in smoke, a truly numbing sense of boredom has long since overtaken what little academic or dramatic interest there was in seeing Sue brought back not so much to life as to a living stage death.

Of all Trevor Nunn's musical productions, and there are four still playing in London from *Cats* and *Chess* through *Les Misérables* to the appalling *Starlight Express*, arguably the most impressive and historic is the one that all too few people have yet managed to see. *Porgy and Bess* is back at Glyndebourne for a second summer in repertoire, which means, in fact, a total of only eight performances between now and the end of the month. Thus far, at £40 a ticket, it has therefore only been seen by about as many people as get to *Cats* on either side of the Atlantic in any given week, and yet amazingly there appear to be no further plans for it beyond a cast recording and maybe one or two concert performances at the Festival Hall early next year.

1987

This is the first ever British staging of the complete *Porgy and Bess*, and under the brisk conducting of Richard Bradshaw it comes in Gershwin's anniversary year as a unique celebration of his one-shot operatic genius. For those of us who knew it mainly from old recordings and the blandly truncated movie and a deadly grand operatic staging by a company at Lincoln Centre a decade or so ago, what Nunn is offering is a total rethink. Against the orchestral wealth of the score he has come up with a tight-knit production of remarkable coherence and intelligence and integrity in which Willard White and Cynthia Haymon give title role performances which I doubt we shall ever live to see improved.

But they are always working within an ensemble: Gregg Baker as the charismatic, murderous Crown, Damon Evans as an unusually subdued, thoughtful Sportin' Life and Marietta Simpson as the earth-mother Maria, all play with tremendous dramatic as well as vocal strength in the setting of John Gunter's timbered, cluttered, balconied Catfish Row, where a supporting cast of fifty are able to create a choral community in which all have identifiable lives and characters.

As with *The Wandering Jew*, it will take about a day of your life to see this five-hour *Porgy*, even assuming there are still Glyndebourne tickets available. But what you will then be left with is the memory of something still more powerful than a soaring opera of love and loss containing about a dozen of the most throat-catching and haunting songs that even Gershwin ever wrote. What you will also be left to cherish is Nunn's discovery that this is a classical tragedy, and when that Gunter set opens up to a blue horizon for Porgy to go on his way to New York in search of Bess, we have a final anthem that is also a monologue of reborn hope. There is greatness here which simply cannot be written off after a couple of brief summer seasons buried deep in the Sussex countryside.

Back in London, *The Colored Museum*, which comes to the Royal Court from Joe Papp's Public Theatre in New York, is a revue that manages to parody almost everything *Porgy* set out to celebrate – there is even a note to the effect that Gershwin could only have written 'Summertime' because he too came from an oppressed race. And although the revue format now seems a bit creaky, what keeps George C. Wolfe's script alive is its constant mockery of racial stereotypes, whether through the agonies of old, black household dramas like *Raisin in the Sun* or the emergence of a new coloured middle class who only have the time and energy to be black on weekends and holidays.

A wickedly funny attack on Josephine Baker for denying her roots and becoming instead more French than Maurice Chevalier is killed by being allowed to run on for about twice its real life. There is a lot that a good director or script editor might have done with some of Mr Wolfe's looser ideas, but I like the air stewardess telling her passengers to fasten their shackles and stop all that drumming, and then a sinister number in which a middle-class reconstructed urban black tries to throw off his old radical past only to have it come back from the trashcan and strangle him. *The Colored Museum* has a lot more to say about new American racial attitudes than many more portentous scripts, and Joe Papp's company of five take us on its guided tour with some savagely good turns.

Japanese Take-away

With the West End premieres of *Follies* and now *Pacific Overtures* (in an English National Opera production by Keith Warner at the Coliseum), this has been the summer in which London finally awoke to the greatness of those Stephen Sondheim scores written and first seen on Broadway more than a decade ago. But where *Follies* has undergone some extensive and faintly weakening second-half revisions to achieve the kind of smash hit existence here that it never enjoyed on home territory, *Pacific Overtures* remains very much as first conceived, and therein lie both its genius and its problems.

The story is of how, in July 1833, a small naval force, under the American Commodore Matthew Perry, sailed into a Japanese harbour, aimed its guns at the mainland and demanded a trade treaty. Such was the opening up of Japan, though as one later American noted, 'We didn't go in – they came out.'

To tell that tale Sondheim and the dramatist John Weidman invented the notion of a mythical and invisible Japanese playwright who, having witnessed about a century of Western musicals, then went home to write a Kabuki operetta based on the Perry invasion. The result was a weird and wondrous blend of ancient and modern zen and zap which ran six months on Broadway and lost its entire investment back in 1976. Since then, however, it has reappeared both off-Broadway and most recently last year in Manchester, where, with smaller scale productions, the underlying themes of colonisation and two-way cultural theft could be better explored.

But what we have at the Coliseum is a return to the broad stage and a fully operatic production: a piece first conceived for Japanese actors who could sing is now played by English singers who can't act, and the lesson of recent years (that Sondheim works better the closer you get to him in the smallest possible setting) has clearly had to be abandoned in the vast open spaces of Ralph Koltai's superb Japanese settings.

Yet this remains that rarity of rarities, a musical which has the courage to think while it sings and dances. To see the ritual lion dance by Graham Fletcher, brilliantly choreographed by David Toguri, as a first-half finale which starts deep in Kabuki and finishes right in the heart of George M.

Cohan's Broadway is actually a better summary of the show than the closing *Next*, which ought to be a chilling litany of the way that Japan reversed the original American takeover by pouring her commercial products into the West. Instead, this has become an uneasy trip to the Tokyo motor show; bikes on a revolving stage do not make the same point as the lyrics here, they merely make them hard to hear.

Certainly, therefore, there are reservations about this *East Side Story*, but they are mainly to do with an opera company's inability to find the ice cold dramatic heart of a musical which is trying to do rather more than celebrate the fact of there being no business like Shogun business. The original director, Hal Prince, once offered to stage this at the National and it was a major mistake not to let him do it there.

Sondheim's cool, crisp, clear songs of wondrous complexity range from the lyrical *Pretty Lady* through an entire biography of one Japanese life in transition (*Bowler Hat*) to a dissertation on the nature of memory and old age (*Someone in a Tree*), and the composer himself once said that *Pacific Overtures* still felt like an assignment, something people ought to see rather than a show to relax into. That may well be true; yet in there is, if not the most popular, then certainly the most complex and ambitious of all his scores, one which deals with life and death and history and invasion and the territorial imperative often in a single number, which is simultaneously a running parody of *Madame Butterfly* and *The Mikado* with additional music by Offenbach and John Philip Sousa.

There is something consistently dazzling about *Pacific Overtures*, and it is not just the headlights of the motorbike on which the lion dancer makes his final appearance en route to the 1988 World's Fair: what is dazzling is the scale on which this imperfect but ever electrifying show was originally conceived. True, you don't come out of the theatre humming its hits, but, as Sondheim has also somewhere noted, the songs you can hum at first hearing are just like all the songs you ever hummed before. There are roughly twenty more performances in the ENO repertoire between now and the end of November, and you'd be unwise not to catch at least one of them. There has never been a show quite like this one and, given the current economics of the musical, there is unlikely to be another: the miracle of *Pacific Overtures* is that it is not *Flower Drum Song* revisited, even if there are a depressing number of people around who still wish that it was.

Court Circular

Before it opened at the Queen's last Tuesday, Jeffrey Archer's *Beyond Reasonable Doubt* had already taken £½ million in advance booking, a non-musical record beaten in recent theatrical history only by Elizabeth

Taylor in *The Little Foxes*. One could therefore as usefully review the gold bars in the Bank of England as a thriller which is thinly covered in dust and comes as a gently languid reminder of the kind of courtroom melodrama that used to play good Saturday matinées at seaside repertory theatres in the days when they could still afford a dozen actors in expensive clothes and two big sets.

It can also be added for the posters that, at a time when the only other thrillers in town are the eternal *Mousetrap* and the appalling *Business of Murder* and a touring revival of *Corpse*, this one is by default the best around. The curious thing about British theatregoers is that they have always preferred their mysteries to be deeply uneventful, otherwise *Sleuth* and *Deathtrap* would still be with us. And although there have been several instances of thrillers being turned into smash hits by the labours of their stars, *Beyond Reasonable Doubt* has a certain eerie fascination in being the only one to be thus transformed by the labours of the *Star* in its advance publicity campaign.

Reviews are not supposed to reveal too much plot, though it can safely be disclosed that as the curtain rises we find Frank Finlay as the Chairman of the Bar Council defending himself on a charge of wife murder. Jeffry Wickham appears for the prosecution before Andrew Cruickshank's avuncular Scots judge. All three give the kind of bravura common-law performances usually only available nowadays on black and white television at about two in the morning. Act One is the trial, and for Act Two we are transported in flashback to Finlay's stately home, where we find his wife (Wendy Craig), a friendly solicitor (David Langton) and an eventual explanation of what really happened. If the first half of the play is a homage to Agatha Christie, the second half is a tribute to Terence Rattigan: venerable jokes about cricket and the bar, with an occasional quote from Dylan Thomas for the intellectuals.

Complete with requisite final twist, Mr Archer's play seems to have been not so much written as assembled from the spare parts of earlier stage thrillers. It is immaculately played, directed (David Gilmore) and designed (Tim Goodchild) but ultimately as dead as the corpse which causes the trial. For all that, this one will (as they say) run and run; not exactly a whodunnit or a howdunnit or a whydunnit, all of which can be worked out early in the first act, nor even a latterday mix of snobbery with violence, but instead an ancient English court circular.

As a complete history of Marxism, *Groucho* (at the Comedy) leaves rather too many questions unanswered; but as an endearing filial tribute to a great comic it works very well indeed, thanks largely to a twenty-four-year-old American actor of remarkable versatility called Frank Ferrante, who plays the title role across seventy years of stage and screen history.

Originally cobbled together last year for Off-Broadway by Robert

Fisher and Groucho's son Arthur Marx, who also directs with the original New York cast, the script falls uncertainly between various stools. It sets out to tell the story of Julius Henry Marx (the Groucho only came from a friendly fellow vaudevillian after the brothers had spent years on the road as variously the Three and Four Nightingales) via several old comic routines and a goodly number of familiar one-liners. But in there somewhere, as Arthur Marx has long been demonstrating in other plays and books about his father, is something vastly more intriguing than just another backstage rags-to-riches saga. There are moments here when we get glimpses of how much more dramatically compelling *Groucho* could be if the authors would decide whether they were writing a nostalgic musical memoir or the tragedy of a man who was always oddly out of his element and unable to handle his own melancholia.

In a two-hour, biographical sketchbook, for which Ferrante is joined by Les Marsden (as both Harpo and Chico) and Marguerite Lowell (as all their women), there is no time to note that Groucho was in fact writing for the *New Yorker* in the year of its birth or that he went on to publish three highly literate autobiographies. There is indeed barely time between Chico on the piano and Harpo at the harp to look at Groucho's lifelong misanthropy or his terror of bankruptcy after the loss of $¼ million on Wall Street, though we do get the final awful octogenarian realisation (beautifully played by Ferrante) that he has never told any of his brothers, let alone his wives, how much he really loved them.

The closing moments of the show are largely drawn from interviews given at the end of his life, and they are both icily sad and blackly funny ('What is responsible for your last three divorces?' 'My last three marriages'); if only this lightning tour of the Marxist philosophy had looked more often at the man and laughed less obsessively at that greasepainted moustache, it could have been a play as well as a hotchpotch of nostalgia. For all that, to misquote a *Variety* headline, Groucho No Longer Sloucho at Box-office.

All Her Yesterdays

The play that brings Maggie Smith back to Peter Shaffer for the first time in more than twenty years, since in fact she confirmed her early West End reputation in his one-act comedies, is a weird and wondrously ramshackle saga of two middle-aged spinsters finally bent on demolishing modern London landmarks in order to reassert the supremacy of the romantic historical past over a present of urban and spiritual blight.

At the opening of *Lettice and Lovage* (Globe) Miss Smith is discovered guiding recalcitrant tourists through the dullest stately home in England; her increasingly fantastic and fictional accounts of what went on there, culminating in death-defying leaps up fifty-foot staircases, bring her to the attention of a grey civil service employer (Margaret Tyzack), who first sacks the outlandish fantasist and then, less plausibly, falls so far under her spell as to end up in hospital with an axe wound when one of their recreations of the execution of Charles I goes a little awry.

In an extraordinarily baroque, rambling comedy of ancient memories and modern mistakes, Mr Shaffer is, I think, telling us that we have destroyed the warmth of history only to replace it with the chill of practicality, but his play goes off at so many eccentric, if usually enjoyable, tangents that we end up, much like the tourists we started with, gazing in awe at a structure riddled with eccentric corridors leading nowhere very specific. It is kind of typical here that the play's most fascinating character, Maggie Smith's mother, who once ran an all-female group of strolling players performing Shakespeare to amazed Dordogne peasants while armed only with a cushion which doubled as Falstaff's stomach and Richard III's hump, is the one we never actually get to meet.

We do, however, get to meet the Margarets, Smith and Tyzack, who duly form themselves into an odd-couple team of amazing and touching credibility: whether acting out the daft charades organised by Miss Smith as Lettice (a growth that, as she notes, was one of God's mistakes; Lovage is merely a herb of miraculous properties) or setting out to wreak urban terror, they are the best double act in town, one much aided at the last by Richard Pearson as an understandably bemused solicitor in Michael Blakemore's marvellously adroit production.

Writing from New York about eighteen months ago, I put it to you that Sam Shepard's *A Lie of the Mind* was, in his own original four-hour production, perhaps a little overlong, but that in there somewhere might be a remarkable play by the man who has long been the Eugene O'Neill of country and western life. Seeing the play again now at the Royal Court in Simon Curtis's splendidly brisk (a mere three hours) and sensitive staging, I am more than ever convinced that what we have here is a Long Day's Journey Into The Popcorn Crackerbarrel.

Centrally the story of Jake, who thinks he has beaten his wife to death, and of Beth, who then recovers, and of their two obsessive, loony backwoods families, this is in a sense a ballad of love and loss, one which meanders through cowboy country looking for some sort of resolution, but coming up only and forever against crashed cars and hospital beds and all the detritus of the American dream turned into nightmare.

Tighter, shorter and sharper than off-Broadway, the Curtis production has Will Patton from the original American cast (though now playing Jake) alongside a strong local team headed by Miranda Richardson, Deborah Norton, Tony Haygarth, Paul McGann and an eerily miscast Geraldine McEwan, who, together, achieve a mythic gallery of mental, physical and romantic ripples at the frontier of a society pockmarked by sudden and random violence. Shepard may come out of O'Neill, but he comes by way of John Steinbeck and Tennessee Williams: his America is an acridly funny, suddenly tragic and ultimately screwed up society of blue jeans and brainrot, where years of inbreeding have produced a *Deliverance* community of mentally damaged farmers often uncertain whether or not they might be their own parents.

It is just, terrifyingly, possible that after Arthur Miller (and with the apparent retirement of Edward Albee) Mr Shepard is now his nation's greatest working dramatist; certainly he is the greatest poet of its backwoods motels. And this production, incidentally, confirms Simon Curtis as the most promising director of his generation, one willing to take on not only Shepard's play but also his own American staging of it and get them both into some kind of coherent shape for overseas audiences.

Elsewhere, a creaking revival of a period drama about a crisis of conscience: at the Savoy, Charlton Heston has joined Frank Hauser's Chichester production of *A Man For All Seasons* and plays Sir Thomas More in a succession of whitening wigs, which are vastly more dramatic than anything going on beneath them. When, a quarter-century ago, Paul Scofield created Bolt's Chancellor on stage and screen, his magical poetry and sense of moral isolation convinced us of a great play; Mr Heston plays More as if only recently descended from Mount Rushmore, and the result is that we are plunged back into an MGM costume drama of Tudor life.

Roy Kinnear manages to raise a few laughs by conceiving the all-purpose Common Man narrator as a mix of Toby Belch and Uriah Heep, while Benjamin Whitrow is superlatively and silkily sinister as Thomas Cromwell.

Rover's Return

To the Mermaid from Stratford's Swan comes Jeremy Irons in a rare and roistering revival of *The Rover* by Aphra Behn, who was this country's first notable female dramatist, always excepting a tenth-century nun called Hrotsvitha, who never seems to get revived anywhere, even by the RSC, despite her being well out of copyright and my frequent reminders that she must really have been where it all started.

What we have here, though, is a Restoration romp from 1677 concerning a group of Cavaliers who, exiled to a Spanish colony during Cromwell's Parliament, start up a series of romantic liaisons with three sisters determined to make the most of carnival time. The play itself leaves a lot to be desired, and is inclined to fall apart somewhat too rapidly after the interval; but by heavily doctoring its text and adding sizeable chunks from its original source (Thomas Killigrew's *The Wanderer*) John Barton has come up with a kind of *Pilgrim's Progress* through foreign romantic disasters, one which allows Mr Irons to define himself as a comical Douglas Fairbanks, admittedly with a voice that veers from Michael Crawford to Ralph Richardson in moments of crisis, rather than the poetic dreamer we have come to expect of him. Taking over from Sinead Cusack as the most famous local courtesan (one who gets an entire billboard to advertise her wares), Stephanie Beacham comes on dressed like an especially exotic wedding cake to do an eccentric impersonation of a period Zsa Zsa Gabor.

What Mr Barton and both his stars have realised about *The Rover* is that it makes no sustained academic sense, but can be hugely enjoyed from moment to moment. Their discovery is principally shared by David Troughton as an Essex booby forever in danger of being deprived of his clothes and his freedom by one of the many more intricate sub-plots. An evening of fireworks and farce may not be precisely the play that Mrs Behn intended, but the spirit of its production admirably conveys her belief in equality among the sexes before marriage coupled with a certain reluctant submission after it. As a large RSC cast buckle their swashes one is reminded of what a useful London home for Swan treats the Mermaid has become, as well as of how sad it would be if the present economic situation causes its loss after January.

It is hard to believe that there ever has been, or perhaps ever will be, a better production of Arthur Miller's *A View From The Bridge* than the one which now comes from the National to the Aldwych Theatre. While his native Broadway, the American theatre he helped to shape and dignify after the war and of which he is unquestionably the greatest living graduate, has turned its commercial back on Miller and is deservedly dying of its own intellectual carelessness, London has always kept him in production (five major premieres and revivals of his work at the National and the RSC alone over the last five years) and now achieves the definitive staging by Alan Ayckbourn of a thirty-year-old play which has not, in the past, been without its problems.

Under the huge and dominant skyline of Brooklyn Bridge, we are introduced to an immigrant domestic tragedy framed within the guidelines of classical Greek drama. Eddie Carbone, played by Michael Gambon, in what has to be the performance of the year, is the self-destructive and yet ever bullish longshoreman, unknowingly in love with his own niece. When that love is first revealed and then threatened by the arrival of a Sicilian 'submarine' who has to be kept in hiding while he attempts an illegal living on the docks, Eddie betrays him to the authorities and brings down on himself the full devastation of a moral code he has never totally accepted or even understood.

Miller's play, which started out as a one-act drama and remains among his tightest scripts, is about the clashes between morality and the law, between romance and incest, between a code of honour and a way of life, but in the end it is always and only about Eddie: 'I mourn him', as his lawyer and the play's narrator says, 'with a certain alarm, because he allowed himself to be wholly known.' And that is the final test of Gambon's mythic and epic performance: across two short hours we do indeed get wholly to know Eddie in a way that we have seldom wholly known Willy Loman or John Proctor, the other two tragic heroes of Miller's best work. A paunchy, powerful obsessive who makes you smell the sweat, as good a man as he had to be, but finally brought down by a self-destructive passion that is animal in its savagery, Eddie goes out like a maimed lion leaving only the wreckage of a family and a waterfront community which could live with everything from the Depression to the immigration authorities, but not with his own incestuous desires.

And for the rest of Ayckbourn's British cast, brought up far from the shadows of Brooklyn Bridge and unacquainted with the code of immigrant conduct or the conscience of a nation in transition, one that Miller alone has always best expressed, this is no less of an achievement: Elizabeth Bell as Eddie's downtrodden wife, Suzan Sylvester as their unlucky niece, Adrian Rawlings as the Sicilian stud, Michael Simkins as his avenging brother and James Hayes as the rueful narrator all give performances which are the distinction and the highlight of this London winter.

Beyond the Farr Horizon

At a time when London's commercial theatre is not exactly overstocked with new plays on major philosophic themes, Ronald Harwood's *J. J. Farr* deserves a welcome (to the Phoenix) for unfashionable courage. Not since Graham Greene gave up agonising about the Catholic dilemma on stage back in the 1950s can there have been a drama so single minded in its determination to discuss the loss of religious faith and its rediscovery, even if that rediscovery leads on to a conclusion that is very nearly as bloodily violent as the offstage events which have caused it.

Harwood's plot is simple enough: the title character, craggily and angrily played by Albert Finney, is an ex-priest who, when kidnapped by Arab terrorists, has returned to the faith as a result of a final sacrament performed for a dying colleague in conditions of appalling horror. Released and back in England as the curtain rises, Farr comes home to a charitable halfway house run for priests who have lost their faith, only to find them oddly unable to deal with his rebirth. For the purposes of the debate that ensues over six short scenes and a fortnight, Harwood has set up five contrasting figures to tackle Farr: there's the butch atheist falling apart at Farr's recantation of atheism (Bob Peck), the wonderfully waspish old gay in a string of pearls (Hugh Paddick), the long-suffering but unforgiving warden (Bernard Lloyd), the sympathetic nursing brother (Dudley Sutton) and the one with a guilty past (Trevor Peacock), all there to represent aspects of loss and all ready to move the chairs into semi-circles for Shavian explorations of the many and varied ways in which God is not mocked.

Clearly a priest who has rediscovered his faith is not about to feel at home in a subsidised limbo apparently reserved for others who have not; but Finney manages to suggest also the alienation of the hostage, his eyes and body forever darting around the stage, always trying to guard a back that has been scarred with something that may very well not be the sign of the cross.

The notion that faith is nothing more than a neurotic device to allay a fear of death is ritually explored, as is the possibility that in the end the moderate and the weak will drive out the strong, as they finally allow Farr to wander off towards the horizon, simply because they can't tolerate the certainties of either absolute faith or total atheism. Deep in Greeneland something is stirring, if only the belief that if you stand in the very middle of the road you won't be hit by cars going in either direction; on the other hand, nor will you get a lift.

J. J. Farr Bob Peck *as Kenneth Lawrie* and Albert Finney *as J. J. Farr*

1987

This is, at times, a play that hovers on the borderlines of its own uncertainties, veering from political thriller to moral debate and back again as if hoping to latch on to something that might get us through the next confrontation. But it is elegantly and sharply written, and the five actors led by Peck who get to challenge Finney for longer or shorter moments manage to catch something of his intense and mesmeric energy, though that alone is what eventually saves Ronald Eyre's thoughtful production from grinding to a total halt. If we are to return to a lost world of articulate, faintly senior-common-room disputation then it is as well to do so in a company as strong as this one.

At the Donmar Warehouse, Cheek by Jowl's touring *Macbeth* is a characteristically inventive and economic studio staging which uses a dozen actors like a Greek chorus to guide us through the action as they double and redouble its central characters. Sometimes the invention kills the source (a latterday female Porter bellowing on about the Stock Market crash does little for the tension of Duncan's murder), but again and again Declan Donnellan's direction comes up with an unusual new idea, be it a blind King or an evil, stammering Malcolm or the arrival of Birnam Wood at Dunsinane conveyed purely by footfalls growing ever louder. Leslee Udwin is a powerful, if faintly alcoholic, Lady Macbeth, while Keith Bartlett offers an opportunist Thane who finally enlists our sympathy by conveying almost chattily his doomed belief in his own immortality. All in all a pressurised, compacted, dark B-movie thriller, and none the worse for that.

At the Apollo, *Dangerous Obsession* is yet further proof that all recognisable forms of human life have now gone out of the English stage thriller. A play deeply buried in the static form of late-night television reruns and desperately lacking any kind of character development or suspense, it opens with a Home Counties lady in a swimsuit having her solarium ('enviable' says the programme, though only, I would guess, to a mad horticulturalist) invaded by an apparently psychotic visitor from her party-going past. They are then joined by her husband, who is the only other character in the cast list, though one fervently hopes when a doorbell later rings that whoever it is, be he only a passing stagehand, will be allowed in for a drink and a bit of a chat. Failing such excitement, it transpires very slowly that a car crash and a possible killing are now to be avenged. Dinsdale Landen, a superb actor here defeated by a part which has been not so much written as assembled from left-over bits of old psycho-movies, plays the stranger whose plan of action often seems rooted in the belief that if he could just manage to bore the other two to death then he wouldn't have to resort to the gun he carries in his briefcase.

Watching three hardworking actors (the others are Carol Drinkwater and Jeremy Bulloch, who both achieve a kind of intermittent adequacy) fervently trying to breathe life back into a script that has died of its own inertia early in Act One, while locked together in a set by Shelagh Keegan where the most exciting possibility is to watch the plants grow, does at least concentrate one's mind on certain suspenseful questions. The main one is whether the management could be had under the Trades Descriptions Act for billing this as a 'gripping new thriller', and, if not, who would pay upwards of £10 a ticket to watch a tacky little triangular conversation piece by a writer (N. J. Crisp) lost in a 1950s video past? Presumably the same people who keep every other thriller in London alive.

Great 'Night' Out

'If music be the food of love, play on' is arguably the most famous and oft-quoted opening line in all Shakespearian comedy. It takes, therefore, a certain amount of courage to start *Twelfth Night* without it, or indeed that whole first scene. Instead, Kenneth Branagh's new production at Riverside Studios plunges us straight into scene two and Viola's shipwrecked arrival: 'What country, friends, is this?' 'This is Illyria, lady,' but it is like no Illyria we have ever seen before. Far from any seashore, all later references to May mornings and sunshine ignored, we would appear to be deep in some park surrounding Anton Chekhov's winter residence. There, taking the play's title quite literally, the designer Bunny Christie offers us snowflakes, half-ruined statues, immense gothic tombstones and a generally ravishing, if melancholic, landscape apparently only waiting for someone to come and paint it as a Victorian Christmas card.

Through the snowflakes wander Aguecheek and Toby Belch and Maria and Feste and Fabian, not figures of the usual slapstick fun, but poets and dreamers and losers apparently all in search of Vanya or at any rate the next train to Moscow: at any moment you expect to hear the fall of trees in some distant cherry orchard. This may not, therefore, be a *Twelfth Night* to appeal to Shakespearian purists; but it is one of the most thoughtful and beautiful of recent years, characterised by a haunting new score by Paul McCartney and Pat Doyle, and crowned by a Malvolio from Richard Briers which is far and away the most comically tragic since Olivier played the role at Stratford all of thirty years ago.

Mr Branagh has all kinds of other ideas about the play: Orsino eventually gets his opening scene, albeit in flashback, and we then get a dropout hippie Feste (Anton Lesser), a Viola (Frances Barber) who is alone the pure innocent abroad in a park where all are trying to betray her, a bully-boy Fabian (Shaun Prendergast) and a Belch/Aguecheek (James Saxon and James Simmons) double act thin enough to hide behind the Christmas tree which masks them from Malvolio.

Everything about this production suggests that the actors are back in

1987

charge, and that what they have done under Branagh's leadership for his own Renaissance company is to restructure an all too familiar text, locate a palm court trio high above the stage and then go to work on an immensely intriguing collection of character studies. True, the Olivia and the Orsino are a little nondescript, and there are moments towards the end when invention and courage seem to flag, but that is a small price to pay for the realisation that Malvolio goes within an act from comic fool to tragic victim, so that his final offstage scream of revenge is worthy of Lear, or that Viola alone retains awareness of a world elsewhere, far removed from all these manic Chekhovian romantic defeatists. It is a rare and wondrous Christmas treat.

The first home-made production at the Bush since its recent fire (one result of which would seem to be a drastic improvement in the comfort of the bench seating) is Jacqueline Holborough's *Dreams of San Francisco*, a wickedly funny play about the five members of a radical touring theatre group who finish up so far removed from the ideas of the sisterhood that they have actually become a nightclub act for tired businessmen. The best thing about Miss Holborough is her ability to juggle a quintet of stereotypes while putting them through an accurate depiction of grue-

Twelfth Night James Saxon *as Sir Toby Belch*, James Simmons *as Sir Andrew Aguecheek*, Francis Barber *as Viola* and Richard Briers *as Malvolio*

some backstage reality, and what she has written here is essentially the feminist *42nd Street*.

Jenny Lecoat plays the ambitious leader of the collective, the only one totally ready to sacrifice all their political or social ideals for a really good contract in London; she is not, however, much helped by a revolutionary saxophonist with a dead dog in a box and nothing against men since she has been one herself, nor yet by a butch electrician, a tap-dancing poet or a vaguely middle-class legit actress appalled to find that at least one of her colleagues believes in liberating socks from department stores without going through the bourgeois ritual of payment for them.

Dreams of San Francisco is about tacky arts centres and life in a transit van and the problems of trying to run a theatre group with no money for audiences who have no interest in political affiliations. It is also, admittedly late in the calendar, the sharpest new comedy of the year and suggests that Miss Holborough has been around that circuit herself and met the sisters who now want to be glitzy torch singers so they can have things like clothes and food. Simon Stokes directs an admirable cast in, sadly, his farewell to the theatre that he has made over the past decade into one of London's best.

1988

A CURIOUS KIND OF YEAR IN AND AROUND THE WEST END, with backstage events often more dramatic than anything going on under the arc lights. This was the year when Sir Peter Hall left the National to take up the management of the Haymarket, only to find there almost as many economic troubles as he had ever encountered on the South Bank; the year when Jeremy Isaacs took over Covent Garden; the year when new (and female) artistic directors took over at Hampstead and at Greenwich; the year when the actors Kenneth Branagh and Derek Jacobi both headed their own separate Shakespeare companies at the Phoenix, with Jacobi's on the route to Washington; the year when the leading West End owners and managers (Stoll/Moss, Maybox and Triumph) all formed new alliances with each other to suggest that in future London shows will have as many producers above the title as those along what is left of Broadway.

It was also the year when the Royal Court celebrated its centenary, when the Playhouse came back to intermittent life under Jeffrey Archer, when redevelopment threats hit the Warehouse in Covent Garden among other fringe theatres, and when the much vaunted supremacy of the English stage musical collapsed in

The Hewison Awards for 1988

Imelda Staunton – 'Uncle Vanya'
Brian Cox – 'Titus Andronicus'
Gemma Craven – 'South Pacific'
Eric Porter – 'Cat on a Hot Tin Roof'

a double of disasters ending in 'ie': *Carrie* and *Winnie*, with *Budgie* not all that much better. Then again there was *Ziegfeld*, which managed at least temporarily to close the London Palladium, though on the 1989 horizon there was happily the prospect of a new, small-scale Lloyd Webber (*Aspects of Love*) as well as a *Butterfly* update to the Vietnam War, *Miss Saigon*, written by the French makers of *Les Misérables*.

Elsewhere it was the year of the solo show: Maureen Lipman triumphing as Joyce Grenfell at her old Fortune home; a superb series of Aids charity Sunday nights from Ian McKellen, Alan Bates and Michael Feinstein; and Adelaide Hall and Elisabeth Welch proving what a lot there was to be said for veteran survival – a theory which might have been disproved by prolonged exposure to Ann Miller and Mickey Rooney in *Sugar Babies* at the Savoy.

But 1988 also brought back to us Alec Guinness (in Lee Blessing's Broadway 'Arms and the Men', *A Walk in the Woods*), Wendy Hiller (in another Broadway triumph, *Driving Miss Daisy*) and Rex Harrison (in *Admirable Crichton*), as well as the rare and wondrous sight of an eighty-four-year-old John Gielgud in *Best of Friends*.

In the classical theatre Jonathan Miller continued to programme the Mirvishes' Old Vic as an assault course in minor academic rediscoveries, while the RSC at Stratford was retrieved from a lacklustre summer by Adrian Noble's epic all-day staging of the *Henry VI/Richard III* plays as *The Plantagenets*. It was also the year of the Prosperos: John Wood at Stratford, Michael Bryant at the National and Max von Sydow at the Old Vic, all breaking their magical staffs at a time when an unusual and alarming number of our directors seemed to have thought autumnal farewells were topical.

Talking of farewells, *42nd Street* and *Follies* and *South Pacific* left us after long London runs, but at £20 or more a ticket it looked as though musicals were still going to make up more than half of the West End mix, if only because they seemed to provide, however nostalgically, the kind of value for money unavailable in a one-set, four-character comedy.

It was a wonderful year for David Thacker at the Young Vic, with superlative revivals of both O'Neill's *A Touch of the Poet* and Miller's *Enemy of the People* translation moving into the West End, but a curiously thin one for topical new drama, with only David Hare's *Secret Rapture* (at the National) and Alan Ayckbourn's *Henceforward* (at the Vaudeville) even attempting to gaze into the Thatcherite local present or future. A headlong flight back to the classical past was even evident in the commercial theatre, where Michael Codron, the only surviving West End manager of real distinction and authority in straight plays, gave us an *Uncle Vanya* (with Michael Gambon) worthy of Olivier's old National, and a Chekhovian anthology at the Aldwych.

1988

In transatlantic terms, the good news was that the traffic had once again become two-way, after seasons in which we seemed to be sending everything and getting nothing back. Otherwise the future seemed more than a little uncertain: the National looked to be in good hands under the new dual management of Richard Eyre (director) and David Aukin (producer), but the RSC was still in a kind of mid-life crisis of uncertain direction; and an insistence by the Thatcher Government that theatre companies come to rely on private sponsors rather than public benefactors had already been shown at Sadler's Wells to be more than a little risky. Hard sponsorship cash was lost there when a company of actors found it impossible to work with the American director nominated by their sponsor.

Not, then, a year to look back on in anger or huge delight: just relief, I guess, that theatrical survival was still generally possible.

Where there's a Will

At the Playhouse until the end of January, and in support of a shelter for Aids victims, Ian McKellen is *Acting Shakespeare* in a marvellously rambling, jokey monologue which manages at one and the same time to be a stage autobiography, a master class in classical playing and a history of Shakespeare and his theatre. Where Gielgud's *Ages of Man* was, thirty years ago, the definitive solo Shakespearian recital, McKellen's is a mix of backstage anecdote and on-stage technique which starts and ends in the most obvious ways (with *All The World's A Stage* and Prospero's great farewell to all his art), but along its two-hour journey manages several surprises, not least by inviting half the audience on stage to act out the collapse of the French army in *Henry V*.

Having toured this show around America for several months, Mr McKellen has arrived at something halfway from a dramatised lecture to a communal celebration. Dressed in a baggy, shiny suit on a stage totally bare except for an armchair, he starts with his own stagestruck childhood in Wigan and Shakespeare's early days in Stratford-on-Avon. From there, via a brisk audience quiz on the names of all Shakespearian musical adaptations, we move on to chatty memoirs of the actor's Cambridge student theatricals in company with the likes of Derek Jacobi and Trevor Nunn, before settling into Hal and Falstaff and a wonderfully lyrical description of Shakespeare's arrival at the Globe. Hamlet's speech of instruction to the players is given in the phrasing of a trendily gay 1980s director, while McKellen also manages a Juliet and even a Mistress Quickly since, as he notes, that was anyway the all-male tradition of the Globe.

A rich and oddly touching history of the survival of the actor through the ages, as well as of Shakespeare himself – since it was, notes McKellen, a couple of actors in the original Globe company who alone managed to get the plays preserved in print – this evening is a spellbinding delight for anyone who has ever cared about the machinery of classical acting. McKellen may still be the oldest Romeo in the business, and one may wish to quarrel with his theory that in the whole of Shakespeare there are no happy marriages (which seems to me to deny the Macduffs and all those Capulets and Montagues who, happy enough at home, only ever fought with rival families); he may even get fractionally dull when he starts the lengthy textual analysis of one *Macbeth* speech, but his lasting passion for the theatre in general and the Bard in particular, his ability to make fun of his own obsessions, and above all his sheer theatrical energy make *Acting Shakespeare* the most enjoyable solo show I have seen since the late Emlyn Williams gave up doing the Dickens.

The yellow brick road now leads directly to the Barbican, where the

1988

RSC has its Christmas treat and one that is likely, I reckon, to turn up there for several decades to come. Ian Judge's staging of *The Wizard of Oz* is in principle nothing new, since local theatres on both sides of the Atlantic have been doing more or less tacky, cut-price versions of the Frank Baum classic since the turn of the century. What is new is his decision to go back to the roots of the 1939 movie and restore all the cut songs as well as most of the original dialogue, so what we have now is a definitive stage musical of *Oz* and one that establishes the story once and for all as, after Mark Twain and *Huck Finn*, the great American fable of peripatetic childhood.

Like our own *Peter Pan*, it is also about flying away to Neverland and then discovering there is no place like home; like *Peter Pan*, it is fantasy about reality, and like *Peter Pan* it is all about people who for one psychological reason or another are terrified of growing up.

But from the opening moment on a bare and dark stage, when Imelda Staunton comes out to sing *Over the Rainbow*, it is clear that we are already home; overcoming those terrible fag-hag memories of Judy Garland at the end of her cabaret career, Miss Staunton gets us straight back to the lost

You Never Can Tell Michael Hordern *as The Waiter*, Irene Worth *as Mrs Lanfrey Clandon*, Terence Wilton *as Valentine* and Jenny Quayle *as Gloria Clandon*

innocence of the 1930s Garland, the child going over the rainbow rather than the woman trying to remember where the hell it led, and from there we are almost immediately into that sudden blaze of colour which, on stage as on screen, denotes arrival in Munchkinland.

Sheila Falconer's choreography and Mark Thompson's sets are a sustained tribute to Hermes Pan and all the Metro musical spectaculars of the years around the war, and from the bare stage of Dorothy's Kansas farmyard they airlift us to an Oz where dozens of children play Munchkins and Jim Carter's Cowardly Lion is an Edwardian explorer. With a nod to the old pantomime tradition, Bille Brown plays in drag the Wicked Witch of the West, managing the not inconsiderable feat of looking and sounding like Dame Edith Evans impersonating Captain Hook. That infinitely nostalgic Yip Harburg/Harold Arlen score is by no means vintage, though we do get a real show-stopper in the long-lost *Jitterbug* number; most importantly, we also get reminded, through a wonderfully reflective and loving treatment, that ding-dong the witch is very much alive and that somewhere over that new neon rainbow the skies really do still seem to be blue.

At the Theatre Royal, Haymarket, Sir Michael Hordern steps elegantly and eccentrically into the shoes of the late Sir Ralph Richardson to play the Waiter in *You Never Can Tell*, one of the comic pit-stops of great septuagenarian classical players, for reasons which presumably have to do with the part being so much better than the play. Bernard Shaw's laboured comedy of a romantic dentist and a pair of teenage twins dealing with their long-separated parents creaks along in a desperately slow production by Toby Robertson from his Theatr Clwyd in Wales, though neither Michael Denison nor even Irene Worth seems to convey any real belief that the play might somehow still be alive and worth reviving; only Jenny Quayle, as an early feminist romantic, occasionally gets the script out of its dust-covered museum casing and suggests that it could still work.

Some Enchanted Evening?

South Pacific is one of only six musicals ever to win a Pulitzer Prize and, after *Oklahoma!*, it established a Broadway record for longevity in the early 1950s. Since that time we over here have known it only from a movie that appears to be made entirely underwater, or else from the occasional underfinanced regional or amateur revival. So Roger Redfarn's new production at the Prince of Wales comes, after almost forty years, as a revelation on several scores, not least that soaring score itself.

From the moment that overture bursts out of the pit, you realise what musicals have lately lost in the name of international high technology and choreography: there are fifteen numbers here, and with the exception of the most intriguing (a song of white-hot racial rage called *You Have To Be Carefully Taught*, which destroys for ever the myth of Hammerstein as a soft and sentimental lyricist), all are classic show-stoppers, from *Cockeyed Optimist* right the way through *Younger Than Springtime* and *Happy Talk* to *This Nearly Was Mine*.

It is true that this production has a faintly bus-and-truck roadshow feel to it, and that Gemma Craven in her perky all-English way is no match for the Mary Martin original; but Emile Belcourt has all the right Pinza operatic qualities for de Becque, Johnny Wade is a plausible Luther Billis and Bertice Reading is nothing less than the definitive Bloody Mary, a great big, black, sinister Mother Courage belting out the songs of Bali Hai.

South Pacific is, at least in its closing thirty minutes, a musical about bigotry and death rather than cockeyed optimism or happy talk or the joys of washing men right out of your hair, and, although there are still problems with a book which all too visibly had its origins in a series of disparate short stories by Michener, a score of dazzling wealth and energy time and again puts subsequent showbusiness composers to shame.

Though in later life, and his own memoirs, Richard Rodgers was inclined to play down the radical aspects of *South Pacific*, it is eminently clear that, long years before Vietnam and Martin Luther King, both Hammerstein and Logan had things they wanted to say about the American military presence overseas and its attitude to locals of another skin colour. Indeed the hero of the show is finally killed offstage because there is no way he can be allowed to marry a native girl, while it is surely some comment on attitudes of the time that the only song not to become an immediate hit is the one which deals with that very problem. The belief that Rodgers and Hammerstein stood for a purely escapist world of singing nuns and lovable children has now to be reconsidered. It is, indeed, arguable that from the death of poor Jud in their initial *Oklahoma!*, through that of the heroes in both *Carousel* and *South Pacific*, they were always concerned with something very much less sunny than a bright golden haze on the meadow.

Despite its moments of visual eccentricity, including the mysterious island of Bali Hai, which now comes complete with a Ziegfeld waterfall and a chorus of belly-dancers apparently recruited from some local nightclub, this remains a hugely welcome reminder of the greatness of a score which marked, after *Porgy and Bess* and *Showboat*, the beginning of the growing up of the modern stage musical; and as Kenneth Tynan said of the original London production, there is really nothing more to do except thank the composer and the lyricist and climb up off one's knees, a little cramped from the effort of typing in such an unusual position of gratitude.

At the Vaudeville, Willy Russell's *Shirley Valentine* is a play for one woman (Pauline Collins) and several unseen supporting characters, which joyously bridges the gap between drama and a solo comic routine. Shirley herself is a forty-two-year-old Liverpool housewife, the St Joan of the fitted kitchen cabinets, who decides that, after a marriage of such tedium she now talks to walls, her only hope is to escape for a short holiday in Greece.

In three monologue scenes we find her frightened of the idea, reluctantly coming to terms with it and eventually settling in Greece for ever; but what really matters here is the sustained mix of character study and comic anecdote with which Mr Russell provides one of the most highly and consistently entertaining evenings in town.

What we also have here, and of course from the same writer, is essentially *Educating Rita's Mother*: Russell is the master Merseyside dramatist of narrowly reclaimed opportunity, and as Shirley gets away from the white wine and the Bruce Springsteen records to find herself and a suntan and even a Greek waiter, instead of a husband who gets jetlagged going to the Isle of Man and culture shocked by a day trip to Chester, you realise that once again the *Pygmalion* routine is going to work.

Shirley Valentine is a rambling, gossipy solo, in which Miss Collins does a great, and I would guess award-winning, comic turn; if we see a better one this year we'll be more than lucky. But Simon Callow's production is also, despite the dying fall of the last act, a masterpiece of sustained energy and delight: in a word, Go. Who else but Willy Russell would have worked out that sex was like a supermarket – a lot of pushing and shoving and you come out with very little at the end?

Poetic Touch

For reasons which remain more than a little obscure, the management of the Young Vic has asked critics not to comment on its current production of *A Touch of the Poet* until it reaches the Theatre Royal, Haymarket, in March. This means that, alas, I can't tell you it is, second only to *A View From The Bridge*, the greatest dramatic evening in town, also about the longest, weighing in at almost four hours. Nor can I tell you that this is the first chance London has ever had to see one of O'Neill's last masterpieces, though I am perhaps allowed to disclose that this is his centenary year and that I can't think of a more fitting tribute.

Presumably I'm also required not to tell you that this is the production in which Timothy Dalton (after an uneasy earlier Shakespearian partnership with Vanessa Redgrave at the Haymarket) finally comes into his own as a major classical player: his vainglorious, alcoholic Irish saloon-keeper, living on memories of soldierly glory in Wellington's army, is a

1988

performance of which John Barrymore himself would have been proud, and one in no way overshadowed by Miss Redgrave in equal strength as the downtrodden wife forever trying to keep those memories alive for fear that the only other alternative is death.

This may be another long night's journey into Irish familial despair, but David Thacker's production is as powerful as his recent Redgrave *Ghosts* at this address, and in Rudi Davies they have found a young actress capable of carrying the immense weight of the play's closing scenes, where she has to come to terms with her own love for a young American aristocrat who also has that fatal touch of the poet.

Perhaps I also ought not to tell you that this is a production which would have glorified the National or the RSC at any time in their history, and I had better also keep to myself the fact that, despite its lyrical rambling verbosity, *A Touch of the Poet* (one of the few surviving scripts from a nine-play cycle about Irish immigrants in the new America of Andrew Jackson, most of which were burnt by the author shortly before his death) reveals an altogether lighter and often sharper O'Neill than the more familiar alcoholic epics. Thacker's cast also includes Amanda Boxer in cascadingly good form as the wealthy mother of the young American drop-out, and John McEnery as the saloon-keeper's disastrously faithful army sidekick. Were I allowed to say anything else about what I would guess to be an award-winning production, I think I would only advise you to get a ticket as soon as possible, either at the Young Vic, where, if the word spreads fast enough, they will have precious few, or in advance for the Haymarket.

Meanwhile I am allowed to tell you what is happening at the Royal Court, where they have moved in from Manchester and the last Edinburgh Festival Ian Heggie's Mobil award-winning *A Wholly Healthy Glasgow*, a somewhat overpraised and oversold little comedy of life in a Scots massage parlour. Buried in its often impenetrable local dialect are some good camp jokes about the fitness racket, and Tom Watson is wonderfully gay as the bent masseur forever trying to get his hands on the living flesh.

Mr Heggie's script has none of the brilliance of Charles Dyer's very similar *Staircase*, nor of Nell Dunn's *Steaming*, but it does suggest, like Michael Frayn's *Alphabetical Order*, the danger of allowing an upright and pure moralist figure (in this case Paul Higgins) loose in a closed world of arcane ritual, and as Barry Humphries might have said on one of his posters, it is a lot shorter and funnier than *Macbeth*.

Gielgud's Friends

At the Apollo, Hugh Whitemore's *The Best of Friends* is an epistolary play in the tradition of *Dear Liar* and *84 Charing Cross Road*, but built this time around three people (Bernard Shaw, the Fitzwilliam Museum director, Sydney Cockerell, and the Stanbrook abbess, Laurentia McLachlan) who for most of their extremely long lives wrote a marathon sequence of letters to each other. Those letters make up the whole of this evening. Mr Whitemore has wisely not attempted to dramatise anything that isn't already in the correspondence, and so what we get is what they wrote about: distant memories of Cockerell's lunch with Tolstoy, Shaw's thoughts on being offered a Nobel Prize ('I can forgive that man for inventing dynamite, but only a fiend incarnate could have invented the prize'), ideas about travel, sex, friendship, careers and God, in which last area the formidable abbess is dominant, never more so than when banishing Shaw from her friendship for several years for having dared to write *The Black Girl in Search of God*.

This is, admittedly, the kind of play you almost expect to have heard in the middle of a radio afternoon, but its overriding importance is that it brings back to the London stage, after a decade away, our greatest living and working actor in a performance of tremendous intelligence and acid charm. John Gielgud's Cockerell is by his own admission a collector of the famous, a man so cautious that he bought his own engagement ring on sale or return, and eventually a museum curator ageing happily in the knowledge that he can still afford an egg with his tea. While Ray McAnally as a jovial Shaw and Rosemary Harris as the abbess are allowed occasional bursts of irritation and anger, Cockerell moves sublimely and gracefully through their friendship, the orchestrator of a rich and rare conversation piece which concludes with him alone in the spotlight, the sole survivor of the trio, noticing that the angel of death seems quite to have forgotten him. It is a solo moment of breathtaking theatrical poetry at the end of an evening of whimsical and wayward charm.

Time has been a lot less charitable to Tennessee Williams than it has to Eugene O'Neill: while *A Touch of the Poet* still blazes with life at the Young Vic after fifty years, *Cat on a Hot Tin Roof* looks, after a mere thirty, like the prototype for some long-lost episode of either *Dallas* or *Dynasty*. This is not the fault of Howard Davies's debut production on the Lyttelton stage of the National, a masterly affair which brings Lindsay Duncan from *Liaisons Dangereuses* to the old Liz Taylor role of Maggie the Cat, while allowing Eric Porter to turn in as Big Daddy an amazingly uncharacteristic performance of immense power, looking even Burlier than Ives.

The problem here is the play itself: those wrought-iron screens are now looking dreadfully overwrought, as Noël Coward once noted, and Williams's hothouse dialogue comes peculiarly close to self-parody. Lines like 'it's avarice, avarice, greed, greed' are inclined in our much cooler era to sound a little repetitive, and though *Cat* still has some marvellous first and second act confrontations, elsewhere it often starts to sound like a Truman Capote gossip column of Deep Southern family warfare. But *Cat* is still essentially the route by which the American theatre progressed from *Long Day's Journey* to *Virginia Woolf*, and its place in the classic repertoire of the National is eventually justified by the performances of Duncan and Porter, as well as those of an entire breed of no-neck monsters, Barbara Leigh-Hunt as their appalling grandmother and Ian Charleson as the latent homosexual husband, forced finally into Maggie's bed to perpetuate the horrendous dynasty. But, in the end, it's Maggie's play, and the Cat herself is a bitchily victorious Blanche duBois up there on the roof in one of the first great American soap-operas.

Once again we have to thank Sam Walters at his hundred-seat Orange Tree Theatre in Richmond for precisely the kind of major theatrical discovery which ought to have been made by the RSC or the National: Harley Granville Barker's semi-autobiographical *The Secret Life*, written over four years from 1919, published to grudging reviews in 1923, but only now to be seen on stage for the first time. It's a country-house drama of immense fascination: ramshackle, overlong, untidy, sprawling and sometimes repetitive, yet centrally concerned with the mysteries of Barker's own life and the forces which caused him to abandon the London theatre that his own early productions had shaped and revolutionised.

The Secret Life lacks the dramatic intensity and immediacy of Barker's earlier *Waste*, which it much resembles, but this is the play Henry James always tried to write and somehow never did. It has a few marvellous scenes, not least because in Sam Walters' thoughtful production Geoffrey Beevers, as the Barker figure, and Vivien Heilbron as his doomed love, give strong performances, ably supported by Michael Elwyn and Angela Browne as figureheads of the England they were intent on escaping for ever.

Carrie on Regardless

A rare week of big American musicals, and we'd better begin with the most controversial. *Carrie*, which plays at Stratford-on-Avon until mid-March, before opening on Broadway at the end of April, is the Royal Shakespeare Company's fifth big-band show in recent years and, though it lacks much of the power and coherence of the other four (*Les Misérables*, *Kiss Me Kate*, *Poppy* and *Wizard of Oz*), it is not entirely the dishonourable disaster that some of my colleagues would have you believe. There is, in fact, no economic or artistic reason at all why the RSC should not tackle original musicals, just as it tackles new drama or old Shakespeare:

musicals are the most vitally important form of all twentieth-century theatre, and the classical company which ignores that deserves to die the lingering death of the Comédie Française or the Berliner Ensemble.

The problem here is Stephen King's book: it did manage to become a successful gothic horror film a decade ago, but now defies all attempts at dramatisation. There is quite simply no plot, unless you count the saga of a latterday middle-American Cinderella going to the high school ball and turning her fingers into flames before the whole ghastly affair degenerates into a kind of laser exhibition.

Despite Ralph Koltai's spectacular set, which can turn itself into gymnasiums and drive-in cinemas and rustic kitchens, and which on the first night frequently threatened to decapitate the show's only other true star, Barbara Cook, nothing on the Stratford stage can rival that chilling movie moment when a hand comes up through a grave during the final titles, and so time and again we are left wondering why a director with the taste and intelligence and courage of Terry Hands should have decided to devote so much time and rehearsal effort to the kind of airport-bookstall shocker that teenagers throw away with their hamburger cartons and empty drink cans.

Debbie Allen's choreography, here as in *Fame*, from which it borrows the great dancer Gene Anthony Ray, has a kind of energy, but not a lot of coherence, while the score, by Michael Gore and Dean Pitchford, allows Barbara Cook as the mad evangelical mother and Linzi Hateley as the telekinetic daughter, a pre-*Oz* Judy Garland with magical powers, a couple of good duets. But nothing can hide the gala kitsch of a gimmicky, flashy and ultimately empty show, set somewhere between *Grease* and a nightmare by Norman Rockwell. By its finale we are faced with a Barbara Cook looking like a country-and-western Lady Macbeth on a staircase apparently designed for Ginger Rogers and several thousand other hoofers; but at no point do we get characters we can care about or a plot that is anything less than patently ludicrous, all of which is a little sad.

Better news at the Cambridge, where five years after its Broadway debut with Minnelli and Rivera we at last get a London look at *The Rink*, Kander and Ebb's edgy, brittle, nervy musical about a mother and daughter also in crisis – though this time only because they are slugging out the future of the family roller-rink in a tacky American fairground. This score has always been an object lesson to the makers of *Starlight Express* in how to do roller-skating musicals, but its real importance lies in a succession of great and glitzy songs, climaxing in one ('All the Children in a Row') which manages to be an entire social history of America in the 1960s. Josephine Blake and Diane Langton may lack the immediate Broadway stardom of their predecessors, but they manage a dynamic, tough and credible double act, while time and time again that blazing score comes to the aid of Terrence McNally's thin plot, one which lurches backwards and forwards through flashbacks to pinpoint the familial troubles between mother and daughter.

The acid edge of Brecht and Weill at their best has always been evident in Kander and Ebb's post-*Cabaret* work, and here a dazzling series of showstoppers takes the roof off a theatre where they deserve to be heard for a long time to come, even if the almost total self-containment of those songs does make for an ultimately irrelevant storyline.

All's Wells

For the first time in almost sixty years, London audiences now have the chance to see the earliest and best of Noël Coward's operettas: *Bitter Sweet* is at Sadler's Wells until March 19. Written and first staged in the late 1920s as an antidote to the Depression, this is an unashamed and lyrical return to the Vienna Woods in which Coward, then at the height of his most controversial fame as the playboy of the West End world, was clearly attempting to prove that he had a heart as well as a head, and a talent for writing lilting, romantic melodies as well as clenched, witty dialogue. The plot is not, therefore, of central importance, though it does have a kind of period fascination: we start at a 1920s London dinner party of the cocktails-and-laughter-but-what-comes-after kind that Coward had already satirised and celebrated in half-a-dozen drawing-room comedies. A young girl is thinking of eloping with a society pianist, and to help her make up her mind, an old lady at the party starts to tell her own story of romantic escape from England. From there we flash back to the Vienna of 1870, where love and death are found amid duels and chandeliers and dear little cafés and all the other surroundings familiar to Lehar and Offenbach and most of the Strausses.

Across half a century, *Bitter Sweet* has only ever been recalled for such classic songs as *Zigeuner* and *I'll See You Again*; there are, in fact, almost twenty others, ranging from the haunting *If Love Were All* (in which I once found the *Talent to Amuse* title for the first Coward biography) through to the gay anthem *Green Carnation* by way of such totally lost numbers as *The Call of Life* and *If Only You Could Come With Me*.

But what is fascinating here is to see how close Coward once came to Ivor Novello and that whole Ruritanian world of uniformed cads and penniless composers, and also how uneasy he was with its most romantic excesses: the schmaltz of *Bitter Sweet* is repeatedly cut through with sharply funny, underplayed lines of dialogue.

Ian Judge's new production has a kind of casual elegance, and it is not his fault that precious few of the splendid Sadler's Wells singers can do much in the way of acting. Time and again a score of amazing and unfamiliar wealth comes to the rescue of a cast which seems very uneasy about the drama, and Valerie Masterson (who alternates Sari with Ann Mackay) looks, like Martin Smith as her composer, deeply relieved when she can lean back into its melodies. But this production has to be seen for Rosemary Ashe, who, as the café singer Manon, gives a performance of immense strength and enchantment, one which makes me long to see the production again on tour in Oxford later this spring, by which time she will have stepped into its leading role. Incidentally, we have one more reason to be grateful to *Bitter Sweet*: while he was writing it, Coward promised the leading role to his childhood friend and co-star Gertrude Lawrence, only later to realise that her light voice would not be able to stand the strain of so complex a score. Instead, he said, he would write her a play. The play was called *Private Lives*.

At the National, Athol Fugard's *A Place with the Pigs* (on the Cottesloe stage) is a curious and very uncharacteristic marital duologue based on the true story of a Soviet deserter who, during World War II, elected to hide out in his own pigsty rather than carry on with the fighting. When the War ended, he decided it would be unsafe to emerge and risk a trial and therefore stayed on amid the pig-swill for another thirty years, becoming, in the end, more and more like the surrounding hogs.

Fugard's play has rare moments of relief, notably when the man disguises himself in female clothing and ventures out for a look at the night sky, but essentially we are locked up in the pigsty with him for a hundred long minutes during which nothing happens and very slowly indeed. This is evidently not intended as another *Animal Farm*, though Fugard has described it as a 'personal parable' and linked it to his own long fight against alcoholism. We are, therefore, perhaps meant to find here the story of a man rediscovering himself through utter reduction to the basics of earth and air, but a distinct lack of drama and unusual lack of character development or insight leads one in the end to wonder irreverently whether it might have been more intriguing to hear the life story of one of the neighbouring pigs. Jim Broadbent does what he can with the hero, while Linda Bassett plays his wife with an understandably increasing irritability.

Like Athol Fugard, Howard Barker is not exactly the first playwright you turn to in search of a cheerful evening out, but his new cycle of ten sketches (*The Possibilities* at the Almeida in Islington) does have at least one brilliant entry: the brief tale of a sinister, itinerant bookseller (Nicholas Woodeson in superb form) who is unwilling to part with a single volume for fear that its contained wisdom might prove intolerable. Written in a style vaguely reminiscent of the sketches that Harold Pinter and Peter Cook used to give to Kenneth Williams back in the 1950s, this, however, stands outside the darkly terror-struck sequence of the others, and, though a versatile cast works well under Ian McDiarmid's sensitive and strong direction, you feel by the end of a none too extended evening that it might have been more fun to spend a weekend with the Macbeths.

Grand National

The first wonder of *The Shaughraun* by Dion Boucicault (now in rare revival on the National's Olivier stage in a splendid and swashbuckling production by Howard Davies) is that neither Fairbanks nor Barrymore ever made a silent movie out of it. Written in 1874, it emerges more than a century later as living proof that theatre doesn't have to be about talking heads. Thanks to a revolving and height-changing drum on the centre of the Olivier stage, which has finally been persuaded to function properly more than a decade after it was first installed, this is a melodramatic evening of clifftop chases and death-defying leaps into the abyss as an amazingly picaresque adventure unfolds through fog and fury.

If you can imagine Shaw's *Devil's Disciple* rewritten by O'Casey and then filmed by the Keystone Cops, you will begin to get some idea of what is afoot here: a Sligo landlord returns from deportation to Australia only to discover that villainous neighbours are after his property, and that he is required to involve himself in a series of military and romantic adventures which usually have him hanging by his fingernails from nearby battlements, while his only friend, the buccaneering shaughraun of the title, is making a speciality of appearing in the flesh at his own funeral celebrations.

The joy of Davies's wide staging is that it never mocks or comments on the action, simply allowing the plot to unfold as the cliffhanger it is, an odd mix of romantic thriller and social farce. In this great rediscovery of a lost classic of the Victorian theatre, Stephen Moore as the villain, Stephen Rea as the titular adventurer, Shaun Scott as the displaced heir and Felicity Montagu as a heroine bearing a remarkable vocal resemblance to the young Maggie Smith all give performances of such joyous and flamboyant theatricality that one almost wishes they had gone all the way and made the show over as a musical.

Australia's most distinguished and prolific playwright David Williamson brings to the Lyric the original native cast of his *Emerald City*, a glossy and waspish comedy about the corrupt awfulness of Sydney showbiz folk when viewed through the eyes of a puritanical Melbourne writer.

Essentially *Faust Down Under*, this is the possibly autobiographical tale of a notable, and hitherto noble, dramatist and screenwriter desperately trying to sell his soul to commercial television, only then to find that rubbish is very much harder to write than it looks. If Melbourne is Perth without the sunshine, then Sydney is New York without the intellect: a city where the whole front page of the evening paper can be occupied by only three words, and those all monosyllabic at that.

The central figures are the writer (Garry McDonald) and his fast-rising publisher wife (Robyn Nevin), both Chardonnay socialists on the cutting edge of middle-class trendiness, and both riddled with compromise and ambivalence about the ethics of private schooling or the need for a bigger apartment on the waterfront at whatever cost to talent and self-satisfaction. But most of Williamson's supporting cast are caricatures of theatrical awfulness, and it is a little hard in the end to care much about what happens to any of them, though I remain sorry we never met an off-stage Polish director whose films start at a crawl and then gallop to a standstill.

Max Cullen's Mike is a Sammy Glick figure of truly wondrous awfulness, rising without trace through the studio politics of Australian film-making, and although in the end this turns out to be a morality tale ('Don't blame the city – the demons are in us') as usual, it is the devil who has all the best of the script. Richard Wherrett's production, on a glitzy, revolving set by Laurence Eastwood, comes as a sharp reminder that Simon Gray doesn't have the monopoly of creative middle-class professional angst.

At Wyndham's, Peter Luke's *Married Love* is an amazingly dusty, creaky and hidebound stage biography of the birth-control pioneer Marie Stopes, which sounds at best like a radio documentary for schools constructed at some time in the middle 1950s. Joan Plowright directs a hardworking cast who, through no real fault of hers or theirs, are totally unable to bring a desperately fragmented and disjointed script to any meaningful kind of theatrical life, so that Susan Hampshire is left as Marie to drift through the action looking like Isadora Duncan with stomach cramps, while John Moffatt gets understandably more and more irritable as the onlooking George Bernard Shaw.

One or two facets of the Stopes life and career are vaguely considered, notably her early feminism and a fatal flamboyance which allowed her to degenerate into an Elinor Glyn heroine seducing young men on bearskin rugs, but a ritual courtroom scene during her libel trial and a disastrously sketchy guided tour of the rest of her long life do not ever manage to rise above the level of lines like, 'You are one of the most eminent scientists in your field,' and 'In my heart I believe God put me here for a higher purpose.'

Her five-year first marriage to an impotent homicidal maniac is dismissed in one briskly offhand conversation with a bicycling Bernard Shaw, and the author seems constantly unable to decide whether Marie was a much-misunderstood revolutionary social engineer or a thoroughly tiresome old bat with a sexual hangup. Either way, she surely deserves a better play than this one.

The Great Gambon

It has become increasingly apparent over the last two years, not least because of the Alan Ayckbourn revival of *View From The Bridge* at the National, that in Michael Gambon we now have a natural leader of the acting profession in this country. His new *Uncle Vanya* at the Vaudeville is in that sense part of a very royal progress towards, if not the mantle of Olivier himself, then certainly that of Ralph Richardson, who was suitably enough the first ever to call him the Great Gambon.

The constant joy and wonder of this new production is the utter control and confidence of Michael Blakemore's staging. It is arguable that Greta Scacchi is a bit dead behind the eyes, but then no one ever said that Yelena had to be more than glacial as she reels around from sheer boredom. Jonathan Pryce as the shambling country doctor Astrov, Jonathan Cecil as the lugubrious neighbour, Imelda Staunton as the doomed Sonya, and Benjamin Whitrow as the treacherous professor, all give performances that would be the envy of any permanent company in this or any other land. The result is a production which should be shown to anyone who believes that the West End at its best cannot challenge the National and the RSC on every level of production and performance. It is, in short, just wonderful, and there is not a lot more to say about it except that Michael Frayn's new translation crowns his Chekhov quartet in glory, and that not since Olivier and Redgrave opened the National with it all of a quarter-century ago has there been a *Vanya*, or indeed a Chekhov, in London to come within a Russian mile of this mournful, magnificent masterpiece.

At the Theatre Royal, Haymarket, Alan Strachan's second production in a decade of *The Deep Blue Sea* comes as another reminder of the blazing and ongoing power of Rattigan's mid-century drama. The story is of Hester Collyer, played now by Penelope Keith in a performance of considerable authority. Separated from an eminent judge (Anthony Bate), she is living with a fatally weak-willed test pilot (David Yelland, in the part that made a star on stage and screen of Kenneth More), and as the play opens she is retrieved by well-meaning neighbours from the suicide which seems to be her only possible solution.

On the original first night in 1952, several critics took the view that all she needed was a good marriage guidance counsellor, which is roughly akin to suggesting that Hedda Gabler would have been fine if she could have located a really expert interior decorator. The whole point of *Deep Blue Sea* is that Hester's survival is a far greater tragedy than her death, and this is a play with roots deep in the truth of Rattigan's own existence.

In essence a triangular piece, cornered by Hester and the two men unable to return her love in anything like its original passion (the wealthy judge she has married and the fatally attractive younger lover), it was derived from a moment in Rattigan's own life when he found himself homosexually trapped between the older and richer Chips Channon and a young suicidal actor. But to have written *The Deep Blue Sea* as a homosexual tragedy in 1952 would have been impossible, so Rattigan gives us Hester instead, and the only real problem with the present casting is that Miss Keith seems altogether too capable to have got herself into this corner, while Mr Yelland, through no fault other than that of the generation gap, finds it difficult to recreate that cheery ex-RAF manner which is so central to a character whose life really stopped in 1940. But in a characteristically meticulous and intelligent production, Strachan has drawn a marvellously detailed performance from John Normington as the sinister neighbour, and proved yet again that Rattigan, like Maugham before him, knew all there was to know about clenched English middle-class moral codes and their appalling dangers.

It is mercifully not often that one is required to survive an evening of such rambling and turgid awfulness as *The Fifteen Streets*, Rob Bettinson's adaptation and staging at the Playhouse of Catherine Cookson's mysteriously bestselling novel of Tyneside life around 1910. A large cast, many of whom seem to be only dimly acquainted with the basic techniques of non-amateur character acting, ritually grind their way through random scenes of life and death and disaster in the kind of show that might once have become one of Lionel Bart's lesser musicals, but is here without even the benefit of an orchestra, let alone a coherent script.

'No good will come of this,' says one of the neighbours early in what promises to be an interminable evening, thereby neatly providing one of the best of the reviews. From the cross-section of characters on stage here, it would seem that Miss Cookson's men are mainly drunk, her women oddly hunchbacked and her children relentlessly adorable, as if auditioning for some kind of period commercial.

The action is not so much slow as frequently stopped, and the dialogue makes *Coronation Street* seem positively Chekhovian by comparison. Every half-hour or so one of the characters, usually a strolling priest or yet another demented neighbour, asks one of the others what has been happening, to which the answer is not a lot: someone gets married, or dies, or gives birth, or falls into the river, or goes to America and everyone else stands around muttering, 'This has got to stop,' which seemed to me an admirable sentiment altogether. The trouble with all this sub-Priestley rubbish is that it has been making a fortune on tour, and well may in London.

1988

Misfortunes of War

Not since Mel Brooks's very memorable *Springtime for Hitler* can there have been a musical of such gothic wartime eccentricity and random awfulness as Robin Hardy's *Winnie* at the Victoria Palace. What we have here are troops of military dancing girls swarming sexily over tanks, while Virginia McKenna sings of *London Pride* and Robert Hardy (no relation to the author) does his justly celebrated impersonation of a cigar-clenching Churchill at the political and air-raided barricades of the wartime city. The thinking would seem to be that patriotism, apart from being the last refuge of the scoundrel, might also be a means of selling off a good many theatre tickets if you haven't really got a book or a score or a plot, or even much of an idea of how else musicals are made.

True, we do get the outlines of a story: in a disused and bombed theatre somewhere in Berlin late in July 1945, a group of English strolling players have mysteriously decided that what Churchill will most need after he wins the next election is to return to Germany and see a tacky musical celebration of how he won the war. Fortunately for him he lost the election, and therefore never had to see the show; we, however, are not that lucky and have to sit through several hours of weird marching displays and musical numbers that would have seemed deeply inadequate on the end of a pier in 1932, let alone in Germany a dozen years later.

Vastly better news at Hampstead, however, where Brian Friel's *Aristocrats* is at last having an English premiere and proving to be a marvellously Chekhovian account of an old country-house family in decline and disarray. There's the uncle who stopped speaking the day he stopped drinking, the no-good son who has gone to work in a German sausage factory, the daughter who has taken to the drink in London, and the one who has stayed at home to play Chopin and look after the dregs of a once great dynasty.

In a rambling, talky evening, during which the only dramatic change is that the family who thought they were re-assembling for a wedding in fact find themselves preparing a funeral, Friel is telling us all manner of home truths about his Irish: their passion for re-inventing their own past lives, their inability to live with any kind of truth except the truth that comes out of a book or a bottle, and yet the lingering power of a Donegal family living in total social and geographic isolation above a village that no longer even knows they are there. Like Dodie Smith and N. C. Hunter and indeed Priestley in this country once, Friel has a classic ability to assemble disparate members of the same clan and then tell each of their stories as part of one huge familial tapestry, and this lyrical and lovely play should be seen not least for the skill with which the director, Robin Lefevre, orchestrates a superlative cast: Sinead Cusack as the alcoholic Alice, Niall Buggy as the semi-detached Casimir symbolically searching for a long-lost croquet lawn now given over to weeds, and William Roberts as the bemused American academic trying to sort out the truth from the fantasy among the branches of a dying family tree, all lead a superb company and deserve a West End transfer.

At the Royal Court, Howard Brenton's *Greenland* starts as a waspish and acid attack on modern London life, full of such recently recognisable characters as a murderous gambling aristocrat and a formidable female moral crusader against sex and violence, but then degenerates in the second half into a wild and woolly vision of some Utopia 700 years hence in which the same characters, having mysteriously become immortal, then drift around in a kind of daft no-man's-land trying to preserve themselves from a slow death by sheer boredom.

The trouble is that, for all its corrupt awfulness, the London of Mr Brenton's political today is far more attractive than the wan idealism of his Utopian tomorrow, and the cast seems to recognise this, so that all the energy and passion displayed in the first half of Simon Curtis's agile production is allowed to drift away into a kind of drugged somnolence in the second. There are here, as in Brenton's earlier *Pravda*, some savagely funny attacks on the way we live now, but the moment he tries to come up with some future alternatives we are left with all the hazy idealism of some left-over 1960s guru. Better perhaps the devils you know than the dreams you've not yet worked through to any coherent conclusion, but Sheila Hancock as the zealot crusader and Jane Lapotaire as the socialist politician and David Haig as the disappearing aristocrat all have their moments.

Utter Joyce

There will be cheering all down Pont Street, and the Home Counties will rise up in celebration from Guildford, yea even unto Leatherhead and Godalming: Joyce Grenfell is back in the West End. Not, admittedly, in person, since she died in 1979, but in a reasonable facsimile thereof cobbled together at the Fortune Theatre as *Re:Joyce!*

Though not exactly a one-woman show, since Maureen Lipman is joined at the piano by Denis King, performing the jovial sidekick role first perfected for Joyce on innumerable tours by the great and good Bill Blezard, this is effectively an evening of Grenfell worship largely comprised of her old songs and monologues, interwoven with extremely brisk biographical linking material by James Roose-Evans, who has also recently published a bestselling edition of her wartime letters. Any attack on Joyce Grenfell, however faint and however qualified, is regarded (as I once discovered to my cost) by the British as second only to an attack on the Queen Mother or polo ponies in the treachery charts.

1988

But certain facts about Grenfell do have to be faced in the light of this celebration, and one of them is that most of her own material was really very sketchy indeed. Wafer-thin speeches about English social misfits or anomalies, and wan little romantic numbers by her faithful composer Richard Addinsell, were turned by Joyce into a kind of greasepaint gold largely because she always retained a curious kind of amateur status, thereby making an audience feel that they could do her show as well as she could. For which reason they loved her far more deeply than any of the more professional revue entertainers who were her contemporaries. But when that material is performed, as here, by an infinitely more experienced and talented and versatile actress, then the result is to highlight the original conjuring trick. The classics are all here, from 'useful and acceptable gifts' through those endless naughty schoolboy routines to the Maud who refuses to come into Tennyson's garden, but the wonder now is how Grenfell got away with them even on Broadway so successfully for so long.

The answer is, of course, that she was somehow all of our aunts, and we never dared to complain when, towards the end, she was getting a bit repetitive and a bit boring. When *Re:Joyce!* concentrates on the wartime Grenfell, and she goes in uniform to slay the enemy with a social monologue ('sugar is unobtainable anywhere in Maidenhead' was her uniquely characteristic comment on the outbreak of World War II), we realise her strength was in adversity. In more peaceful times one might have hoped she could have found herself one or two better writers, but there is a huge on-going love for her among those who have always preferred the ladies and gentlemen to the players, and I suspect that *Re:Joyce!* will be at the Fortune, and in Miss Lipman's suitcase, for several years to come. She has even managed to perfect that maddeningly arched eyebrow of surprise with which Grenfell used to acknowledge the applause of the faithful, and Alan Strachan's agile production has done both ladies proud.

Phoenix Rising

Not since Olivier was at the height of his National Theatre management twenty years ago has a troupe of actors been so spectacularly and successfully led from within as the Renaissance Company under Kenneth Branagh. Opening a new Phoenix Theatre season of three Shakespearian classics, all directed by other actors (Judi Dench, Derek Jacobi and Geraldine McEwan), *Much Ado About Nothing* can be taken perhaps as a statement of the company's aims. It is in the best sense both spare and sparse: a group of fifteen actors, working against a minimal setting on an evidently tight budget, seem under Dame Judi Dench to have reached no very startling or original new thoughts about the play, but are united in a determination to get back to the basic text and do it as sharply and clearly and simply and swiftly as possible. So this is in no way a director's evening, though Dench has visibly passed on some of her own rare comic timing in Shakespearian plots to Samantha Bond, a wily and assured Beatrice up against the faintly seedy Benedick of Branagh himself.

This is a production which first opened on a studio stage in Birmingham, and might still look better somewhere a little smaller than the Phoenix, but it is peopled by actors who seem relieved not to be constrained by anything too definite in the way of a set or a period or a philosophy. They are young and a little raw around the edges, but the verse speaking is crystal clear, and there is a lyrical amiability about the staging which suddenly makes one realise for how many years Shakespearian comedies have been shrouded in the darkness that usually comes from a director trying to tell us something about them. What we have here is not exactly Shakespeare for schools, but it does seem to me to mark a shift of emphasis and an absolute faith in the line-by-line qualities of the text, one which points up, albeit unintentionally, the desperate gimmickry and intellectual exhaustion of the current RSC *Much Ado* at Stratford.

At Greenwich from Toby Robertson's Theatr Clywd in Wales, a wonderfully joyous rediscovery: *Captain Carvallo* was, in a Laurence Olivier production back in 1950, the play that first established Peter Finch on stage and made the name of its author Denis Cannan, who went on to become Peter Brook's writer on *US* and *The Ik*. Since then it would appear to have disappeared almost entirely, only now to surface looking and sounding like Shaw's *Devil's Disciple* as rewritten by the young Peter Ustinov.

Carvallo is set in the middle of this century, in the middle of Europe, and at the end of a long war. Further precise details are unnecessary for a philosophic comedy about patriotism and love and the problems of blowing up people you quite like; but instead of the whimsical and fey debate that might have been expected, what Cannan actually wrote was a sharp-edged satire on the sexual deceits and moral compromises of warfare, in which there are no winners or losers, no heroes or villains, but merely a lot of men in each other's trousers trying to sort out extra-marital affairs and daily survival amid the bombs.

Coming so soon after World War II, the play at first might have seemed like an Englishman's answer to *Schweik* or *Jacobowsky and the Colonel*. In fact, it's both more farcical and more academic than either of them, an elegantly and wryly sardonic, languid and literary comedy of military manners, quite superbly played by Neil Stacy (as a biology professor desperate to be seen doing the right thing), Oliver Parker (as the swashbuckling partisan), Angela Thorne (as the romantic housewife) and

1988

Derek Smith (as her idiotic husband). Robertson's production has a superb stage confidence, living forever on the borderlines of romantic comedy and manic farce, and it ought not to be another forty years before this enchanting script is again retrieved from its mothballs.

If a play has lain unrevived for not just forty years but four entire centuries, there is usually a fairly good reason and with *Bussy d'Ambois* the reason is evidently that it is largely unplayable. As usual one has to admire Dr Jonathan Miller's courage in programming his current Old Vic season as though examining audiences for their chances of first-class honours degrees in difficult texts at some singularly obscure university drama department, but the decision to revive *Bussy*, at least in this way, borders on the purely perverse.

A melodrama by George Chapman (he of the Homer translations) based on the life of a soldier at the court of the French Henri III around 1575, the play resolutely refuses to deal with the many adventures of Bussy's picaresque life, dwelling instead and at some length on the one incident of court intrigue which led to his death. Those expecting another *Changeling* or *Duchess of Malfi* or *'Tis Pity* should be warned that what we end up watching here is *Andromaque* without the jokes: endless speeches about the nature of love and betrayal, but no dramatic energy or activity.

David Threlfall in the title role starts out intriguingly like an Iago with moral scruples, but his final death scene goes on nearly as long as Miller's own celebrated parody of a Shakespearian death in *Beyond the Fringe*, and not even Sara Kestelman's tortured countess can make one believe that this particular text should ever have been taken off the library shelf.

Hall Over Now

Sir Peter Hall ends his management of the National Theatre, as he began it in 1974, with a revival of *The Tempest*; but where then we had the melodic majesty of John Gielgud's elegiac Prospero, we now have the arid, academic Michael Bryant performance, one of faultless line-readings and superb intelligence, but fatally short on sheer dramatic intensity.

Someone somewhere seems to have dedicated 1988 as the year of *The Tempest*: already we have John Wood as a Stratford Prospero, the Japanese at Edinburgh, and now we also get Max von Sydow in the role for Jonathan Miller at the Old Vic. Logically Hall's should have been the great climax of and farewell to his years at the National, but in fact it's an oddly low key and uninvolving affair, perhaps better seen in the original studio conditions than moved into the vast open spaces of the Olivier stage.

This is minimalist late-Shakespeare, stripped quite literally to the bone – Ariel even flies down on one from the heavens – and determined not to give an inch to the autumnal melancholy of what many have, albeit wrongly, seen as Shakespeare's own farewell to his craft. But the price of schoolroom discipline has always been a certain lack of magic. True, we get the circle of sand with which Hall surrounded his earliest *Troilus* at Stratford almost thirty years ago, but, beyond that and a fiery Miranda from Shirley Henderson (replacing Hall's own daughter, who has withdrawn from the production), there is precious little to focus the attention. A chorus of apparently moonwalking mutants, a bloodsoaked Caliban from Tony Haygarth and a tetchy Sebastian from Basil Henson all surround Bryant as if expecting a final breakthrough into mesmeric stardom; whereas the lesson of the fifteen years that he has shared with Hall on the South Bank is that he lacks the authority of Prospero.

Hare's Breadth

The central importance and achievement of David Hare, whose seventh and latest play for the National Theatre in the Lyttelton is *The Secret Rapture*, lies in the way that he seems uniquely prepared to write of the human cost of current British politics. Among his major contemporaries, Alan Ayckbourn does indeed write about the darker realities of modern family life in Britain, and Caryl Churchill in *Serious Money* writes of the corruption of the City; but Hare alone relates public to private morality.

His new play is in a Chekhovian sense *Two Sisters*: one is a Thatcherite junior minister, the other a saintly designer prepared to sacrifice first her work and ultimately her life for the love of others. Around the crucial and superb performances of Penelope Wilton and Jill Baker as the sisters, Hare has drawn portraits of their abusively alcoholic stepmother (Clare Higgins), a husband (Paul Shelley) determined to do business the way Christ would have done business, and a lover (Mick Ford) in the grip of an ultimately fatal romantic obsession. What we then get, across two acidly well-written hours, is a modern morality play about England.

Howard Davies's spare and subtle production, played against equally powerful scenic backgrounds by John Gunter, brilliantly balances the private and the public issues: we never forget that this is a play about a family trapped between two funerals, nor do we lose sight of an outside world in which people as well as companies can be totally and brutally asset-stripped. On its highest level *The Secret Rapture* is always about love and hate and good and evil; its triumph is never to stay in that unworldly atmosphere, but instead to relate every moral issue to the reality of the way we now lead our daily lives. It is beyond question the best new play of the year.

This being the time of *The Tempest*, we now have at the Old Vic the Jonathan Miller version with Max von Sydow, a sonorous and cadaverous

1988

Prospero, who seemed on the first night remarkably unsure of the plot, given that he has been playing the role in Sweden since 1953 among all those Bergman movies.

Miller's masterstroke in this *Tempest*, as in the one he directed some fifteen years ago, is the curtain-call notion that after Prospero breaks his staff and forsakes his magical powers, these are inherited by Ariel and Caliban in a burst of colonial rebellion. But beyond that he doesn't seem to feel strongly about the play, giving it a languid production of huge intellectual confidence and authority, but not a lot of action. There is also some curious casting: the comedian Alexei Sayle, one of nature's Calibans, is in fact Trinculo; while Rudolph Walker's monster is unusually dapper, temperamentally more at home with the marooned courtiers than the wilder beasts of the island. But Rudi Davies's Miranda is the strongest we have had all year, and Carl Davis has created a romantic score only faintly at odds with the academic nature of the rest of the evening. The only remaining question arising from von Sydow's lugubrious reading is why Bergman never got around to the movie version: few Prosperos can ever have been seen through a glass quite so darkly.

English Roses

After a winter and indeed a summer of considerable discontent at their Warwickshire base it is good to find the Royal Shakespeare Company back on form with *The Plantagenets*, a nine-hour saga carved and sometimes hacked out of the three parts of *Henry VI* and *Richard III*. It is arguable that the RSC is always at its best in epics: from *Wars of the Roses* and *The Greeks* through *Nicholas Nickleby* to *Les Misérables*, there is something immensely reassuring about a company of forty advancing towards the footlights to play out some vast dramatic national anthem of blood and death and restoration.

True, this one is a little rough around the edges: Charles Wood's severe editing leaves us with a magnificent opening section (*Henry VI*) before declining into a somewhat somnolent *Edward IV* and then rising again to the heights of *Richard III*, though even here Adrian Noble as director seems willing to sacrifice a totally cohesive production for some spectacular isolated moments.

What is best about these *Plantagenets* is the way they give spirit and energy and purpose back to an acting troupe which has for too long lacked all of that. What is alarming is the way they show up the ongoing RSC weakness in character acting and verse speaking, so that after the demise of David Waller early in the day we are left with no courtiers or attendant lords of any weight or authority. We do, however, get Penny Downie ageing across nine hours from the young bride to the old crone Queen

Margaret, Anton Lesser as a campy and idiosyncratic Richard, Ralph Fiennes as an unusually powerful Henry VI and Oliver Cotton doing a splendid treble as Suffolk, Cade and Buckingham. We also get the stunningly bronzed settings of Bob Crowley.

The Goodness of Guinness

In the cultural and intellectual desert that has been this past year on Broadway, Lee Blessing's *A Walk in the Woods* shone out like a neon-lit oasis. Here was a play which had the courage to form itself into a two-man duologue, and to tackle abstract notions about the nature of peace, notions which most producers other than the great and good Lucille Lortel would have at least tried setting to music.

Now the play comes to the Comedy Theatre in London with a new cast, consisting of Alec Guinness (in his first West End appearance for a decade) and the archetypal man in the grey-flannel suit, Edward Herrmann, and although it is true that there have been certain losses in the Atlantic crossing, there have also been considerable gains. On one level, this is a play that belongs in that grouping of *The Odd Couple* and *I'm Not Rappaport* and *Driving Miss Daisy*, Broadway hits in which two people of apparently impossibly and irreconcilably different backgrounds and attitudes are brought towards a kind of understanding of each other in the name of common humanity. But Mr Blessing wants us to understand something more than that: in a wry, subtle, laconic duologue, he wants to make the point that negotiations are in the end only about negotiators, and that the life or death of the planet is simply the life or death of the men who inhabit it. If you have forgotten what the theatre of civilised debate was once all about, if you have not lately come across a script in which the ideas mattered more than the plot or the characterisation, then *Walk in the Woods* is the play to remind you of what we have lost.

Not that Guinness is exactly self-effacing: in the role of the veteran Soviet negotiator, strolling through the Geneva woods with his American opposite number to test out the possibilities of arms reductions, he may well lack all the Russian bear-like qualities of Robert Prosky, who originated the role in New York; but he brings instead a kind of wily survival. Guinness is the only actor I know who, while talking about walking on eggshells, can also show you what it is like to walk on eggshells, and his performance is a sort of summary of Soviet cunning over the years, brought up forever sharply against the idealist innocence of Herrmann's not-so-ugly American.

Ronald Eyre's production has the courage of its own inactivity, so we appear at times to be watching a radio play; but as the men always doomed to make recommendations rather than decisions, the men who know from the outset they are only as good as the next election campaign, Guinness and Herrmann achieve a masterly balance. One of the curious virtues of Blessing's script is that, although written pre-*glasnost*, and therefore already technically out of date, it achieves a kind of timelessness by insisting on the petulant bickering of its participants. Lines such as, 'If mankind really hated war there would be millions of us and two soldiers,' or, 'History is only geography over time,' suggest a weird mix of Bernard Shaw and Henry Kissinger; but the play gradually acquires a life of its own, so that by the end we desperately and futilely want a treaty to be signed, not so much for the sake of the world as for that of its two signatories – men we urgently want to end their lives and careers with some sense of achievement and satisfaction. What we are left with, of course, since Mr Blessing is nothing if not a realist, are a couple of men paid to say no and look good while doing so amid the endless and awful neutrality of Swiss timber forests.

On the Cottesloe stage of the National, a new production of Strindberg's *The Father* has the virtue of a scathing adaptation by John Osborne, whose line in chauvinist rage and marital loathing has always seemed to

A Walk in the Woods Edward Herrmann *as John Honeyman* and Alec Guinness *as Andrey Lvovich Botvinnik*

mark him out as a natural Strindbergian for our times. This David Leveaux staging started out with Anton Rodgers in the title role, but, due to rehearsal differences, now stars Alun Armstrong as the Captain, driven to madness and a straitjacket by doubts over the true parentage of his child, while Susan Fleetwood, in wonderfully glacial form, plays the wife who is the authoress of all his woes.

In a very strong studio setting by Annie Smart, *The Father* is played for two hours without a break as an intense chamber-piece about the overthrowing of a man and a mind through sexual and social doubt. But what Osborne has superlatively realised is that it is a play entirely driven by its own internal anger, a kind of greasepainted rage, which this superb new translation sustains with nightmarish intensity. Strindberg himself saw the script as a staging-post on the road to suicide, a shadow-play which would work only if tackled with extreme subtlety, and there are moments here when Mr Armstrong, writhing around in a cage full of female tigers, seems dangerously close to the kind of Victorian melodrama that its author most feared. But Osborne's timeless horror of rampant women pulls him back time and again from that brink, and the result is a period *Virginia Woolf* of dazzling power.

Future Indefinite

Alan Ayckbourn's comedies have been getting darker by the year, but *Henceforward* (at the Vaudeville) has to be the bleakest yet. Somewhere out along the furthest reaches of the London Underground, in a no-go area inhabited by marauding bands of murderous feminists, there lives a composer so withdrawn from his own family and past that he can now only communicate with a domestic robot and a series of electronic music-makers. A life of compact disc creation would seem to have so compacted him that, when he has to present a façade of acceptability in order to reclaim his own daughter, he is forced to rent a girlfriend whose idea of a little light conversation is to ask, 'Your wife, is she dead at all?'

Ian McKellen as the semi-detached composer, and Serena Evans as the inane rentagirl, play the first half alone as an increasingly chilly black farce, getting even blacker after the interval when the McKellen character turns the girl into a robot and then sets her on his ex-wife (an icy Jane Asher) in a nightmare parody of domestic bliss. What Mr Ayckbourn would have us know is that the future is going to be much like the present only nastier, and that, if an artist retreats into his own art, then he must expect to have just tape-recordings for company. But the brilliance of *Henceforward* is the way that it works within the conventions of West End comedy to come up with a subversive, futurist, mechanical farce about isolation and introversion, one which looks at moments as though Noël

1988

Coward has been asked to rewrite the myth of Frankenstein. A world of robots in which child welfare officers come complete with personal alarm systems running down their spines is perfectly suited to Ayckbourn's mastery of acute social embarrassment, and his own production is nothing short of superb.

At the new Baylis Theatre within Sadler's Wells, a sharp lesson in the dangers of the Thatcherite belief that commercial sponsorship can or should replace centralised Arts Council funding for the stage. A production of *The Madwoman of Chaillot* was to have been directed there by Sharon Gans. When she withdrew during rehearsals after 'artistic differences' with the cast, so did her American sponsor, leaving the Baylis in a cash crisis within weeks of opening what promises to be a welcome and much-needed halfway house from the West End to the experimental fringe.

True, this *Madwoman* (in a production now directed by Nick Hamm, the Baylis's resident artistic director) is not as successful as his initial *House of Blue Leaves*, partly because Giraudoux's wartime classic is now looking very much the worse for wear. The postwar years have not been kind to the particular and peculiar form of fey French period whimsy, best exemplified by Anouilh and Giraudoux, and though it must have been hoped that a fable of capitalist greed and disaster might look topical in a London still recovering from stockmarket collapse, it in fact looks more like something that a Gallic J. M. Barrie might have cobbled together around the turn of the century.

Eleanor Bron in the title role brings a kind of academic gravity to a part requiring wild eccentricity at the very least, and though the rest of the female casting is very strong (Selina Cadell, Celia Imrie), the company seems to have established no house style with which to conquer a rambling and difficult play, full of false leads and baroque diversions, but unable at last to say as much in almost three hours about a money-grubbing society as Alan Ayckbourn can say in three lines.

Manfred Karge is the German dramatist who made his name over here with *Man to Man*, the play about the transvestite labourer disguised to take over her late husband's job; and now also to the Royal Court from Edinburgh's Traverse Theatre comes *The Conquest of the South Pole*, the tale of how four unemployed young Germans set out to dramatise Amundsen's famous Polar expedition, seeing in it some sort of metaphor for their own precarious existence in a backwater town.

The translation is again by Tinch Minter and Anthony Vivis, and once more has an eccentric kind of urgency, as Karge, a natural heir to Brecht himself, tackles issues of social unrest within the familiar framework of heroic tales from the past. The overall impression is that of a cabaret rather than a drama, with fragmentary character sketches overlapping to form a collage of youthful despair at the ways of a changed world in which it is no longer possible to have adventurous heroes or even famous losers like Shackleton. Instead of Polar adventurers we now have poleaxed teenagers, defeated even before they set out on any journey by a social system which seems to have no place for them, except as statistics within a dole queue.

Karge writes a manic, heightened kind of prose which often seems just waiting for the musical settings of a latterday Kurt Weill. But he is well served by Stephen Unwin and a Scots-sounding cast, who have found certain regional affinities with a Germany in which rampant disaffection among young people with the state systems has led only to the outrage of Karge's fantasies for a dead end.

The Hollow Crown

To the Phoenix Theatre, only recently vacated by Kenneth Branagh's Renaissance Company, now comes another example of actor power: Derek Jacobi with his own company in a kingly double of *Richard II* and (after Christmas) *Richard III*, productions in part financed by the Kennedy Centre in Washington, which is where they will end up later next year.

For a definition of blazing Shakespearian stardom, you would do well to start here: Jacobi takes Richard II not so much as the traditional poet king but rather as the actor king, a man forever testing his own theatricality against those around him, hoping almost to the last that yet another great speech might get him out of prison and back to his usurped throne. Jacobi's command of the verse, his ability to switch from gay despot to defeated husband within a few dozen lines, is immensely impressive and powerful, which is more than can be said for his surroundings. Denied the economic resources of a subsidised permanent company, Clifford Williams has gone for an uncharacteristically plodding production, in which other players are apt respectfully to back upstage whenever Jacobi opens his mouth, much after the fashion of minor character actors on a Donald Wolfit tour of the 1950s. Only Robert Eddison, as the dying John of Gaunt, gives a performance able to challenge the supremacy of Jacobi. Elsewhere a slow-starting and at best workmanlike rendering of the text only ever comes to life when its star is moving into another of the classic tirades. There is a lot to be said for star actors moving back into positions of centre-stage authority in Shakespeare, but their productions still need a point of view, and that is oddly lacking here.

Rather more experimental Shakespeare at the Warehouse in Covent Garden, where Declan Donnellan's award-winning Cheek by Jowl Company give us the fourth *Tempest* this year. After John Wood (Stratford),

Max von Sydow (Old Vic) and Michael Bryant (National), Timothy Walker's punkish Prospero is full of surprises, not least during the opening storm scene which he, usually offstage at the time, orchestrates as a director in dark glasses.

Donnellan's determination would seem to be never to let us think we know the play, and never to let it drift into mere recital or repetition: every scene and every character has been rethought, the King of Naples has even changed sex, and much of the second half now seems to be taking place backstage at some nightmarish Victorian music-hall, presided over by Stephano and Trinculo. Those still expecting an isle full of noises, or a poetic ringmaster breaking his magical staff, or even a Shakespearian farewell to classical greatness, will all be disappointed. Instead, we have a revolutionary rethinking of the text, which is often inclined to backfire into mere gimmickry, but equally often manages, through its own manic energy and invention, to give us fresh insights into an over-familiar island.

The idea of setting the whole play backstage, so that Prospero is forever directing his islanders and their invaders in a series of magical charades, might have worked better in the hands and company of Peter Brook. Cheek by Jowl are young and talented, but even they seem a little hesitant at some of the improvisations thrust on them, and none of the players, not even Cecilia Noble as a beautiful black Miranda, seems to have the confidence to retrieve the verse from group vocal exercises. If you know the play very well, these variations on its themes may hold the attention since the production is extremely brisk; if not, wait for the RSC revival to come into the Barbican from Stratford early next summer.

Already into the Barbican Pit from last year by the Avon, John Caird's production of *A Question of Geography*, by John Berger and Nella Bielski, has lost none of its chilly Gulag intensity. Set in Stalin's labour camps during the last summer of his life, it tells across three hours of one mother, heartbreakingly well-played by Harriet Walter. Reunited with a teenage son after fifteen years' separation, she establishes a kind of domestic happiness with him and the camp doctor before being torn from them and sent back into stricter confinement.

Unlike *Ivan Denisovich*, the Berger/Bielski script focuses on the minute details of life on the fringes of the camps, where a kind of underprivileged normality could be achieved in between visitations from the threatening guards. In long, rambling monologues and the reading of letters from ages ago and far away, an almost Chekhovian picture of postwar Russian life is assembled, during which the terror is not of distant trees being chopped in some cherry orchard, but of whole lives being wasted or destroyed in sub-human conditions.

The RSC's long-held belief that all shows in their claustrophobic London Pit should last at least three full hours once again weakens the impact of a script in desperate need of cutting by at least half an hour. But there are haunting performances from Mark Dignam as the old violinist, Clive Russell as the doctor and Linus Roache as the teenager, who alone can still think about some sort of a future.

1989

THE YEAR THAT SAW THE PASSING OF THE 1980S also saw the passing of two great British theatrical giants, Lord Olivier and Sir Anthony Quayle, the ongoing occupation of the West End by huge new musicals (*Miss Saigon*, *Aspects of Love* and the catastrophic *Metropolis*) and the rediscovery of Shakespeare's Rose Theatre on a Bankside site alongside the one where Sam Wanamaker has, through twenty years and with rather less publicity, been reconstructing Shakespeare's Globe.

It was also a year of major performances in relatively minor plays (Denholm Elliott as the waspish old actor in David Mamet's *A Life in the Theatre*, Sheila Hancock as the lesbian school principal in Andrew Davies's *Jean Brodie-esque Prin*) and of an unexpected Arts Council increase in subsidy levels of eleven per cent, one which suggested that, as it drew near to the end of its third and current term, Thatcher's Conservative administration might at long, long last have begun to see the wisdom of putting slightly more money into the whole of British theatre than one small German town annually gives its opera house.

It was a year in which the National Theatre established the extremely strong producer-director partnership of David Aukin and Richard Eyre, a year in which the Royal Shakespeare Company flailed around in search of a leader, following the abrupt resignation of Terry Hands and general company uneasiness over Barbican life, and a year in which Nicholas Hytner proved himself as the hottest young director in town with a remarkable double of *Miss Saigon* (the Boublil/Schonberg Vietnam update of *Madame Butterfly*) and *Ghetto* (Joshua Sobol's harrowing account of Polish Jews being forced to form an acting company for the entertainment of their Nazi oppressors).

It was the year in which John Wood returned after a decade in the United States to a remarkable London triple of *The Tempest*, *The Master Builder* and *The Man Who Came to Dinner*, and in which Trevor Nunn also impressively returned to his RSC roots with a small-scale production of *Othello*, starring Ian McKellen as Iago and, as Othello, the Porgy of Nunn's Glyndebourne revival of the Gershwin opera, Willard White. Nunn also courageously cast his wife Sharon Lee-Hill in the London premiere of *The Baker's Wife*, Stephen Schwartz's great scoring of the Pagnol film about French village life, which was very coolly received by critics long accustomed to Nunn's more spectacular musical ventures with Andrew Lloyd Webber.

New plays were precious few and far between, though the year did end at the Barbican Pit with Stephen Poliakoff's *Playing With Trains*, a savagely waspish indictment (somewhere between *Citizen Kane* and *The Master Builder*) of the British terror of inventions and inventors. Prior to that, the best new plays around had been Timberlake Wertenbaker's *Our Country's Good* and Martin Sherman's *A Madhouse in Goa*, a double bill about American dreams turning into nightmares on Greek islands, in which Vanessa Redgrave gave one of two superb 1989 performances. The other was in Peter Hall's rare staging of *Orpheus Descending*, which then triumphantly transferred to Broadway alongside Hall's other West End classical hit, the Dustin Hoffman *Merchant of Venice*.

This was also the year that saw the closing of the Royal Court's studio Theatre Upstairs, but the rise from the ashes of its own fire of the Tricycle in Kilburn.

It was the year in which Deborah Warner triumphed at the Barbican with *Titus Andronicus* and *King John*, but then moved disappointingly to the broad open spaces of the Olivier stage at the National with the Fiona Shaw version of *The Good Person of Sichuan*. It was the year when Steppenwolf came triumphantly to town with John Steinbeck's *Grapes of Wrath*, and when Leonard Bernstein came to the Barbican for two nights only to premiere and record his long-awaited concert version of *Candide*.

1989

Surprise hits of the year included *The Tempest* remade as a rock musical and Peter O'Toole impersonating to perfection the vodka-stained character of the journalist Jeffrey Bernard. Steven Berkoff came from the Edinburgh Festival to the National with a mesmeric and balletic reinterpretation of Oscar Wilde's *Salome*, Maria Aitken came from Glasgow to the Garrick in Philip Prowse's electrifying staging of *The Vortex*, and in the wake of the Kenneth Branagh and Derek Jacobi Shakespeare seasons at the Phoenix, Alan Bates and Felicity Kendal established another commercial classical stronghold at the Strand with new productions of *Ivanov* and *Much Ado About Nothing*.

All in all, a year when Shakespeare had nearly as many West End hits as Lloyd Webber, and maybe none the worse for that, though musicals still generated much of the West End's electricity, not least because of Jonathan Pryce's breathtaking performance as the hustler-pimp finding his American dream turning into the nightmare of *Miss Saigon*.

Down in Old Tennessee

Though already in economic and artistic dispute with the owner-management of his new home at the Haymarket, Sir Peter Hall brings that theatre a rare touch of transatlantic classical courage with *Orpheus Descending*, the script that Tennessee Williams first wrote back in 1940 as *Battle of Angels*, but is now best known as a movie entitled *The Fugitive Kind*. Described by Williams himself as 'the tale of a wild, spirited boy who wanders into a conventional community of the South and creates all the commotion of a fox in a chicken coop', it was the first of his plays to get a professional production (in Boston), and retains a kind of fascination for the early glimpses it affords of Blanche duBois and Big Daddy and all the other doomed, emotional vagrants of his later and better plays.

True, those wrought-iron screens are already dreadfully overwrought, and the mood in Two River County is ripe for a lynching as soon as the curtain rises on a traditional assembly of Williams's characters on the run from their own lives. Julie Covington as the young Blanche figure, Miriam Margoyles as the God-fearing painter, the Canadian actor Jean-Marc Barr in the Brando role of the guitar-strumming drifter and, above all, Paul Freeman as the evil, dying husband are gathered around Vanessa Redgrave, as the Italian owner of a dry-goods store, already orphaned by the Ku Klux Klan and now about to unleash another bloodbath around her own passionate encounters.

A rare example of great company acting within a commercial West End proscenium arch, Hall's production comes as a sharp reminder of how early in his twenties Williams acquired the mythic, poetic and operatic greatness that was to characterise *Streetcar*.

For those of us who have long believed, sometimes unfashionably, that in *Forty Years On* and then *The Old Country* Alan Bennett wrote two of the best postwar British plays, the good news at the Lyttelton is that he has come back to the theatre with another classic: *Single Spies* is a double-bill made up of *An Englishman Abroad* (his television drama about the real-life meeting in Moscow between the actress Coral Browne and the double-agent Guy Burgess in 1958) and a new play, *A Question of Attribution*, which confronts another spy, Anthony Blunt, with the present Queen at a moment in the 1970s when she, but few others, had discovered his treacherous past.

Prunella Scales plays both Miss Browne and the Queen in performances of cascadingly gracious theatricality. Bennett himself plays Blunt, with Simon Callow as Burgess, and the two men also share the direction of one-act sketches of dazzling invention and brilliance about the nature of treachery and loneliness. Bennett writes his central characters lengthy monologues of dry, bitchy introversion in which can be discovered a lot of the truth about the England of E. M. Forster and Philip Larkin and men for whom internal exile was a permanent condition of life itself. But he also has a sharp eye and ear for historical eccentricity: whether discovering that both Burgess and Browne were jilted by Jack Buchanan, or inventing wonderfully random royal chats with an all-knowing Queen for whom heaven will be something of a come-down, Bennett's treacherous writing deserves a West End transfer.

At the Duke of York's, Tom Stoppard's *Artist Descending A Stair* is an old radio play from 1972 given a first and lively staging by Tim Luscombe: like the later Stoppard *Jumpers* and *Real Inspector Hound*, this is a murder mystery turned into a linguistic parody puzzle, but here concerned with three avant-garde artists and the blind girl who comes to live with them. The play moves back in time from 1972 to 1914 and then comes forward again in an intricate pattern of overlapping or conflicting memories, but in the end is a surprisingly simple tale of friendships established and betrayed. Across eighty no-interval minutes, Alan MacNaughton and William Lucas and Peter Copley and Sarah Woodward play it quite beautifully.

Single Spies Simon Callow *as Burgess*, Prunella Scales *as HMQ* and Alan Bennett *as Blunt*

The seasonal musical at the Orange Tree in Richmond is a 1960s curiosity by Anthony Newley and Leslie Bricusse which achieved a respectable Broadway life with Newley himself in the lead, but closed on a British road tour before reaching London. This is, therefore, the local premiere of *Roar of the Greasepaint – Smell of the Crowd*, and, despite an agile new production by Kim Grant, they were wise not to open it even in the West End of a quarter-century ago. Though it has a vastly better score than the same team's more successful *Stop the World I Want To Get Off*, as neither Bricusse nor Newley ever seem to have had the faintest idea of plotting or construction, and always declined to use a librettist, we are left with a ramshackle charade resembling a *Waiting For Godot* singalong in which a winsome young tramp slugs it out with an elegant old bully.

History Boards

No Royal Shakespeare Company director has had a better season than Deborah Warner: two of her productions, *Titus Andronicus* and *Electra*, are having sold-out seasons now at the Barbican Pit, while a third (*King John*) is shortly to arrive from Stratford. In so far as it is possible to talk about characteristic productions by a director not yet thirty (and intriguingly non-university trained, on a drama school stage management course) then *Electra* is typical Warner: an intense, almost religious experience on a bare stage through which runs a river turning slowly to blood as the awful events unfold. It is hallmarked by what might be called the Barbican barbarity of *Titus*, but also by an absolute belief in simplicity and textual purity. The production even stars Peter Brook's wife, Natasha Parry, as Clytemnestra in a staging Brook himself would, one feels, recognise and admire.

A hundred-minute, no-interval powerhouse of blood and vengeance, *Electra* is about grief feeding on hate: the Kenneth McLeish translation is as bare, spare and intense as the staging, and its star is Fiona Shaw, who gives a performance of extreme thin-lipped emotional power. But the key here is economy of thought, movement, deed: the whole show appears compressed to its absolute minimum, as the children of the cursed house of Atreus attempt to come to terms with whatever the Gods have in store for them. Piers Ibbotson is a strong Orestes, but essentially the evening belongs to Miss Shaw and Miss Warner, who give it an energy and a driving sense of purpose which makes one long to see them work together again on one of the major main-stage Shakespeares.

On the Cottesloe stage of the National, Brian Friel's Irish Field Day Company have a production of his new *Making History* with another of the company's directors, Stephen Rea, cast in the central role of Hugh O'Neill, an Irish chieftain in the reign of the first Elizabeth. But the play's title is in fact ambiguous: O'Neill did indeed make history, as a turncoat rebel and pioneer of Irish links with the Vatican, but it also refers to the way that history itself can be remade by those who happen to be writing it with the needs of a specific audience in mind. Thus another leading character here is Archbishop Lombard (Niall Toibin), a historian who is determined to rewrite O'Neill's career even in the man's own lifetime, so that it will resemble a more traditional tale of Irish patriotism. In fact, O'Neill was an infinitely complex man, much married and terminally uncertain of which side he was supposed to be joining in what war against whom. He died the death of neither a traitor nor a hero, just that of an old exile in Rome desperately trying to turn his ancient historical involvements into the money for another drink and some more memories of the time when he seemed to be at the centre of his nation's already turbulent history.

Rea brilliantly conveys the vacillation and the uncertainties of a man who suddenly finds himself trying to be a hero for a less than heroic cause, and Friel's play is essentially a lengthy debate about the differences between history as it appears on the printed page, and history as it is when you have to negotiate it from day to day. But this is also of course a play about Ireland, and about the moment in around 1600 when O'Neill had to decide whether to deal or fight with the English who were already his in-laws and his invaders.

The Field Day Company has already toured *Making History* through their native Ireland, and are admittedly not at full National strength as a team of character actors: but Rea and Toibin are well contrasted as the political pirate and his staid chronicler, while the issues raised by the play about Irish co-existence with either England or Europe have a kind of eternal topicality. It is arguable that the period of history treated by the play, the time of the Flight of the Earls, was what conditioned modern Ireland and it is therefore important to examine the truth as against the myth of O'Neill, who married into an English settler family in Ireland and was always half inclined to sell himself to Elizabeth rather than local authorities.

O'Neill himself calls the official version of his history nothing more than a 'florid lie' and is trying, as the play and his life end, to inject a little of the truth about his marital status and his political ambiguities before the myth takes total control. A treacherous opportunist and a womaniser, he was also true to his own eccentric nobility and was finally only defeated by his own attempts to remain loyal to both Belfast and London, for which he was generally vilified as the Northern Lucifer. Whether a Gaelic rebel or trotting beside the Tudors (it was Queen Elizabeth herself who made him an Earl), O'Neill symbolised a modern confusion over expediency and loyalty rather than the older and simpler virtues of revolt, and, in questioning the veracity of this history, Friel has himself taken certain liberties with the chronology of his life. But against a complex local background of party and church politics, the play stands as an investigation into truth: as Shaw's General Burgoyne always said when asked what history would say of his executions, 'History, sir, will tell lies as usual.'

The Play of the Movie

On the Lyttelton stage of the National, David Mamet's *Speed-The-Plow* is looking a lot stronger than on Broadway; true, this is still basically a one-joke sketch about studio executives running amok, and vastly less detailed in its analysis of California movie dreaming than a play like Christopher Hampton's *Tales From Hollywood*. But Gregory Mosher's London production seems much tighter and better than the currently re-cast Manhattan version minus Madonna; and there is a breathtaking staccato energy about Mamet's dialogue, here as in his better plays, *Glengarry Glen Ross* and *American Buffalo*. In *Speed-The-Plow* no sentence is ever truly finished, no deal finalised, no contract signed, no movie made; but the quickfire intensity of the power-gaming is all. Two old buddies, a clean-cut studio executive (Colin Stinton) and his shambling, but no less ambitious, sidekick (Alfred Molina), fall out over an apparently naive young secretary (Rebecca Pidgeon) and whether to make a surefire blockbuster or a more ecologically worthy picture about the perils of radiation.

So much for plot. What Mamet is essentially writing here is a morality play about power and virginity and sex and the moral epilepsy that more than one critic has always found at the heart of his plays. In that sense, *Speed-The-Plow* is a brisk fable, highlighted by sudden bursts of verbal or physical assault and by great comic dexterity. Whether he is noting that in Los Angeles one wrong deal will turn your name into a punchline overnight, or merely that no film is made which you can't summarise in a single line for television guides, Mamet is savagely energetic in his loathing of a movie business in which he clearly sees a metaphor for America's moral and spiritual decline. What will be really funny is when they try filming that one out West.

Back in 1924, *The Vortex* was the country house party drama that changed the shape of the West End and, more than any other, Noël Coward's career as actor and dramatist and director. The first truly contemporary play of its era, dealing with drugs and nymphomania and, perhaps, even sub-textual homosexuality, it dragged the British theatre into the twentieth century amid a good deal of critical reluctance and official threats of censorship. Not since Wilde's *The Importance of Being Earnest* thirty years before had any play had so marked an effect on the social life of London, and, at the time of its premiere, *The Vortex* was attacked in almost identical dustbin-drama terms that were applied to Osborne's *Look Back in Anger* thirty years later. It had precisely the same scandalous success, and a similar effect on the theatre around it: scripts of the 1920s can quite clearly be identified as pre-*Vortex* or post-*Vortex* in their attitudes to what is permissible on stage.

So where does that leave us sixty-five years further down the line? With a rare and major revival at the Garrick of Philip Prowse's hothouse production from the Glasgow Citizens, of which the three stars are: Maria Aitken as the nympho-mother; Rupert Everett as her drug-addict son; and Mr Prowse's own amazing settings, characterised by full-length bedroom mirrors and the sort of interior decor that makes Marie Antoinette's Versailles look like a triumph of quiet good taste.

The script itself is untypical early Coward, neither stiff-upper-lipped nor very jokey: but, like *Easy Virtue* (seen at this same theatre last year), it sets out to dynamite the upper middle classes from within the barricades of their own cocktail parties, only turning at the very last into an intensely moralistic update of the closet scene from *Hamlet*, in which the son tries to alert the mother to her own human vanities before ending up with her on the bonfire of them.

At the Young Vic, Arthur Miller's *Two-Way Mirror* is a double bill of short plays for two characters both played by Helen Mirren and Bob Peck. In *Some Kind of Love Story* she is a paranoid hooker with a strong belief in the conspiracy theory of recent American history, and he is the jaded cop who loves her and has to draw from her the truth about a five-year-old murder. In *Elegy for a Lady* she is a fashionable boutique owner and he is a married man looking for a gift for his dying mistress. Both plays are about the distortions of time and memory and the agonies of unequal or unrequited love; but where the second is an elegiac tone-poem for the stage, the first is a raw emotional thriller which brings Miller surprisingly close to the echoes of Tennessee Williams.

That Miller is the greatest living American dramatist there can be no doubt, despite Broadway's shameful inability even to name a theatre after him, let alone keep his classics in constant revival. But, of these new scripts, the first is the kind you wish Rod Steiger could have filmed with Marilyn Monroe in the middle Fifties, while the second is an infinitely more cerebral and distant piece, full of anguish and regret, but more liable to have been filmed through a glass darkly by Ingmar Bergman.

Auld Lang Syne

The problem with *Metropolis* at the Piccadilly is not just that it doesn't really work as a 1989 stage musical; the problem with *Metropolis* is that it never really worked as a Fritz Lang film either. In 1927 it had a cast of 37,000 people (extras were cheap in Germany at the time), and a budget of 7 million marks, which virtually bankrupted the UFA studios when the film proved less than a box-office triumph. Sixty years later, it has cost £3 million to stage with a cast of merely thirty, and what was wrong with the original is still wrong. Luis Buñuel called the Lang production 'two movies glued together by their bellies'. The new staging by Jérôme Savary from a score by Dusty Hughes and the producer Joe Brooks has in a way solved that problem of a divided identity, with two quite separate stories stuck together in all the wrong places.

The star of the evening is undoubtedly Ralph Koltai's set, a vast tubular affair framed by the kind of glass-walled lifts you see in California hotel lobbies. On its upper levels lives John Freedman (played by Brian Blessed) as the master of the world, a performance he would seem to have modelled on equal parts Orson Welles and Sydney Greenstreet at a time very late in their careers when they had taken to appearing in truly appalling science fiction B-to-Z movies.

On its lower levels live the workers, a team of slaves who provide the Freedman city with all its energy, but precious little of its music. The score has a kind of all-purpose adequacy but no real energy or identity, so that the songs sound as though they could have been written for *Chess* or *Starlight Express* or *Time* or any other recent West End musical where it was felt that scenery and volume could take the place of plot and purpose.

And while above the ground the worker is being transformed into a robot, so as to cause less dissension among the slaves, below ground a batch of lovable children, apparently on loan from *Annie*, are setting off on an ecological quest for the greenery they have hitherto been denied.

Metropolis is therefore about everything and nothing: themes of social injustice and the need for poetic individuality are buried within the kind of gothic horror story that even Boris Karloff and Peter Lorre would have had doubts about filming, except as a parody of the genre.

Judy Kuhn, on loan from Broadway, has a winning voice and a kind of musical energy that transcends some of her weaker numbers, but even she is defeated by dialogue apparently cobbled together on the backs of envelopes during technical rehearsals for the overwhelming set changes.

The score at best resembles *Modern Times* set to music by Abba, but lyrics like 'We're the cream / We're the crust / We're for pleasure / We're for lust' do not inspire the belief that we have here any challengers for Stephen Sondheim.

To the Lyric on Shaftesbury Avenue from a long off-Broadway run comes *Steel Magnolias*, Robert Harling's soap-operatic account of life and death in a beauty parlour of the deep South. An all-female cast of six led by Rosemary Harris and Maggie Steed and Vanessa Redgrave's daughter

Joely Richardson are directed by the actress Julia McKenzie, who, here as in her earlier production of *Stepping Out*, has managed to create a closed community world where gossip and smiles through the tears are the main dramatic bindings.

If you can imagine a folksy small town tragi-comedy written by an unholy alliance of Carson McCullers, Thornton Wilder and Tennessee Williams, then you will have some idea of what to expect.

In the course of the evening all the women get their hair done several times, one of them gets married and pregnant and dies, another gets transformed from a true curmudgeon into a mildly lovable old battle-axe, but that's about it for action.

The only men are heard offstage, usually firing guns at harmless animals or neighbours, and a warmly touching and lyrical if rather heart-tugging script is regularly retrieved from unforgivable sentimentality by the sheer waspishness with which the clients regard each other across the mirrors.

Women whose lives have been experiments in domestic terror are matched against beauticians longing for escape to Baltimore, hairdo capital of the world. Underneath every manicure there are nails just waiting to tear into the neighbours.

Set in the kind of community where nothing much happens and very slowly at that, but where if anything moves you either stuff it, shoot it or marry it, this randomly chatty little play about women who think that Sherlock Holmes is some kind of housing project manages to hover on a perpetual tightrope between laughter and tears before finally coming down to the inevitably tear-jerking reconciliation of apparent social opposites, bonded at last by the death of one of their number.

Jean Boht, Stephanie Cole and Janine Duvitski complete a strong team of beauty parlour regulars who appear to have had certain crucial parts of their brains blown away by the dryers.

Aspects of Success

What matters most about Andrew Lloyd Webber's *Aspects of Love* (at the Prince of Wales) is that it marks the coming of age of the English stage-musical. For this is not a scenery show, or a dance extravaganza, or even a collection of rock-pop hits cobbled together along a familiar storyline. Rather it is a lyrical, heartbreakingly romantic chamber piece, through-sung and deeply faithful to David Garnett's 1955 novel from which it derives its slender plot and, more importantly, its mood of bitter sweet regret for dangerous and sometimes impossible liaisons.

Aspects of Love tells of a young boy bringing a penniless actress to the home of his uncle in the south of France, only to have the uncle fall in love with the girl while he eventually falls for the uncle's daughter. Stated so briefly, the story has a darkly uneasy aspect of relative values gone adrift. But the brilliance of the scoring and of Trevor Nunn's production is the way that it returns time and again to familiar themes of lost and betrayed and rediscovered love among people often separated by a generation and at least one marriage, but locked together by their passionate belief in passion itself.

Mindful that musical audiences are still hungry for some sort of spectacle, Maria Björnson's stunning if sometimes overly lavish sets can open up to entire French landscapes and Italian studios, while a fundamentally domestic five-character plot is highlighted by occasional circus or fairground scenes to allow a sudden chorus. But the intimacy is all, and in the quietest of duologues lie some of the most breathtaking moments, notably one in the second half when the old *roué* uncle sings to his daughter of his desire to be the first man she'll remember and the last that she'll forget. For that number alone, *Aspects of Love* richly deserves the £7 million that it has already taken in advance bookings well into next year. But even more importantly, the success of a show like this means that we at last have in this country the possibility of a truly adult and complex musical theatre.

Aspects is a cynical, edgy, and at the same time charming piece in which the sophistication narrowly outweighs the sentiment. It opens on a backstage dressing-room and never moves far away from the world of the actress at its centre, brilliantly played by Ann Crumb, with Michael Ball as the lover she eventually loses to her daughter, and Kathleen Rowe McAllen, another Broadway import, as the flamboyant Italian mistress. But the performance of the night is that of Kevin Colson, stepping in for Roger Moore to a difficult score and wonderfully suggesting on stage the kind of elegant romantic decay that on screen one used to associate with the likes of David Niven and Maurice Chevalier.

Yet the musical that *Aspects of Love* most resembles, in its theatricality and its dark, aching romanticism and the complexities of its score (which Lloyd Webber co-wrote with the lyricists Don Black and Charles Hart) is Sondheim's *A Little Night Music*. There is a poetic purity here not often found in current big-band shows, as well as a magical energy of music and mood that could well lead to a whole new world of intelligent and intimate adult singalongs.

At the Shaftesbury, trailing clouds of glory and several awards from a long Broadway run, David Henry Hwang's *M. Butterfly* is the story of a French diplomat who fell in love with a Chinese Opera star and lived with her for twenty years apparently without realising that she was both a man and a spy.

John Dexter's extravagant and splendid production, here as in New

York, is a suitably operatic affair, using the parallels Hwang sets up with Madame Butterfly as the basis for a spectacular staging rich in the images of Chinese and Japanese theatre. Just as *Royal Hunt of the Sun* and *Equus* were sometimes more Dexter than Shaffer in their ultimate epic theatricality on stage, so *M. Butterfly* spreads out from its text to suggest a huge panorama of East-West sexual and social and political relationships, most of them mistaken and misguided from their outset.

Anthony Hopkins, in the role of the trusting diplomat, has a butch heartiness that makes the plot a little harder to accept, for all its documentary base, than on Broadway, where I saw David Dukes give a performance of intriguing ambisexuality, leaving open the question whether the diplomat in truth knew all along that his beloved singer was a man. Equally, G. G. Goei as the transvestite spy is a little less subtle than his New York counterpart, so we have a play that, while still very strong indeed, has been oddly coarsened by its Atlantic crossing and one or two miscast minor roles. All the same, this is that comparative Broadway rarity, a major new drama that tackles issues of sexual and cultural mismatching with a fragmented, acerbic intensity and dark intelligence.

Ivory Merchant

What is remarkable about the Dustin Hoffman *Merchant of Venice* at the Phoenix, which has already become the most heavily booked Shakespearian revival in the history of the West End, is that it is not really the Dustin Hoffman show at all.

His Shylock must be one of the most self-effacing of recent times, a shy and halting, hesitant figure who seems almost embarrassed by his first-act demand for a pound of the merchant's flesh. It is only when armed with his courtroom knife some acts later that Hoffman manages to acquire anything like the mesmeric theatricality that we have come to expect from the role as played by the likes of Olivier and O'Toole and Redgrave. But this is no bad thing. Shylock is a part wonderfully suited to Hoffman's situation as an American movie outsider (although he has worked on the US stage) joining a troupe of resident local classicists to make his London and Shakespearian debut after a year or so of master classes with Sir Peter Hall.

Not only is his American English probably closer to Shakespeare's own than our latter-day tongue here, but as Shylock has a mere half-dozen scenes he is able to maintain his separation and with it his alienation from the rest of Hall's team, several of whom have been together since his days at the National. So this is Shylock versus the world, and Hall has made another decision that works in Hoffman's favour: he has given the play its centre in Belmont, a romantic if rather chilly country landscape of loves won and lost, against which the ugly racism of Venice seems almost a sub-plot, one that Hoffman's very low key and low voiced Shylock can more easily control because it again seems to be faintly at a tangent to the rest of the action.

Such a reading puts Portia stage centre at all times, since she alone dominates Belmont and the courtroom, and Geraldine James, looking like a young Vanessa Redgrave, gives a performance of faultless if faintly Thatcherite bossiness, whether stripping Shylock of all his potential revenge or upbraiding her husband for giving a wedding ring away to herself.

This is a cool, thoughtful *Merchant*, elegantly played against pillars of the Rialto by a cast that seems to have little interest in radical re-interpretation of a familiar text and still less in underlining (as in some recent revivals) the inherent violence of the anti-Semitism. True, Shylock gets spat upon a lot, but in a casually social kind of way, as if that was the way one always greeted Jews. The ruling classes, led by Leigh Lawson as the merchant Antonio, Nathaniel Parker as Bassanio and Michael Siberry as Gratiano, are superbly in command of the verse but lack a certain tension, as though the whole problem of the pound of flesh is a tiresome irritant rather than a real threat to life. But this too is what you get with a polite Shylock: his final departure from the courtroom, manhandled by a bunch of local thugs, and not for the first time, goes almost unnoticed as the Belmont mafia get back to their country pursuits.

An oddly gentle and even tranquil rendering then, on such a night as this. But underlying it is a sense of melancholy, and the suggestion that even in deep Belmont countryside the meaning of what the others have done to their alien back in Venice will eventually darken all their lives.

In the meantime, we have Hoffman to thank for adding yet another commercial Shakespeare season to a West End that currently seems more classical than ever before. Audiences here are beginning at last to demand something other than musicals, even away from the subsidised houses.

Vintage Grapes

After several seasons in which it has seemed that the stage traffic across the Atlantic has been almost solely westward, it is good to report a London summer once again alive to the sheer wealth of the American theatre. The most welcome of all American imports in recent times has been the arrival at the National Theatre of Steppenwolf, the Chicago theatre company, as part of Thelma Holt's International Theatre Season with its epic fiftieth anniversary staging of John Steinbeck's *The Grapes of Wrath*.

Steppenwolf brings all its intensity and ensemble strength to the story of the Joad family crossing from Oklahoma to California after the dust-bowl disaster. Not since *Nicholas Nickleby* has there been so classic an example of a great national book becoming an equally great national theatrical event.

In *The Grapes of Wrath* a company of thirty-five, led by Gary Sinise as the quietly rebellious son Tom (the role with which John Ford once confirmed the movie stardom of Henry Fonda) bring to heart-breaking and heart-stopping life the great set-piece moments of drama in the narrative, while all the time reminding us of its underlying biblical humanity and its terrible topicality half a century on into a new time of peril for America's farming communities.

From the arrival of Jim Casy (Terry Kinney), the itinerant lapsed preacher, across three hours to the breathtakingly final silhouette of the abandoned mother, having endured the burial of her stillborn child, now using her milk to suckle an old and dying man, this Frank Galati adaptation and production is a marvellously evocative pageant from a powerhouse of the American regional theatre, one that faces up to the bleak humour as well as the social anger of the original novel.

A harmonica band occasionally accompanies the pilgrims as they set off in an already broken down jalopy to cross the country in hopes of fruitpacking work in a Far West that becomes less inviting with every mile that they approach it. Along the way there are moments of triumph and defeat, deaths and births and reunions, battles with the authorities and with landowners determined to keep the migrants off their territory; there is also the growth of a kind of union solidarity as banks foreclose on tenant farmers and labour is exploited, so that by the time Tom gets to his unforgettable 'I'll be there' speech, this has become a journey into the minds and hearts of men as well as a vision of a country in economic and social turmoil.

And just as, in Steinbeck's repeated theme, all men have to become part of one great being before they can properly function as individuals, so all of Steppenwolf becomes one great voice to chorus this howl of American heartland pride and rage on the long trail to California. There is a raw strength here, and an understanding of what it means to be a stage company, which ranks them with the best in the world.

Dog's Dinner

An all-American week at the Royal Shakespeare Company's Barbican home: a new Richard Nelson satire on visiting academics in the studio theatre, while on the main stage there is a fiftieth-anniversary production of George S. Kaufman and Moss Hart's *The Man Who Came to Dinner* with John Wood as Sheridan Whiteside, the critic whose hip injury forces him to stay with, and subsequently scare the living daylights out of, a small-town Ohio family by drastically reorganising their domestic and social lives.

Whiteside was rather more than loosely based on the now almost forgotten critic and pundit Alexander Woollcott, and one somehow expects an accordingly gargantuan figure: Monty Woolley created the part on Broadway and film (though Woollcott himself later took to playing it on the road between his own lecture tours) and my father, Robert Morley, first played it here, which is why this column is signed with the christian name it is, since I was born on the first night at the Savoy in 1941.

Better perhaps to declare that interest before venturing to suggest that Wood may be miscast. An essentially aquiline and elegantly slender actor of undoubted brilliance in everything else he touches, he here seems physically and vocally at odds with the bullying, ranting Whiteside. As conceived by Kaufman and Hart, the man is a monster and not always a very sacred one at that. As played by Wood, he looks more like Bernard Shaw in a mild rage. There is something fundamentally very cadaverous about this performance, where it needs to be bloated, and that is not the only problem.

For though the RSC has had the intelligence to import Gene Saks from Broadway to give the Barbican company a sense of the original style and pace required for the wisecracks, he and they have been defeated by the sheer width and depth of the main Barbican stage, which makes the small town Ohio living-room look like the deck of an ocean liner and kills much of the farce stone dead simply by the time it takes for one character to reach another.

Then again, programme notes are required to explain to modern audiences thirty or so characters who get passing mentions in the script, from Dorothy di Frasso ('said to be Gary Cooper's mistress') all the way through to William Beebe, 'inventor of the Bathysphere' and doubtless worth a good laugh in 1939, but now just another name in what the audience was beginning to regard as a telephone directory of the famous dead.

Then there are the characters who actually make appearances on stage: not only Woollcott but thinly disguised variants on Noël Coward, Harpo Marx and the axe-murderess Lizzie Borden, all adding to the impression that what we have here is not so much a play as a brisk tour of Madame Tussaud's devised for audiences who wished to hear nothing much more than the dropping of some very noisy names.

If *The Man Who Came To Dinner* wears its age much less well than such earlier Kaufman and Hart hits as *You Can't Take It With You* and *Once in a Lifetime*, it is perhaps in the nature of a one-joke play. Once the celebrated lecturer has fallen over the Ohio doorstep and forced himself upon the

1989

unlucky owners, there is really very little for him to do except wheel himself around their home while trying to stop his secretary running away with a local journalist.

Celebrities do indeed drop in, as do choirboys and tame penguins and mad professors, but the famous name jokes are apt to get a little repetitive almost three hours into a very long evening, and because the plot has nowhere to go, each new visitor is merely the cue for another set conversation-piece in which period gossip and backstage insults are ritually traded. Whiteside needs perhaps to be played by a performer rather than an actor (one can only hope that this is not being read by a fatherly eye). He has to be larger than life in a Falstaffian sense, and there also needs to be something a little chilly about him, so you can believe that he'd willingly have had his mother burned at the stake in order to get a light for his cigarette.

Wood remains oddly lovable even in his rudest moments, and for an actor used to working within companies, another problem of the star vehicle is that he has no equals on stage, only a few visiting stooges and the resident family to insult, all of whom are really only set up in the first place so that he can effortlessly knock them down with his wheelchair.

Estelle Kohler is, however, suitably theatrical as the actress and Desmond Barrit manages a wonderful extra Marx Brother known as Banjo. For the rest, the feeling is of a classical company doing their best to have a summer romp for the visiting tourist but somehow unable to throw themselves lightly or briskly or wholeheartedly enough into a tricky Broadway period piece.

Downstairs in the Pit, talking of the tourist trade, Richard Nelson's *Some Americans Abroad* is an elegantly satirical look at the annual migration of campus academics to the cultural heights of Stratford and the National Theatre. Some familiar transatlantic targets of professorial pretension are hit accurately enough, but beneath the glib and witty surface, something rather nastier is going on here: one of the academic tourists is about to lose his teaching job, another is accused of touching up one of his female students in the back of a rented car en route to Stratford.

Real life has an unfortunate habit of peering through the late-night moral debates and the culture-vulture itinerary, and the contrasts between lofty intellectual ideal and seedy collegiate realities of sex and power are wittily highlighted in a fragmentary sequence of table talks as the group winds its timetabled way for credits around the landmarks of England's culture.

Anton Lesser as the wiry, manic leader of the faculty, Oliver Cotton as the accused sex fiend and Simon Russell Beale as the tutor desperate for tenure lead a strong cast in Roger Michell's agile production, one due I suspect for a longer commercial life in the West End.

Ghetto-Blaster

In a very strong week for London drama, the National Theatre's *Ghetto* is an epic Nicholas Hytner production on the Olivier stage of Joshua Sobol's heartbreaking play about life among Lithuanian Jews on their way to the death camps in 1943. For two years, under Nazi guard, they performed for their captors, finding in comedy and song ways of speaking the unspeakable and facing the inevitable.

Sobol's script raises many other issues apart from the possibilities of escaping from life into theatre. It asks about collaborators like Gens (John Woodvine), the chief of Jewish police who did deals with the Nazis over the deaths of his own people so that others might have a chance of survival, and about the right of any of us who were not there to judge those who escaped or those who died, or even those who made a profit within the eccentric economics of the community.

This is an evening of pure, chilling theatre in which not only Woodvine as the anguished ghetto leader but Alex Jennings as his silkily sadistic Nazi overlord and Maria Friedman as the songbird of the community give hauntingly memorable performances against Bob Crowley's forbidding scenic reminders of life under an inhuman occupation.

Part of a ghetto trilogy originally seen in Sobol's native Israel, this London premiere comes after widely acclaimed productions in a dozen cities from Berlin to Los Angeles; but it is hard to believe that it has ever been given a stronger or more directly challenging staging.

Iris Murdoch is back in London after twenty years with *The Black Prince*, her own dramatisation of her novel (at the Aldwych).

On one level the story of a peculiarly unfortunate tax inspector (Ian McDiarmid, in what will prove one of the award-winning performances of the year) who falls in love with a teenage girl and finishes up in prison for a murder he never committed, Murdoch's play is in fact a literary conundrum based on reflections of *Hamlet* (the other Black Prince of the title) and a sardonic mix of death and deceit.

Around the tax man are assembled a doomed but best-selling novelist (Simon Williams), a suicidal sister (Norma West), a doctor brother (John Fortune) and a ghastly ex-wife (Deborah Norton), all of whom have their own agendas for life or death and all of whom impose upon the central figure until a monastic prison cell becomes his only retreat from debates on the nature of art and truth and life itself. A chain of moral failures leads to mayhem, marriage and murder in roughly that order, but *The Black Prince* is also about redemption through love and art: the discovery, says Murdoch, of what one has always known. As in the best of Simon Gray and Tom Stoppard, there is a constantly shifting balance between the life of the mind and the activities of those onstage, and as in all the best theatre the great laughs are also the most shocking in their utter truth. *The Black*

Prince is likely, alongside *M. Butterfly*, to become the snob hit of the season.

At the Cambridge, *Sherlock Holmes: the Musical*, although new to the stage, has the curious look of a show that has been locked in a time vault for twenty or thirty years. Relentlessly cheerful cockney singers and jovial dancing priests lead us into a world I had thought demolished by Stephen Sondheim and Andrew Lloyd Webber and the coming of the thoughtful or innovative song-and-dance evening. But here it all still is, preserved in all of its awful tourist-coach-party predictability: from a spectacular start up on the Reichenbach Falls, the musical drops straight into turgid knee-jerking singalong with lyrics that start 'Without kings there can be no crowns' and then go on unflinchingly to 'Without ups there can be no downs,' except that the latter are rather more in evidence than the former.

The author, composer and lyricist is Leslie Bricusse, whose music for the words of Anthony Newley a couple of decades back gave us *Roar of the Greasepaint* and *Stop the World*. But he now badly needs the help of a co-writer or three, and the best of his songs (*London Is London*) has already been used in at least one movie musical. His plot, though not a lot worse than that of the non-musical *The Secret of Sherlock Holmes*, currently at Wyndhams, is no better either. We get the usual odd-couple Holmes and Watson, with Ron Moody looking craggy as the detective and Derek Waring looking inane as the doctor, while only Liz Robertson as Moriarty's murderous daughter manages to emerge, from show-stoppers designed to stop a show that has never really started, with anything like dignity or distinction.

Sherman Tanks

If you can imagine Terence Rattigan's *Separate Tables* rewritten by a curious alliance of Gore Vidal and Tennessee Williams, you will have some idea what to expect of Martin Sherman's *A Madhouse in Goa* at the Lyric, Hammersmith.

Two short plays, linked (as were Rattigan's) by at least one central figure, are concerned with a man who could have wandered in from Williams, only then to find himself severely satirised on arrival by Vidal. These are Sherman's points of reference, and though his new play has been – shamefully – grudgingly received, it seems one more indication of a rich London summer of intelligent new dramas.

Sherman's man is a writer (Rupert Graves) whom we first meet on a Greek island after he has been chasing his melancholy around Europe for several months. There he comes across an older woman (Vanessa Redgrave), not exactly Mrs Stone having her Roman Spring. Instead, she seems a kind of cultural Auntie Mame who carries around her own little bell for summoning waiters and is only displaced by an elaborate and unbelievable blackmail plot designed to have her vacate her favourite terrace table so that it may be used by the king of Greece. So far, so Rattigan, even allowing for a gay little sub-plot in which the writer is seduced by a mercenary waiter.

But as this first play (*A Table for a King*) gives way to the infinitely chillier second one (*Keeps Raining All the Time*) we have moved forward a quarter of a century, to 1990. The writer is now a brain-dead wreck, living on a volcanic island, watching in angry silence as the world breaks up around him. The role is taken on by Arthur Dignam, allowing Graves to reappear as a manic Hollywood producer who believes that Christ is his director, while Redgrave turns up as an ageing flower child from the 1960s who has now become the minder of the old writer.

To move in one evening from a sunnily romantic terrace to an apocalypse of Aids, terrorism and cancerous death suggests, and not for the first time, that Sherman is among the most ambitious of contemporary dramatists, and his tricky, treacherous, intermittently manic play is wonderfully and coherently directed by Robert Allan Ackerman, he who has only recently emerged from the Broadway calamity of *Legs Diamond* and must have been more than a little relieved to find a script in which the words actually added up to ideas.

Walk on the Wilde Side

Like the young Orson Welles, Steven Berkoff is an impresario of the ego: he acts, writes, directs himself in a succession of theatrical happenings, often funded by his own movie appearances as a saturnine villain in James Bond or Eddie Murphy escapades. Again like Welles, he tends to provoke either slavish devotion or deep distaste from his audiences. Now, to the National Theatre's Lyttelton stage from this year's Edinburgh Festival, comes his adaptation of Oscar Wilde's rarely revived *Salome*. Written in 1892 in French for Sarah Bernhardt, who played it four years later in Paris, the play was banned in Britain until 1931, when it was given a first public production in a translation by Wilde's lover, Lord Alfred Douglas. Since then it has seldom been dug out of the closet, largely because the tale of Salome dancing for Herod to obtain the head of John the Baptist has been reckoned almost unplayable on account of its deep purple poetry.

Berkoff has stripped away all the ornate trappings and given us a bare-stage 1920s cocktail party at which the full horror of the story is revealed to a group of white-faced guests. What Berkoff has realised, of course, is that here, as in many of his better-known works, Wilde had, beneath the flowery language, a sharply defined sense of pure drama.

1989

With a running time of barely ninety minutes, *Salome* now unfolds like a kind of thriller as we wait to see whether the dance of the seven veils will be performed, and what is to be the price Herod finally has to pay for it. In the title role Katherine Schlesinger mimes her stage act without the need to take off a glove, while Berkoff and Carmen du Sautoy sit on their thrones as uneasily as Claudius and Gertrude watching Hamlet's play.

What Berkoff has also seen, I think, is the lead that Wilde gave to such twentieth-century playwrights as Noël Coward. Coward like Berkoff stripped away Wilde's exaggerated theatrical mannerisms and found a way of paring comedy down to its bones. *Salome* is, of course, no laughing matter, but Berkoff performs much the same act of reduction to essentials. As the black-tie party slowly disintegrates into a slanging match between Herod and his termagant wife, so in a single spotlight John the Baptist watches them from his prison cell, the only character in the drama to be played for real by Rory Edwards, who thus becomes quite literally the spectre at the feast of his own murder.

I had totally forgotten, in the thirty or so years since I last read the play, its breathtaking last-line twist, and the way that Berkoff now makes the whole charade work as a chilly political thriller is magnificent. His staging is visually stunning, and his own performance as an arrogant Herod brought almost to self-destruction by his obsessive need to see his stepdaughter perform.

Someone Like You is a new and first musical by Petula Clark, for which she has written all the music and in which she stars as an Englishwoman searching for her wastrel husband in the United States just after the Civil War. It is now on a pre-London tour.

For those of us who think of Clark as a somewhat bland romantic singer in the Julie Andrews image (both began their careers in London radio and as child stage stars just after World War II) her show comes as a revelation and delight. Like *The Hired Man*, *Someone Like You* has a craggy, grainy intensity. It tackles such issues as slavery, feminism and racial intolerance with a cool intelligence.

Clark and her director Robin Midgeley have wisely cast two of the great recent discoveries from *Les Misérables*: Dave Willetts, who was the second Valjean before replacing Michael Crawford as *The Phantom of the Opera* and Clive Carter, who was the second Javert. Both have magnificent voices, and as they fight over Clark they also manage to fight out the Civil War in microcosm. At times a musical *Gone With the Wind* and at others something very much more political, this is a highly energised and superbly played (at least by its three principals) musical.

Well Baked

Unquestionably the greatest American musical never to have reached Broadway, *The Baker's Wife* is now at the Phoenix, completing a quintet of West End musicals directed by Trevor Nunn (the others being *Cats*, *Starlight Express*, *Aspects of Love*, all by Andrew Lloyd Webber, and the Boublil/Schonberg *Les Misérables*) and in this case starring his wife, Sharon Lee Hill, in the title role.

Like Harold Rome's 1955 *Fanny*, to which it owes a huge if not unacknowledged debt, *The Baker's Wife* is based on a classic French film by Marcel Pagnol and is the story of a small community in crisis. The plot could hardly be simpler: the new baker in town loses young wife to lover, is then unable to bake, and in order to get their croissants back his neighbours make it their business to reunite the uneasy couple.

Across three hours, the story is apt to grow a little thin, but what saves *The Baker's Wife* time and again is a score of huge and magical delight, the work of Stephen Schwartz, who wrote *Godspell* and *Pippin* and has here come up with song after song of tremendous gallic enchantment, all of which sound like Piaf or Trenet in top form. Even so, the show closed pre-Broadway in Boston a decade ago, apparently because of a clash between composer and director about the kind of musical it was meant to be, and this production still bears the traces of the original problem. The book by Joseph Stein, who also wrote *Fiddler on the Roof*, just cannot sustain so rich and vibrant a score and, although Nunn has as usual done his utmost to make this a company show, it is still left with about twenty characters in search of a plot.

Lee Hill is a little wan as the faithless wife, but James Villiers (croaking rather than singing his numbers, in the firm tradition of Rex Harrison and David Tomlinson) makes a wonderfully irritable mayor and Alun Armstrong is mesmeric as the cuckold baker.

Not all of the new songs sound to me like improvements on the original score, but there are still so many masterpieces here, including the *Meadowlark* that has become a standard Broadway audition piece, that *The Baker's Wife* finally wins over even the most fervently anti-French sentiments. As in *Les Misérables*, a far more sombre and revolutionary musical, Nunn has created for the West End stage an entire and plausible French community, one brought to life here by the choreography of David Toguri, which is never less than subtle and stunning. In New York this has become, with Sondheim's *Anyone Can Whistle*, one of the most famous 'lost' musicals, and it would be good to see Nunn get it on Broadway at last.

Elsewhere, it has been a week of *Hamlet*. Shakespeare seems to reach London now not as single spies, but in battalions. Last year we had three *Tempests* and four *Twelfth Nights* running simultaneously, and now we have a trio of *Hamlets*. At the National, Ian Charleson has replaced Daniel Day-Lewis in Richard Eyre's statuesque production, the Barbican has last season's Stratford revival, while to the Old Vic comes Yuri Lubimov's Russian production with Daniel Webb.

Of the three, Lubimov's is far and away the most radically inventive. He starts the play with the Act Five gravediggers and later he deletes Fortinbras altogether. The real star here is the arras behind which Polonius is eventually murdered. Through the production it swoops and whirls around the stage, forming rooms or corridors or battleground horizons, while the cast shares out the evening to such an extent that most of them, line by line, take over Hamlet's most famous soliloquies.

Rather like the old, gimmicky Charles Marowitz Shakespeares of the 1960s, Lubimov's is quick, jokey, exaggerated in a circus way, and performed in near-workshop conditions by a hard-pressed cast, of whom only Webb and the Polonius of Richard Durden are truly notable. This is an English-language replica of the production with which Lubimov made his name at the Taganka in Moscow more than twenty years ago, and it remains an event rather than the radical new interpretation that was evidently intended.

On the main Barbican stage, Ron Daniels's modern-dress version has Mark Rylance as an unusually mad prince in a more conventional reading of the text, played out against sets by Anthony McDonald that look like a homage to all the films of Ingmar Bergman. Peter Wight is a nervy Claudius, capturing the mood of high neurotic intensity that drives the play.

Up at the newly restored and no longer fire-damaged Tricycle in Kilburn, Nigel Williams's *Nativity* is a seasonal update of the Bethlehem story, designed as a savage indictment against Thatcher's Britain, but emerging as a rather folksy little fairy tale about an unwanted child. Nabil Shaban is, as usual, charismatic in the part of the villainous landlord, but elsewhere Chris Bond's production seems defeated by Williams's characteristically well-written but ultimately shaky fable for our time.

Salute to the Player King

As all-star theatrical matinées go, it had to be the greatest in living memory: in order of first appearance at the altar or lectern of Westminster Abbey there could be found Douglas Fairbanks, Michael Caine, Maggie Smith, Paul Scofield, Derek Jacobi, Ian McKellen, Dorothy Tutin, Frank Finlay, Albert Finney, Sir John Mills, Dame Peggy Ashcroft, Sir John Gielgud and Sir Alec Guinness. Even the understudies were impressive, with Peter O'Toole standing in for Jean Simmons during a somewhat kitsch opening pageant. All in honour of the man billed in the programme as Baron Olivier of Brighton, thereby making Sir Laurence sound like one of the jokier characters from his own superb gallery of period eccentrics.

Next year, his ashes will be laid alongside those of Irving and Garrick in Poets' Corner, since the Abbey has only ever allowed about one actor per century to darken its portals and has yet to bring itself even to consider an Actors' Corner. True, they recently permitted a plaque for Sir Noël Coward, but even Irving only got in there by happy accident, though he was the first player ever to get a knighthood (just as Olivier was the first

Sir Laurence Olivier

ever to get a peerage, not to mention the Order of the Yugoslav Flag with Golden Wreath). When Sir Henry died in 1905 he was refused the Abbey as a last resting place until the Dean of the day had his eyesight saved by a renowned oculist. In return, the Dean offered the oculist anything his heart desired and the oculist said he wanted Irving to lie in the Abbey.

No such special dealing has been necessary for Olivier, though it was John Osborne in a letter to *The Times* who first called for the rare honour to be accorded him. And although there are still those of us who believe, despite all recent obituaries and tributes, that history may well judge Gielgud to have been the greatest actor of their shared and remarkable generation, with Redgrave and Richardson in hot pursuit, there can be no doubt that Olivier was the one uniquely plugged into the heart of his time and nation.

Henry V was thus the theme of Friday's service, though its poetic highlight was Gielgud's superlative echo of Hamlet's dying speech, in itself another kind of valedictory.

The voice of Olivier himself, starting the St Crispian quietly enough and then building to the well-known operatic crescendo of 'We few, we happy few' made this a Shakespearian gathering, though in biographical terms it remained an oddly chilly and soulless affair. Sir Laurence the actor was saluted time and time again: Alec Guinness, in a line from his address which sounded more like a personal warning to Kenneth Branagh, noted unarguably enough that no one is ever going to be the second Olivier for the simple reason that he was unique and irreplaceable. But of Olivier the man there was almost no trace: no mention of his private life, no word of reminiscence from his first or third wives (Jill Esmond and Joan Plowright), who were both silently present, no mention of his children, though all were there, no reference to Vivien Leigh. This was purely a salute to the Player King, and on that level, as directed and choreographed for the Abbey by Patrick Garland, it worked well enough.

All the ushers were drawn from the ranks of Olivier's first National Theatre company of 1963, and the opening parade ended in the laying on the High Altar of such treasures as his Order of Merit, hotly followed by his Oscar, as if to emphasise the noble and the commercial aspects of the late Lord. Then came models of his National and Chichester theatres, the crown from *Richard III* and the laurel wreath of *Coriolanus*.

Also laid on the altar was the sword of Edmund Kean, once presented to Olivier by Gielgud. Years later, someone asked Sir Laurence to whom in his turn he would be handing it on: there was an icy pause before Olivier replied, 'To no one. It is mine.' And now, presumably, it will live in the Abbey, as if to emphasise Sir Alec's point about Olivier having no theatrical heirs apparent or actual. Because of his *Henry V* and his theatre management, Olivier did indeed transcend the usual thespian career patterns, and the Abbey in its memorial service was rightly acknowledging the monumental historic importance of the man without whom we might still have no National Theatre.

Garland's production was superbly lit and orchestrated, right down to the bit-part players in the aisles, while even the bells that pealed out over Parliament Square afterwards sounded like a Walton theme from *Richard III*. The casting was equally astute: Finney, who had been thrown into fame by understudying the 1959 Olivier *Coriolanus* and having to go on for the great man; O'Toole, whose Hamlet albeit shakily opened the National at the Old Vic in 1963; Caine, who said once to me on the set of *Sleuth* that acting opposite Olivier was like trying to play opposite God. But it was Dame Peggy Ashcroft, Olivier's Juliet more than half a century ago, who showed up the rest of Garland's Abbey cast by working without a script, speaking, instead of reading, the *Lycidas* that Olivier so loved. And far from the usual rent-a-celebrity gathering into which actors' memorial services so often degenerate at other churches, this was undoubtedly an hour of classic theatricality. On Broadway nowadays they reckon that the best performances and the best audiences are all to be found at memorial services, and as usual we may not be so far behind. Ticket touts endorsed this one, or tried to, and crowds started forming outside the Abbey well before 9 a.m. to reserve the best pavement space for autographs and flashbulbs.

None of the living great or good seemed to be absent, though one couldn't help in those holy premises noting the absence of some select dead: surely Richardson and Redgrave deserve their foot or two of Abbey flooring, and if only Sir Ralph had lived to fire one of his celebrated first-night rockets from the roof, the ceremony would have been complete. As it was, there were in the old MGM slogan 'more stars than in the heavens', and the clergy were firmly relegated to the very back of the set. Olivier himself, like Sybil Thorndike a vicar's child, might perhaps have cast them in better roles: as it was, the urge to stand and applaud has never been harder to suppress near an altar.

But no curtain calls were taken, and we left the Abbey as we always left Olivier's performances, knowing everything about the player, but nothing about the man inside the costumes. The man we were recalling was Henry V and Richard III: it still was not Sir Laurence himself. The old conjuror has gone to his grave with all of that mysterious magic intact and unexplained.

Index

Abba, 140
Accrington Pals, 27
Ackerman, Robert Allan, 115, 228
Ackland, Joss, 41, 48, 75
Ackland, Rodney, 78
Acting Shakespeare, 180
Adams, Jonathan, 80
Adams, Polly, 50
Addinsell, Richard, 130, 197
Adler, Christopher, 73–5
Admirable Bashville, The, 65
Admirable Crichton, 178
Adrian Mole, 98
Aeschylus, 12
After the Ball is Over, 102
Aitken, Maria, 15–16, 52, 102, 107, 128, 211, 217
Aladdin, 53
Albee, Edward, 94
Alexander, Bill, 64–5, 158–9
Alfreds, Mike, 127, 161–2
Allam, Roger, 118, 159
Allen, Debbie, 188
Allen, Sheila, 144
All My Sons, 26, 36–8, 90
American Buffalo, 79
American Clock, The, 145–7
Anderson, Kevin, 132–3
Anderson, Lindsay, 69–70
Andrews, Anthony, 131
Andrews, Harry, 59
Annals, Michael, 86
Another Country, 6, 38, 130
Antony and Cleopatra, 21
Anyone Can Whistle, 123
Archbishop's Ceiling, 124
Archer, Jeffrey, 2, 165–6, 177

Aren't We All?, 86–8
Are You Lonesome Tonight?, 98
Aristocrats, 195–6
Arlen, Harold, 182
Armstrong, Alun, 118, 204, 230
Artist Descending a Stair, 213
Ashcroft, Dame Peggy, 10, 62, 70, 234
Ashe, Rosemary, 190
Asher, Jane, 129, 204
Aspects of Love, 178, 209, 219–20
Aspern Papers, 79
Astoria, 39
As You Like It, 91, 124
Atkins, Eileen, 28, 29
Atkinson, Rowan, 79
Attenborough, Michael, 145
Audley, Maxine, 102
Aukin, David, 5, 26, 179, 210
Aunt Dan and Lemon, 113–14, 128
Avian, Bob, 157
Ayckbourn, Alan, 6, 155, 170, 193
  Chorus of Disapproval, 99, 111–12
  Henceforward, 178, 204–5
  Intimate Exchanges, 79
  Sisterly Feelings, 10
  Way Upstream, 40

Babes in Arms, 78
Bacall, Lauren, 109
Bad Language, 65
Bagnold, Enid, 139
Bailey, Robin, 160
Baker, Gregg, 163
Baker, Jill, 200
Baker, Sean, 149
Baker's Wife, The, 210, 230

235

INDEX

Balcony, The, 157–8
Ball, Michael, 220
Bamber, David, 80
Bannen, Ian, 31–2, 53
Barber, Frances, 55, 174
Barker, Harley Granville: *The Secret Life*, 187; *Waste*, 98, 107–8
Barker, Howard, 190–1
Barnum, 27, 32–4
Barr, Jean-Marc, 212
Barrit, Desmond, 225
Barry, Julian, 74–5
Bartlett, Keith, 172
Barton, John, 10, 12–14, 107, 169–70
Barton, Steve, 147
Bassett, Linda, 190
Bate, Anthony, 193
Bates, Alan, 53, 59, 126–7, 178, 211
Baum, Frank, 154, 181
Battley, David, 70
Beacham, Stephanie, 170
Beale, Simon Russell, 225
Beastly Beatitudes of Balthazar B, 27
Beaumont, Francis, and Fletcher, John, 138–9
Beaumont, Penelope, 44
Beck, Michael, 109
Beethoven's Tenth, 52
Beevers, Geoffrey, 187
Behn, Aphra, 169–70
Belcourt, Emile, 183
Bell, Elizabeth, 171
Benefactors, 85–6, 135
Bennett, Alan, 130
　An Englishman Abroad, 212–13
　Kafka's Dick, 124
　A Question of Attribution, 212–13
　Single Spies, 6, 212–13
Bennett, Michael, 140, 156
Berger, John, 207
Berkeley, Busby, 40–1
Berkoff, Steven, 97, 211, 228–9
Bernard, Jeffrey, 211
Bernstein, Leonard, 210
Best Little Whorehouse in Texas, The, 27

Best of Friends, 178, 186
Best People, The, 87
Betrayal, 50
Bettinson, Rob, 194
Beyond Reasonable Doubt, 165–6
Bicât, Nick, 14
Bielski, Nella, 207
Big in Brazil, 78, 79
Biko, 78
Biograph Girl, The, 10
Bitter Sweet, 189–90
Björnson, Maria, 220
Black, Don, 220
Black Prince, The, 226–7
Blake, Josephine, 188–9
Blakely, Colin, 37
Blakemore, Michael, 26, 37–9, 86, 135, 168, 193
Blessed, Brian, 218
Blessing, Lee, 178, 202–3
Blethyn, Brenda, 86
Blezard, William, 133, 196
Blithe Spirit, 128–30
Blockheads, 78
Blood Brothers, 6, 53, 58
Blythe, Domini, 44
Boht, Jean, 219
Bolt, Robert, 169
Bond, Christopher, 58, 104–5, 231
Bond, Edward, 41
Bond, Samantha, 198
Boublil, Alain, 6, 117
Boucicault, Dion, 191
Bowe, John, 145
Bowles, Peter, 142–3
Boxer, Amanda, 119, 185
Boy Friend, The, 90
Bradley, David, 159
Bradshaw, Richard, 163
Bradwell, Mike, 65
Branagh, Kenneth, 5, 88, 154, 177, 197–8, 206
　Henry V, 105–6
　Twelfth Night, 174–5
Breaking the Code, 124, 149–50
Breaking the Silence, 79, 94–6, 98
Brecht, Bertolt, 44, 210

236

INDEX

Brenton, Howard:
   Greenland, 196; *Pravda*, 103–4, 196; *The Romans in Britain*, 2, 9, 10
Brewer, Linda-Mae, 91, 93
Bricusse, Leslie, 214, 227
Bridge, Andrew, 137
Briers, Richards, 174
Brightman, Sarah, 147
Broadbent, Jim, 190
Bron, Eleanor, 110, 127, 205
Brook, Faith, 90
Brooks, Joe, 218
Brothers Karamazov, 27
Brown, Bille, 182
Browne, Angela, 187
Browning Version, The, 10
Bryant, Michael, 5, 63–4, 134, 146, 178, 199
Bryceland, Yvonne, 41
Bryden, Bill, 10, 69, 78, 106–7
Budgie, 178
Bufman, Zef, 46
Buggy, Niall, 195–6
Bulloch, Jeremy, 173
Burge, Stuart, 38
Burgess, Anthony, 64
Burrows, Abe, 44
Burton, Richard, 21
Bury, John, 101
Bussy d'Ambois, 199
Buxton, Judy, 14

Cadell, Selina, 110, 127, 205
Cadell, Simon, 129
Café Puccini, 133
Cage aux Folles, La, 124, 139
Caine, Michael, 234
Caird, John, 20, 116, 149, 207
Callow, Simon, 27, 97, 124, 184, 212
Camille, 98
Candide, 210
Cannan, Denis, 198–9
Captain Carvallo, 198–9
Cargill, Patrick, 102
Carousel, 78
Carr, Jane, 73, 92

Carr, Pearl, 156
Carrie, 154, 178, 187–8
Carter, Clive, 228
Carter, James, 45
Carter, Jim, 182
Cartwright, Jim, 124
Cashel Byron's Profession, 65
Cat on a Hot Tin Roof, 186
Cats, 27, 30, 39, 84
Cavander, Kenneth, 12, 13
Cecil, Jonathan, 193
Chalk Garden, The, 139
Channon, Paul, 40
Chapman, George, 199
Chapman, Robin, 6, 130–1
Charles, Maria, 156
Charleson, Ian, 45, 57, 93–4, 187, 231
Chekhov, Anton:
   The Cherry Orchard, 69–71, 127–8; *Seagull*, 27, 99, 105; *Uncle Vanya*, 178, 193; *Wild Honey*, 79, 92–3
Cherry Orchard, The, 69–71, 127–8
Chess, 124, 140–1
Childe Byron, 27
Children of a Lesser God, 26
Chitty, Alison, 67
Chkhikvadze, Ramaz, 12
Choderlos de Laclos, 125
Chorus of Disapproval, A, 99, 111–12
Christie, Bunny, 174
Church, Tony, 14, 108
Churchill, Caryl:
   Serious Money, 2, 154, 161; *Top Girls*, 54
Circe and Bravo, 141–2
Clark, Dave, 136
Clark, Petula, 229
Clyde, Jeremy, 50
Cocktail Party, The, 143–4
Codron, Michael, 5, 135, 178
Colbert, Claudette, 79, 87
Cole, Stephanie, 219
Coleman, Cy, 34
Coleridge, Sylvia, 65
Collier, Ian, 16
Collins, Pauline, 184

237

INDEX

Colored Museum, The, 163–4
Colson, Kevin, 220
Common Pursuit, The, 78, 89–90
Congreve, William, 79
Conolly, Patricia, 29
Conquest of the South Pole, The, 205–6
Cook, Barbara, 188
Cookson, Catherine, 194
Cooney, Ray, 52–3
Copley, Peter, 213
Coriolanus, 100–1
Cork Report, 123, 153
Corn is Green, The, 108
Cornwell, Charlotte, 93
Costigan, George, 58
Cotton, Oliver, 85–6, 202, 225
Counsell, Elizabeth, 74
Country Girl, The, 52, 68–9
Courtenay, Margaret, 156
Courtenay, Tom, 11, 16–17, 70, 78, 82–3
Covington, Julie, 45, 57, 79, 103, 212
Coward, Noël, 10, 14–15, 128
   Bitter Sweet, 189–90
   Blithe Spirit, 128–30
   The Vortex, 211, 216–17
Craig, Wendy, 166
Craven, Gemma, 112, 183
Crawford, Michael, 27, 32–4, 147–8
Crawley, Bob, 149
Crisp, N. J., 174
Cross, Beverly, 112
Crowden, Graham, 20
Crowley, Bob, 202, 226
Cruickshank, Andrew, 166
Crumb, Ann, 220
Cullen, Max, 192
Cummings, Constance, 107
Curran, Paul, 147
Curry, Tim, 52, 57, 133
Curtis, Simon, 124, 168–9, 196
Cusack, Niamh, 115
Cusack, Sinead, 195
Cyrano de Bergerac, 64

Da Costa, Liz, 150
Daglish, Neil, 146

Dahl, Roald, 120–2
Daisy, 52
Dale, Jim, 33–4
Dalton, Timothy, 47, 184
Dancin', 30
Dangerous Obsession, 173–4
Daniels, Ron, 95, 158, 231
Dark River, 78
Daubeny, Peter, 6
David, Joanna, 70, 150
David, John, 116
Davies, Andrew, 209
Davies, Howard, 44, 61, 125, 186, 191, 200
Davies, Irving, 75
Davies, Oliver Ford, 14
Davies, Rudi, 185, 201
Davis, Carl, 201
Day Well Spent, A, 34
Day-Lewis, Daniel, 231
de la Tour, Frances, 5, 11, 53
Dean, Isobel, 150
Dear Anyone, 52
Deep Blue Sea, 27, 193–4
Dekker, Thomas, 27
Dench, Judi, 5, 23, 49, 52, 107–8, 151, 197–8
   as Cleopatra, 155
   Lady Bracknell, 41, 57
   Mother Courage, 79
Denison, Michael, 182
Dexter, John, 10, 27, 56, 143, 220–1
Dexter, Sally, 133
Dickens, Charles, 10, 19–21
Dickson, Barbara, 58
Dignam, Arthur, 228
Dignam, Mark, 208
Dining Room, The, 53
Dionisotti, Paola, 162
Don Juan in the Russian Manner, 92
Don, Robin, 91, 93
Donleavy, Brian, 27
Donnellan, Declan, 173, 206–7
Downie, Penny, 201–2
Doyle, Pat, 174
Dreams of San Francisco, 175–6

238

INDEX

Dresser, The, 11, 16–17
Drinkwater, Carol, 173
Driving Miss Daisy, 178
De Sautoy, Carmen, 229
Duchess of Malfi, The, 27, 109–10
Duet for One, 11
Dukes, David, 221
Dunaway, Faye, 141–2
Dunbar, Adrian, 148
Duncan, Lindsay, 125, 186–7
Dunlop, Frank, 22
Dunn, Nell, 26, 185
Durden, Richard, 231
Duvitsky, Janine, 219
Dyer, Charles, 185

Early Days, 11
Eastwood, Laurence, 192
Ebb, Fred, 60
Eddison, Robert, 143, 206
Edgar, David, 20, 52, 61
Edmond, 128
Educating Rita, 18–19
Edward II, 124
Edward IV, 201
Edwards, Rory, 229
Eggar, Samantha, 105
Electra, 214
Elegy for a Lady, 217
Eliot, T. S., 143–5
Elliott, Denholm, 209
Elliott, Michael, 10, 78
Ellis, Antonia, 72–3
Elwyn, Michael, 187
Emerald City, 191–2
Emperor, The, 155
Enemy of the People, 178
Englishman Abroad, An, 212–13
Entertainer, The, 142–3
Espert, Nuria, 124
Euripides, 12
Evans, Damon, 163
Evans, Serena, 204
Everett, Rupert, 38, 117
Eyre, Richard, 5, 45–6, 179, 210, 231
Eyre, Ronald, 59, 60, 139, 202

Fahey, Jeff, 132–3
Falconer, Sheila, 182
Falkland Sound, 53, 62–3
Falls, Robert, 108
Family Voices, 48
Farago, Peter, 128–30
Farrah, 119
Fatal Attraction, 120–2
Father, The, 203–4
Fathers and Sons, 160–1
Feinstein, Michael, 178
Fenton, James, 117
Ferrante, Frank, 166–7
Fiander, Lewis, 133
Fiennes, Ralph, 160, 202
Fierstein, Harvey:
    La Cage aux Folles, 124, 139; *Torch Song Trilogy*, 114–15, 139
Fifteen Streets, The, 194
Filippo, Eduardo de, 52, 63–4
Findlay, Deborah, 159
Finlay, Frank, 71, 166
Finney, Albert, 52, 78, 124, 132, 171–3, 234
Fisher, Robert, 166–7
Fleetwood, Susan, 204
Fleming, Lucy, 59
Fletcher, Graham, 164
Follies, 155, 156–7, 178
Fool for Love, 78, 79, 93–4, 98
Ford, Mick, 200
Ford-Davies, Oliver, 62
Fortune, John, 226
42nd Street, 98, 110, 178
Fosse, Bob, 30
Fox, Edward, 118
Francis, Clive, 89
Fraser, Bill, 70
Frayn, Michael, 12, 79, 92–3, 185, 193; *Benefactors*, 85–6
Freed, Donald, 141–2
Freeman, Paul, 212
Friedman, Maria, 226
Friel, Brian:
    Aristocrats, 195–6
    Fathers and Sons, 160–1
    Making History, 214–16

239

INDEX

Friel, Brian – *cont.*
   Translations, 26, 31–2, 42
Fugard, Athol, 53, 190
Fulford, Christopher, 135
Fuller, Toria, 107
Funny Thing Happened on the Way to the Forum, A, 123

Gaetani, Raimonda, 64
Galati, Frank, 223
Gale, John, 59, 112
Galileo, 10
Gambon, Michael, 10, 41, 67, 99, 112, 155, 170–1, 178, 193
Gans, Sharon, 205
Garden, Graeme, 79
Gardner, Geraldine, 73
Garland, Judy, 98, 115–16
Garland, Patrick, 59, 91–2, 233–4
Gems, Pam, 116
Genet, Jean, 157–8
Genius, The, 53
Gershwin, George, 162–3
Ghetto, 210, 226
Ghosts, 124, 148
Gielgud, Sir John, 5, 6, 178, 180, 186, 233
Gigi, 98
Gilbert and Sullivan, 10
Gill, Peter, 10, 67, 93
Gilmore, David, 166
Giraudoux, Jean, 205
Gish, Lillian, 10
Gish, Sheila, 59, 79, 81, 144
Glass Menagerie, The, 107
Glengarry Glen Ross, 52, 69
Glenister, Robert, 160
Goei, G. G., 221
Golden Boy, 78
Golden Girls, 78, 88
Goldman, James, 156
Good, 27, 39, 42–4
Goodall, Howard, 6
Goodchild, Tim, 166
Goodman, Henry, 158
Good Person of Sichuan, 210
Gordon, Hannah, 52, 68–9

Gore, Michael, 188
Gorky, Maxim, 119–20
Gough, Michael, 87, 150
Grant, Deborah, 34
Grant, Joyce, 161
Grant, Kim, 214
Grapes of Wrath, The, 210, 222–3
Graves, Rupert, 227
Gray, Dolores, 157
Gray, Simon, 26, 78, 89
Greeks, The, 10, 12–14
Green, Benny, 65
Greenaway, Peter, 79
Greene, Justin, 80
Greenland, 196
Grenfell, Joyce, 196–7
Grey, Joel, 134
Griffiths, Richard, 61
Grimes, Frank, 23, 70
Grossmith, George and Weedon, 151
Groucho, 166–7
Grout, James, 109
Guard, Pippa, 159
Guinness, Sir Alec, 178, 202–3, 233;
   as Shylock, 91–2
Gunter, John, 163, 200
Gurney, A. R., 53, 93
Guys and Dolls, 40–1, 44–6, 57, 98
Gwilym, Mike, 14, 48, 132

Haig, David, 103, 196
Hall, Adelaide, 178
Hall, Sir Peter, 5, 21, 26, 44, 46, 48–9, 52, 74–5, 100–1, 124, 126, 177, 199–200, 210, 212, 221
Hamlet, 5, 21, 41, 230–1
Hamlisch, Marvin, 52, 74–5
Hamm, Nick, 205
Hampshire, Susan, 192
Hampton, Christopher, 64, 65
   Les Liaisons Dangereuses, 125–6
   Tales from Hollywood, 53, 65–7
Hancock, Sheila, 110, 127, 196, 209
Hands, Terry, 5, 64, 115, 157, 188, 210

INDEX

Happiest Days of Your Life, 78
Harburg, Yip, 182
Hard Feelings, 54–5
Hardy, Robert, 195
Hardy, Robin, 195
Hare, David, 99
   Pravda, 103–4
   Secret Rapture, The, 178, 200
Hare, Doris, 56
Harling, Robert, 218–19
Harris, Rosemary, 37, 56, 186, 218–19
Harrison, Rex, 52, 56, 87–8, 178
Harrison, Tony, 106–7
Hart, Charles, 147, 220
Hart, Moss, 223–4
Harwood, Ronald, 11, 16–17
   Interpreters, 118–19
   J. J. Farr, 171–3
   Tramway Road, 78
Hastings, Michael, 102–3
Hateley, Linzi, 188
Hauser, Frank, 169
Havergal, Giles, 10
Havers, Nigel, 48
Hawthorne, Nigel, 64–5
Hayes, James, 171
Hay Fever, 52
Haygarth, Tony, 168, 200
Hayman, David, 134
Haymon, Cynthia, 163
Head, Anthony, 127
Head, Murray, 140
Healy, David, 45, 156–7
Heard, John, 113
Hearn, George, 139
Heartbreak House, 52, 55–6
Heggie, Ian, 185
Heilbron, Vivien, 187
Helen, 13
Hellman, Lillian, 6, 10, 46–7
Hello Dolly!, 35, 36, 52, 78
Henceforward, 178, 204–5
Henderson, Shirley, 200
Henry IV, 47–8
Henry V, 78, 105–6
Henry VI, 178, 201–2

Henry VIII, 60–2
Henson, Basil, 104, 200
Herbert, Ian, 3
Herman, Jerry, 139
Herman, Ray, 158
Herrman, Edward, 102–3, 202–3
Her Royal Highness?, 27
Hersey, David, 83
Herzberg, Paul, 81
Heston, Charlton, 169
Hicks, Greg, 101
Higgins, Clare, 200
Hill, Dave, 150
Hiller, Danny, 58
Hiller, Wendy, 79, 178
Hinge and Bracket, 10
Hired Man, The, 6, 98
Hodge, Patricia, 85–6
Hoffman, Dustin, 210, 221–2
Holborough, Jacqueline, 175–6
Holt, Thelma, 6, 155, 222
Home, William Douglas, 101–2
Hopkins, Anthony, 97, 99, 103–4, 154, 221
Hordern, Sir Michael, 52, 57–8, 182
Horovitch, David, 131
Hörvath, Ödon von, 66–7
Hoskins, Bob, 44
House of Bernarda Alba, 124
Howard, Alan, 10, 42–4, 100
Howard, Leslie, 42, 112
Howard, Pamela, 91
Huggett, Richard, 27
Hughes, Dusty, 65, 218
Hugo, Victor *see Misérables, Les*
Humphries, Barry, 41
Hunt, Linda, 113–14
Hunt, Marsha, 147
Hunter, Kelly, 74
Hurt, John, 105
Hutchings, Geoffrey, 71
Hwang, David Henry, 220–1
Hyde, Jonathan, 110
Hytner, Nicholas, 82, 124, 210, 226;
   The Scarlet Pimpernel, 112–13

Ibbotson, Piers, 214

INDEX

Ibsen, Henrik, 124, 148
Importance of Being Earnest, The, 14, 78
Imrie, Celia, 205
Infernal Machine, 124
Ingham, Barrie, 146–7
Inner Voices, 63–4
Insignificance, 41
Interpreters, 118–19
In the Belly of the Beast, 108
Intimate Exchanges, 79
Iphigenia in Aulis, 13
Irons, Jeremy, 169–70
Isaacs, Jeremy, 177
Ivanhoe, 211

J. J. Farr, 171–3
Jackson, Glenda, 11, 78, 79, 99
Jacobi, Derek, 5, 21, 52, 64, 124, 149–50, 177, 197, 206
James, Geraldine, 222
James, Peter, 10, 123–4
James, Polly, 88
Jameson, Louise, 28
Jarvis, Martin, 48–9
Jayston, Michael, 15–16
Jean Seberg, 73–5
Jefford, Barbara, 160
Jenn, Stephen, 141
Jennings, Alex, 226
Jesson, Paul, 63
Jeweller's Shop, The, 6
Jewett, Christopher, 93
Jew of Malta, The, 157
Johnson, Celia, 70, 91, 118
Johnson, Teddy, 156
Johnson, Terry, 41
Jones, David, 149
Jones, Freddie, 11, 17
Jones, Gemma, 62, 96
Jones, Griff Rhys, 79
Judge, Ian, 181, 189–90
Judy, 98, 115–16
Jumpers, 78, 82–3
Jungle Book, The, 79
Juno and the Paycock, 22–3
Jury, Chris, 55

Kafka's Dick, 124
Kancheli, Gia, 12
Kander and Ebb, 188–9
Kane, Richard, 135
Karge, Manfred, 205–6
Karlin, Miriam, 115
Katis, Diana, 55
Kaufman, George S., 223–4
Kaut-Howson, Helena, 119
Kay, Charles, 108, 113
Kean, Marie, 23
Keegan, Shelagh, 174
Keep Raining All the Time, 228
Keith, Penelope, 52, 193–4
Kelly, Peter, 80
Kempson, Rachel, 144
Kendal, Felicity, 35, 50, 135, 211
Kenwright, Bill, 68
Kern, Jerome, 98
Kernan, David, 98
Kerr, Deborah, 108
Kessler, Lyle, 132
Kestelman, Sara, 146, 199
Kind of Alaska, A, 48
King, David, 59
King, Denis, 65, 196
King, Stephen, 188
King John, 210, 214
King Richard II, 10, 206
King Richard III see *Richard III*
Kingsley, Ben, 20, 99, 115
Kingston, Mark, 18–19
Kinnaird, Cora, 70
Kinnear, Roy, 110, 169
Kinney, Terry, 223
Kipling, Rudyard, 79
Kiss Me Kate, 154
Kitchen, Michael, 79
Kohler, Estelle, 225
Koltai, Ralph, 164, 188, 218
Korberg, Tommy, 140
Kramer, Larry, 132, 134–5
Kretzmer, Herbert, 117
Kuhn, Judy, 218
Kyle, Barry, 88, 138

La Rue, Danny, 52, 78

INDEX

Lambert, Anne Louise, 57
Lambert, Annie, 13
Landen, Dinsdale, 36, 173
Landor, Jennifer, 55
Langton, David, 166
Langton, Diane, 188–9
Lapotaire, Jane, 52, 149, 196
Laurents, Arthur, 139
Lawrence, Gertrude, 14–15, 190
Lawson, Leigh, 127, 222
Laye, Dilys, 158
Lecoat, Jenny, 176
Lee-Hill, Sharon, 210, 230
Lefevre, Robin, 69, 142, 195
Legrand, Julie, 127
Lehrer, Tom, 10
Leigh, Adele, 156
Leigh-Hunt, Barbara, 187
Lennon, 98
Lerner, Alan Jay, 124
Lesser, Anton, 41, 149, 174, 202, 225
Le Touzel, Joshua, 38
Lettice and Lovage, 155, 167–8
Leveaux, David, 204
Liaisons Dangereuses, Les, 123, 125–6
Lie of the Mind, A, 155, 168–9
Life in the Theatre, A, 209
Lipman, Maureen, 178, 196–7
Little Foxes, The, 6, 41, 46–7
Littler, Emile, 27
Lloyd, Bernard, 172
Lloyd, Hugh, 110, 127
Locke, Philip, 67
Loesser, Frank, 44
London Theatre Record, 3
Lonsdale, Frederick, 86–8
Lortel, Lucille, 202
Lowell, Marguerite, 167
Lubimov, Yuri, 231
Lucas, William, 213
Luce, Richard, 2
Lucie, Doug, 79
  Hard Feelings, 54–5
  Progress, 131–2
Luke, Peter, 192
Lumley, Joanna, 129

Lupone, Patti, 118
Lyndon, Richard, 140
Lynne, Gillian, 31, 75, 147

M. Butterfly, 220–1
McAllen, Kathleen Rowe, 220
McAnally, Ray, 186
McAuliffe, Nichola, 79, 133
Macbeth, 9, 21–2, 44, 173
McCallum, Joanna, 92
McCartney, Paul, 174
McCowen, Alec, 10, 21, 79, 143–4, 160
McCoy, Horace, 158
McDiarmid, Ian, 67, 106, 191, 226
McDonald, Anthony, 231
McDonald, Garry, 192
Macdonald, Robert David, 80, 134
MacDonald, Stephen, 132
McEnery, John, 185
McEnery, Peter, 19, 135
McEwan, Geraldine, 5, 52, 57, 168, 197
McGann, Paul, 168
McGuinness, Frank, 124, 145
McInnerny, Tim, 104
Mackay, Ann, 190
McKellen, Ian, 93, 97, 99, 109–10, 127–8, 178, 180, 204, 210; as Coriolanus, 100–1
McKenna, Siobhan, 124
McKenna, Virginia, 195
McKenzie, Julia, 44–5, 57, 155, 156–7, 219
Mackie, Lesley, 116
McLeish, Kenneth, 214
McNally, Terrence, 189
MacNaughton, Alan, 213
Made in Bangkok, 135
Madhouse in Goa, A, 210, 227–8
Madwoman of Chaillot, The, 205
Makarova, Natalia Romanovna, 79
Making History, 214–16
Malkovich, John, 132
Mamet, David, 52, 69, 92
  Edmond, 128
  A Life in the Theatre, 209
  Speed the Plow, 179, 216

243

INDEX

Man and Superman, 27
Man for All Seasons, A, 169
Man Who Came to Dinner, The, 210, 223–5
Mandragola, 78
Mantle, Doreen, 90, 119
Margoyles, Miriam, 212
Marks, Alfred, 73
Marlowe, Christopher, 157
Married Love, 192
Marsden, Les, 167
Marx, Arthur, 167
Mason, Brewster, 93
Massey, Anna, 41, 48, 49
Massey, Daniel, 27, 79, 88, 96, 107–8, 156–7
Master Builder, The, 210
Master Class, 79, 80–1
Master Harold and the Boys, 53
Masterson, Valerie, 190
Matalon, Vivian, 78
Matthews, Francis, 87
Mayall, Rik, 79
Maydays, 52
Mayer, Louis B., 116
Mayes, Dermot, 20
Me and My Girl, 98
Measure for Measure, 79
Medoff, Mark, 26
Melia, Joe, 44, 158
Mercer, David, 11
Merchant of Venice, The, 91–2, 210, 221–2
Merrick, Simon, 69
Metropolis, 209, 217–18
Michell, Roger, 225
Middlemass, Frank, 142
Midgeley, Robin, 229
Miles, Sir Bernard, 69–71
Miller, Ann, 178
Miller, Arthur:
  All My Sons, 26, 36–8, 90
  American Clock, 145–7
  Archbishop's Ceiling, 124
  Enemy of the People, 178
  Two-Way Mirror, 217
  A View from the Bridge, 155, 170–1

Miller, Jonathan, 6, 41, 178, 199, 200–1
Miller, Max, 142
Minnelli, Liza, 60
Minter, Tinch, 205
Mirren, Helen, 217
Mirvish, Ed, 6, 39
Misalliance, 148–9
Misérables, Les, 6, 98, 99, 107, 116–18, 154
Miss Saigon, 178, 209, 210, 211
Mitchell, Julian, 6, 38, 130
Moby Dick, 78
Moffatt, John, 119, 192
Molina, Alfred, 216
Molloy, Molly, 141
Molnar, Ferenc, 79
Montagu, Felicity, 191
Moody, Ron, 52, 227
Moon for the Misbegotten, 53
Mooney, Paul, 142
Moore, Stephen, 73, 191
Morahan, Christopher, 95
Morgan, Priscilla, 28
Morgan, Wendy, 127
Morning's at Seven, 78, 90
Mosher, Gregory, 216
Mother Courage, 79
Mousetrap, The, 40, 121
Mr and Mrs Nobody, 151
Mrs Warren's Profession, 98
Much Ado About Nothing, 211
Murcell, George, 59
Murdoch, Iris, 226–7
Murphy, Gerard, 48, 107, 138
Mutiny, 98
My One and Only, 91
Mysteries, The, 98
Mystery plays, 106–7

Napier, John, 12, 20, 47, 84, 117, 136–7
National Theatre, 1
Nativity, 231
Nederlander, James, 39
Nelson, Richard:
  Principia Scriptoria, 124, 149

244

INDEX

Some American Abroad, 225
Nerd, 79
Nevin, Robyn, 192
Newley, Anthony, 214
Nicholas, Paul, 31
Nicholas Nickleby, 10, 19–21, 98
Nichols, Peter, 12, 28–9
  Passion Play, 28–9, 42, 50
  Poppy, 40, 53, 71–3
  Privates on Parade, 72
Night and Day, 103
Niven, David, 112
Noble, Adrian, 106, 178, 201
Noble, Cecilia, 207
Normal Heart, The, 132, 134–5
Normington, John, 45, 194
Norton, Deborah, 168, 226
Not About Heroes, 53, 132
Nunn, Trevor, 5, 10, 20, 22, 31, 44, 47–8, 84, 107, 116, 124, 140–1, 162–3, 210, 220, 230

O'Brien, Edna, 27, 29–30
Observe the Sons of Ulster Marching Towards the Somme, 124, 144–5
O'Callaghan, Richard, 62
O'Casey, Sean, 22–3
Ockrent, Mike, 19, 28, 64, 156
Odets, Clifford:
  The Country Girl, 68–9
  Golden Boy, 78
Ogilvy, Ian, 89, 130–1
Oklahoma!, 10, 12
Oliver!, 52
Oliver, Stephen, 20
Olivier, Laurence, 5, 135–7, 142; death and funeral, 6, 209, 231–5
Oman, Julia Trevelyan, 151
One of Us, 6, 130–1
O'Neill, Eugene:
  Moon for the Misbegotten, 53
  A Touch of the Poet, 178, 184–5
On the Razzle, 34–6
On the Spot, 79
On Your Toes, 79
Orczy, Baroness, 112–13

Orphans, 124, 132
Orpheus Descending, 210, 212
Osborn, Paul, 90
Osborne, John, 6, 203–4, 233
  The Entertainer, 142–3
  A Patriot for Me, 53, 58–60
Othello, 99, 115, 210
Other Places, 41, 48–9
O'Toole, Peter, 9, 21–2, 211, 234
Our Country's Good, 210
Overheard, 27
Oxenford, John, 34

Pacific Overtures, 72, 123, 155, 164–5
Pacino, Al, 79
Pack, Roger Lloyd, 93
Pack of Lies, 52
Paddick, Hugh, 172
Page, Louise, 78, 88
Paget, Nicola, 87
Paige, Elaine, 31, 140
Pal Joey, 10
Papp, Joe, 132, 163–4
Parker, Nathaniel, 222
Parker, Oliver, 198–9
Parry, Natasha, 214
Pasco, Richard, 160, 161
Passion Play, 28–9, 42, 50
Paterson, Bill, 45
Patriot For Me, A, 53, 58–60
Patton, Will, 168
Peacock, Trevor, 172
Pearce, Joanne, 142
Pearson, Richard, 168
Peck, Bob, 111, 172, 173, 217
Peg, 78
Pennell, Nicholas, 29
Peter Pan, 52
Petersen, William, 108
Petherbridge, Edward, 21, 57, 97, 109–10, 127
Phantom of the Opera, 124, 147–8
Phedra, 79, 99
Phillips, Leslie, 70
Phillips, Robin, 30
Pickford, Mary, 10
Pidgeon, Rebecca, 216

245

INDEX

Piercey, Jennifer, 88
Pigott-Smith, Tim, 5, 86
Pinter, Harold, 26, 86, 89, 109, 141
   Betrayal, 50
   Other Places, 41, 48–9
Pitchford, Dean, 188
Place with the Pigs, A, 190
Plantagenets, The, 178, 201–2
Platonov, 92–3
Playing with Trains, 210
Plenty, 39
Plowright, Joan, 70–1, 79, 124, 192
Pogson, Kathryn, 114
Poliakoff, Stephen:
   Breaking the Silence, 79, 94–6, 98
   Playing with Trains, 210
Poppy, 40, 53, 71–3
Porgy and Bess, 162–3
Porter, Eric, 186–7
Possibilities, The, 190–1
Potter, Dennis, 53
Pownall, David, 80–1
Pravda, 97, 99, 103–4, 196
Prendergast, Shaun, 174
Prin, 209
Prince, Hal, 105, 147, 156, 165
Principia Scriptoriae, 124, 149
Private Lives, 10, 14–15
Privates on Parade, 72
Progress, 90, 131–2
Prokoviev, Sergei, 80–1
Prowse, Philip, 110–11, 211, 217
Pryce, Jonathan, 5, 99, 193, 211

Quarshie, Hugh, 138
Quayle, Anna, 91, 92
Quayle, Sir Anthony, 5, 102, 209
Quayle, Jennifer, 16, 131, 182
Quartermaine's Terms, 26
Question of Attribution, A, 212–13
Question of Geography, A, 207–8
Quick, Diana, 132
Quilley, Denis, 120, 121, 139

Raffles, 79
Rattigan Terence, 10, 40, 93; *Deep Blue Sea*, 27, 193–4

Rawlings, Adrian, 171
Ray, Gene Anthony, 188
Ray, Robin, 133
Re: Joyce!, 196–7
Rea, Stephen, 191, 214–15
Reading, Bertice, 11, 183
Real Thing, The, 49–50, 82, 86
Reardon, Michael, 138
Reddington, Ian, 55
Redfarn, Roger, 182
Redgrave, Sir Michael, 6, 68, 79
Redgrave, Vanessa, 99, 124, 148, 184–5, 210, 212, 227–8
Rees, Roger, 19, 50
Renaissance Company, 197–8
Rice, Tim, 98; *Chess*, 124, 140–1
Richard, Cliff, 135–7
Richard II, 10, 206
Richard III, 5, 10, 12, 78–9, 97, 99, 178, 201–2, 206
Richardson, Joely, 219
Richardson, Miranda, 168
Richardson, Sir Ralph, 6, 11, 52, 63–4, 71
Rickman, Alan, 65, 125–6
Rigg, Diana, 56, 156–7
Rigoletto, 41
Rink, The, 188–9
Rivals, The, 52, 57–8
Riverside Studios, 39
Roache, Linus, 208
Road, 124
Roar of the Greasepaint – Smell of the Crowd, 214
Roberts, Rachel, 11
Roberts, William, 196
Robertson, Liz, 52, 227
Robertson, Margaret, 70
Robertson, Patrick, 28
Robertson, Toby, 182, 198–9
Rodgers, Anton, 28, 29
Rodgers, Richard, 9–10, 78, 99, 183
Rodway, Norman, 22–3
Rogan, John, 22, 145
Rogers, Paul, 48–9
Rolfe, Guy, 67
Romans in Britain, The, 2, 9, 10

INDEX

Rooney, Mickey, 178
Roose-Evans, James, 196
Rose, 11
Rose, Geoff, 134
Rose Theatre, 209
Rosenthal, Jack, 26
Ross, Steve, 79
Rough Crossing, 79
Rover, The, 169–70
Runyon, Damon, *see Guys and Dolls*
Russell, Clive, 208
Russell, Ken, 90, 92
Russell, Willy, 18–19, 58, 124
   Blood Brothers, 6, 53, 58
   Shirley Valentine, 184
Rustaveli (Russian theatre company), 12
Rutter, Barrie, 45
Ryall, David, 101
Ryan, Madge, 87
Ryecart, Patrick, 57
Rylance, Mark, 162, 231

Sachs, Leonard, 156
Sacks, Oliver, 49
Saks, Gene, 224
Salome, 211, 228–9
Saroyan, William, 79, 88–9, 90
Satton, Lon, 84
Savary, Jérôme, 218
Savident, John, 75
Saxon, James, 174
Sayle, Alexei, 201
Scacchi, Yelena, 193
Scales, Prunella, 212
Scarlet Pimpernel, The, 98, 112–13
Schlesinger, John, 56
Schlesinger, Katherine, 229
Schofield, Andrew, 58
Schofield, David, 62, 147
Schonberg, Claude-Michel, 6, 117
Schwartz, Stephen, 210, 230
Scott, Shaun, 191
Seachange, 78
Seagull, The, 27, 99, 105
Seberg, Jean, 52, 73–5
Secret Life, The, 187

Secret Rapture, The, 178, 200
Serious Money, 2, 154, 155, 161
Serjeant Musgrave, 78
Seven Brides for Seven Brothers, 110–11
Shaban, Nabil, 231
Shaffer, Peter, 126–7, 155, 167–8
Shannon, Michael, J., 107
Shaughraun, The, 191
Shaw, Fiona, 126, 210, 214
Shaw, G. B., 1
   Cashel Byron's Profession, 65
   Heartbreak House, 52, 55–6
   Man and Superman, 27
   Misalliance, 148–9
   You Never Can Tell, 182
Shaw, Martin, 68
Shawn, Wallace, 113–14, 128
Sheen, Martin, 134
Shelley, Frank, 92
Shelley, Paul, 200
Shepard, Sam:
   Fool for Love, 93–4
   A Lie of the Mind, 168–9
Shepherd, Jack, 52
Sher, Antony, 52, 64–5, 115, 154
   as Malvolio, 159
   Richard III, 78–9, 97, 99
Sheridan, R. B., 52, 57–8
Sherlock Holmes: the Musical, 227
Sherman, Martin, 210, 227–8
Sherrin, Ned, 133, 151
Shirley Valentine, 124, 184
Shoemaker's Holiday, 27
Shostakovich, Dmitri, 80–1
Shrapnel, John, 13, 14
Siberry, Michael, 222
Silver, Philip, 29
Simkins, Michael, 171
Simmons, James, 174
Simon, Josette, 88
Simpson, Marietta, 163
Simpson, N. F., 63
Sinden, Donald, 112–13
Singin' in the Rain, 52, 98, 110
Single Spies, 6, 212–13
Sinise, Gary, 133, 223

247

INDEX

Sisterly Feelings, 10
Sleep, Wayne, 31
Smart, Annie, 204
Smash, 26
Smith, Derek, 199
Smith, Dame Maggie, 15, 27, 29–30, 79, 118–19, 124, 155, 167–8
Smith, Martin, 190
Sobol, Joshua, 210, 226
Some Americans Abroad, 225
Some Kind of Love Story, 217
Someone Like You, 229
Sondheim, Stephen, 11
   Anyone Can Whistle, 123
   Follies, 155, 156–7, 178
   A Funny Thing Happened . . . 123
   Pacific Overtures, 72, 123, 164
   Sweeney Todd, 11, 104–5
Song and Dance, 52
Sophocles, 12
Sound of Music, The, 27
South Pacific, 178, 182–3
Speed-the-Plow, 216
Stacy, Neil, 59, 198
Stafford-Clark, Max, 54, 103, 113, 161
Stapleton, Maureen, 47
Starlight Express, 77–8, 83–5, 98
Staunton, Imelda, 158, 181–2, 193
Steaming, 26
Steed, Maggie, 218–19
Steel Magnolias, 218–19
Stein, Joseph, 230
Steinbeck, John, 210, 222–3
Stephens, Robert, 15, 63–4
Stevens, Ronnie, 59
Stevenson, Juliet, 96, 126
Stewart, Patrick, 48, 127
Stilgoe, Richard, 84
Stinton, Colin, 216
Stock, Nigel, 59
Stokes, Simon, 176
Stoppard, Tom:
   Artist Descending a Stair, 213
   Jumpers, 78, 82–3
   Night and Day, 103

On the Razzle, 34–6
Real Thing, 41, 49–50, 82, 86
Rough Crossing, 79
Storey, David, 11
Strachan, Alan, 10, 16, 81–2, 107, 131, 193–4, 197
Strange Interlude, 78, 90
Streetcar Named Desire, 79, 81–2
Streets of London, The, 10
Stride, John, 68–9
Strindberg, August, 203–4
Stubbs, Imogen, 138–9
Sturridge, Charles, 105
Sturua, Robert, 12
Suche, David, 99, 115
Sue, Eugene, 162
Sufficient Carbohydrate, 53
Sugar Babies, 178
Summer, 41
Sumpter, Donald, 159
Surrey, Kit, 158
Sutton, Dudley, 172
Suzman, Janet, 13, 14, 99, 119–20
Swan Theatre, Stratford-upon-Avon, 137–8
Sweeney Todd, 11, 104–5, 116
Sweet Bird of Youth, 109
Sylvester, Suzan, 171
Syms, Sylvia, 142

Table for a King, A, 228
Tales from Hollywood, 53, 65–7
Talk of the Town, 39
Tartuffe, 64–5
Taylor, C. P., 27, 39, 42–4
Taylor, Elizabeth, 6, 41, 46–7
Taylor, Gwen, 54
Tempest, The, 199–200, 200–1, 206–7, 210, 211
Terry, John, 135
Thacker, David, 124, 148, 178, 185
Thaw, John, 61
Thee and Me, 10
They Shoot Horses, Don't They?, 157–8
Thomas, Michael, 50
Thomas, Sian, 162

INDEX

Thompson, Brian, 53
Thompson, Mark, 182
Thorndike, Daniel, 64
Thorne, Angela, 198–9
Threepenny Opera, The, 133–4
Threlfall, David, 199
Tiller, Stephen, 54
Time, 135–7
Time of Your Life, The, 79, 88–9, 90
Tinker, David, 63
Titus Andronicus, 210, 214
Toguri, David, 45, 75, 133, 158, 164, 230
Toibin, Niall, 215
Tom and Viv, 79, 102–3
Tomelty, Frances, 135
Tomfoolery, 10
Toms, Carl, 130, 161
Top Girls, 54
Top People, 78
Torch Song Trilogy, 114–15, 139
Touch of the Poet, A, 178, 184–5
Towb, Harry, 45
Toye, Wendy, 78
Tramway Road, 78
Translations, 26, 31–2, 42
Troughton, David, 170
Trumpets and Raspberries, 79
Turgenev, Ivan Sergeievich, 160–1
Turing, Alan, 149–50
Turner, John, 141
Turning Over, 53
Tutin, Dorothy, 27, 139
Twelfth Night, 5, 79, 158–60, 174–5
Two Into One, 79
Two Noble Kinsmen, The, 138–9
Two-Way Mirror, 217
Tynan, Kenneth, 4, 11, 89, 139, 183
Tyzack, Margaret, 90, 103, 168

Udwin, Leslee, 92, 173
Uncle Vanya, 178, 193
Unwin, Stephen, 206
Ustinov, Peter, 27, 52, 118

Vahey, Brien, 144
Vassa, 99, 119–20

Victoria Station, 48
View From the Bridge, A, 155, 170–1
Villiers, James, 230
Virginia, 27, 29–30
Vivis, Anthony, 205
Voces de Malvinas, 63
Von Sydow, Max, 178, 199, 200–1
Vortex, The, 211, 216–17
Voss, Philip, 162

Wade, Johnny, 183
Wadham, Julian, 63
Wadsworth, Andrew, 58
Wagner, Robin, 141
Wale, Terry, 115–16
Walk in the Woods, A, 178, 202–3
Walker, Rudolph, 201
Walker, Timothy, 207
Waller, David, 201
Walter, Harriet, 159, 207
Walters, Julie, 19, 78, 79, 82–3, 93–4
Walters, Sam, 78, 187
Wanamaker, Sam, 68, 209
Wanamaker, Zoe, 88
Wandering Jew, The, 161–2
Wandor, Michelene, 162
War at Home, 79
Ward, Eliza, 14
Ward, Simon, 56, 144
Waring, Derek, 227
Warner, Deborah, 210, 214
Warner, Keith, 164
Warren, Marcia, 129
Waste, 98, 107–8
Watch on the Rhine, 10
Waterhouse, Keith, 151
Watson, Tom, 94, 185
Way of the World, The, 79
Way Upstream, 6, 40
Webb, Daniel, 231
Webber, Andrew Lloyd, 2, 6, 27, 30–1, 77–8, 98
  Aspects of Love, 178, 219–20
  Cats, 84
  Phantom of the Opera, 124, 147–8
  Starlight Express, 77–8, 83–5

249

INDEX

Webster, John, 27, 109–10
Weidman, John, 164
Welch, Elisabeth, 98–9, 178
Welland, Colin, 27
Wells, John, 27
Wells, Ken, 31
Wertenbaker, Timberlake, 210
West, Lockwood, 17
West, Norma, 226
West, Timothy, 21–2, 79, 80–1
Wherrett, Richard, 192
White, Orna, 71, 72
White, Willard, 163, 210
Whitehead, Paxton, 56
Whitelaw, Billie, 14, 28, 29, 67
Whitemore, Hugh:
   The Best of Friends, 186
   Breaking the Code, 149–50
Whitrow, Benjamin, 28, 29, 135, 169, 193
Wholly Healthy Glasgow, A, 185
Wickham, Jeffry, 119, 166
Wight, Peter, 231
Wild Honey, 79, 92–3
Wilde, Oscar, 211, 228–9
Wilder, Thornton, 34–5, 90
Wilkinson, Colm, 99, 118
Wilkinson, Tom, 148
Willetts, Dave, 228
William, David, 38
Williams, Clifford, 87, 150, 206
Williams, Emlyn, 108
Williams, Hugh, 70
Williams, Michael, 79, 151
Williams, Nigel, 231
Williams, Simon, 89, 226

Williams, Tennessee:
   Cat on a Hot Tin Roof, 186–7
   The Glass Menagerie, 107
   Orpheus Descending, 210, 212
   Streetcar Named Desire, 79, 81–2
   Sweet Bird of Youth, 109
Williamson, David, 191–2
Wilson, Paul, 140
Wilson, Sandy, 90, 92
Wilton, Penelope, 200
Winnie, 178, 195
Winter Journey, 68
Withers, Googie, 139
Wizard of Oz, The, 154, 181
Wolfe, George C., 163–4
Wolfit, Sir Donald, 11, 16
Wood, Charles, 201
Wood, John, 5, 178, 210, 223–5
Wood, Peter, 35, 36, 50, 57, 145;
   The Threepenny Opera, 133–5
Woodeson, Nicholas, 190
Woodvine, John, 21, 226
Woodward, Peter, 65
Woodward, Sarah, 213
Worth, Irene, 101, 182
Woza Albert!, 53
Wright, Teresa, 90

Yates, Peter, 119
Yelland, David, 193–4
Yonadab, 126–7
York, Susannah, 120–1
You Never Can Tell, 182

Ziegfeld, 178